Revitalizing an Established Program for Adult Learners

ALISON RICE, EDITOR

TESOL Language Curriculum Development Series

Kathleen Graves, Series Editor

 TESOL Teachers of English to Speakers of Other Languages, Inc.

Typeset in Adobe Garamond with Frutiger Display
by Capitol Communication Systems, Inc., Crofton, Maryland USA
Printed by United Graphics, Inc., Mattoon, Illinois USA
Indexed by Pueblo Indexing and Publishing Services, Pueblo West, Colorado USA

Teachers of English to Speakers of Other Languages, Inc.
700 South Washington Street, Suite 200
Alexandria, Virginia 22314 USA
Tel 703-836-0774 • Fax 703-836-6447 • E-mail tesol@tesol.org • http://www.tesol.org/

Publishing Manager: Carol Edwards
Copy Editor: Ellen Garshick
Additional Reader: Sarah J. Duffy
Cover Design: Capitol Communication Systems, Inc.

ISBN 9781931185448
Library of Congress Control No. 2007904838

Contents

Series Editor's Preface

The aim of TESOL's Language Curriculum Development Series is to provide real-world examples of how a language curriculum is developed, adapted, or renewed in order to encourage readers to carry out their own curriculum innovation. Curriculum development may not be the sexiest of topics in language teaching, but it is surely one of the most vital: At its core, a curriculum is what happens among learners and teachers in classrooms.

Curriculum as a Dynamic System

In its broadest sense, a curriculum is the nexus of educational decisions, activities, and outcomes in a particular setting. As such, it is affected by explicit and implicit social expectations, educational and institutional policies and norms, teachers' beliefs and understandings, and learners' needs and goals. It is not a set of documents or a textbook, although classroom activities may be guided, governed, or hindered by such documents. Rather, it is a dynamic system.

This system can be conceptualized as three interrelated processes: planning, enacting, and evaluating, as depicted in the figure.

Planning processes include

- analyzing the needs of learners, the expectations of the institution and other stakeholders, and the availability of resources
- deciding on the learning aims or goals and the steps needed to achieve them, and organizing them in a principled way
- translating the aims and steps into materials and activities

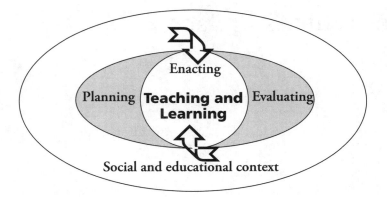

Teaching and learning processes include

- using the materials and doing the activities in the classroom
- adjusting them according to learners' needs, abilities, and interests
- learning with, about, and from each other

Evaluation processes include

- assessing learners' progress toward and achievement of the aims
- adjusting the aims in response to learners' abilities and needs
- gathering information about the effectiveness of the aims, organization, materials, and activities, and using this information in planning and teaching

These processes create a system that is at once stable, rooted in what has gone before, and evolving as it responds to change, to new ideas, and to the people involved. People plan, enact, and evaluate a curriculum.

The Series: Educators Bringing About Change

In these volumes, readers will encounter teachers, curriculum developers, and administrators from all over the world who sought to understand their learners' needs and capacities and respond to them in creative, realistic, and effective ways. The volumes focus on different ways in which curriculum is developed or renewed:

- Volume 1: Developing a new curriculum for school-age learners
- Volume 2: Planning and teaching creatively within a required curriculum for school-age learners
- Volume 3: Revitalizing a curriculum for school-age learners
- Volume 4: Developing a new course for adult learners
- Volume 5: Developing a new curriculum for adult learners
- Volume 6: Planning and teaching creatively within a required curriculum for adult learners
- Volume 7: Revitalizing an established program for adult learners

The boundaries between a program and a curriculum are blurred, as are the boundaries between a curriculum and a course. *Curriculum* is used in its broadest sense to mean planning, teaching, and evaluating a course of study (e.g., a Grade 2 curriculum or a university writing curriculum). A *course* is a stand-alone or a specific offering within a curriculum, such as a computer literacy course for intermediate students. A *program* is all of the courses or courses of study offered in a particular institution or department, for example, the high school ESL program.

The overarching theme of these volumes is how educators bring about change. Change is rarely straightforward or simple. It requires creative thinking, collaboration, problematizing, negotiation, and reflection. It involves trial and error, setbacks and breakthroughs, and occasional tearing out of hair. It takes time. The contributors to these volumes invite you into their educational context and describe how it affects their work. They introduce you to their learners—school-age children or adults—and explain the motivation for the curriculum change. They describe what they did, how they evaluated it, and what they learned from it. They allow you to see what is, at its heart, a creative human process. In so doing, they guide the way for you as a reader to set out on the path of your own curriculum innovation and learning.

This Volume

This volume provides accounts of 11 English language programs in Australia, Canada, Korea, Turkey, and the United States. These programs have sought solutions to issues such as increased competition for declining numbers of students, changing student populations and demands, and institutional requirements to better prepare future undergraduate or graduate students. The authors present strategies for long-range planning and situation and needs analysis as well as practical ideas for creating collaborative teams and solutions for working with stakeholders who, for a variety of reasons, are uncomfortable with change. The contributors provide valuable and frank insights into the complex process of innovation and provide the reader with thoughtful models for revitalizing an established program.

Dedication

This series is dedicated to Marilyn Kupetz, a gifted editor, a generous mentor, and a discerning colleague. The quality of TESOL publications, including this series, is due in no small part to her vision, attention to detail, and care.

Kathleen Graves

English Language Programs and Change: Be Prepared

1

ALISON RICE

An organization which fails to adapt and move with the times is one which will fall behind and eventually expire. (White, 1991, p. 19)

In the past few years, the world has learned some economic hard truths. "The world is flat," says Friedman. "People now have the communication and innovation tools to compete, connect and collaborate from anywhere" (Friedman, 2006, p. 25). He argues that suppliers of goods and services are no longer limited by national or temporal boundaries and that economic rewards and security will go to those who encourage creative thinking, flexibility, education, and openness to novel ideas. English language programs, whether ESL or EFL, supply an important service. Are they also subject to global market competition? If so, as program directors, coordinators, or faculty, do we need to develop business savvy as well as our academic knowledge?

The title for this volume in the Language Curriculum Development Series, *Revitalizing an Established Program for Adult Learners,* clearly reflects TESOL's belief that English language teaching (ELT) programs cannot remain stagnant. And so, although the chapters focus on curriculum change and development, the authors, most of whom hold administrative positions in addition to having teaching duties, implicitly agree with Friedman. It is clear that they are well aware that today's students are courted by many programs and that political and economic realities affect the number of students who enroll each semester and, thus, ultimately, their programs' survival.

Additionally, English programs are often seen not only as service programs to their institutions and local community, but also as sources of students and revenue. Whether for-profit or nonprofit, they must, at the very least, cover expenses in order to remain viable. The authors speak to this when they discuss mandates to adapt to new enrollment trends, improve service to their students and stakeholders, create new and innovative products, and find new markets—the faster, the better.

To accomplish these goals requires immense effort and persistence, and even so, success is not assured. A Delphi Group (2006) white paper on the topic of innovation states discouragingly that the introduction of innovative processes or products is not the natural or automatic result of "creatively thinking about a market challenge." Indeed, the report continues, "this is far from the truth. Most often innovation ends up involving high measures of serendipity and simple brute force" (p. 2). Even worse, Markee (1997, p. 6), quoting a 1981 study by Adams and Chan, writes that, at least at the time of their research, up to 75% of all educational innovations were ultimately unsuccessful. Why is this so? What can TESOL educators do to ameliorate this harsh assessment, as "brute force" is certainly not part of the TESOL culture?

Numerous authors (e.g., Curtis, 1999; Stoller, 1997; White, 1991) have looked at the process of change in education, and in language education in particular, in an attempt to find out why some innovations succeed while others fail. The consensus: School-based change can be frustrating, complex, time-consuming, difficult, exhausting, and energy draining. Moreover, implementation of new program procedures or curricula is expensive, both monetarily and emotionally. Stoynoff (1991) lays out the problem:

> *Any change in the status quo necessitates a reallocation of the increasingly limited resources in an institution. Resources such as space, money, and release time are scarce commodities in most schools. The implementation of a significant change or innovation of any kind is an immediate threat to secured positions and established allocation patterns in the organization. In most cases, it requires reductions in one area to fund disbursements in another. (p. 10)*

Teacher or student resistance can also hinder a proposed innovation. Not surprisingly, new, supposedly improved ways of thinking and novel or revamped procedures urged by program directors or higher levels of institutional administration are not necessarily viewed as better by the users, who often find proposed change unrealistic, if not threatening. Here Curtis (1999) provides some hopeful insights, spotting two positive themes running through the published literature:

- Effective, targeted support for teachers through the change process, based on their self-identified support needs, positively affects the likelihood of acceptance of new procedures or policies.
- Effective support through the change process plays an important role in teachers' professional development.

So what can change agents do to promote buy-in? Curtis (1999) stresses listening to teachers' ideas—their input, based on classroom experience, and involvement in all stages of educational change can make the difference between true acceptance and implementation of an innovation versus superficial, short-term lip service and quick reversion to older habits. Honesty and trust between administration and teachers are absolutely vital—teachers need clear and truthful explanations of higher-ups' reasons for wanting change. Curtis cites Churchill et al. (1997) when pointing out that teachers who sense ulterior motives for educational initiatives (e.g., motives related to economic savings for the program rather than to the introduction of superior pedagogy) are likely to resist. Above all, Markee (1997) stresses that "teachers must perceive change to be relatively advantageous to them if they are to accept it" (p. 15). These points, discussed more fully below, are exemplified in this volume by Rawley and Roemer (chapter 5) as well as Beuster and Graupensperger (chapter 2), who discuss issues of faculty buy-in or lack thereof, and of crises caused by lack of trust.

In my own role as director of a large, urban intensive English program (IEP), I have been strongly influenced by Stoller's (1997) appeal to program directors to serve as "catalysts for change and innovation." Strong leadership, she declares, will let us "enhance many aspects of our programs, creating greater job satisfaction among faculty and staff, better learning conditions for students, improved reputations for our programs, and more effective management of program resources" (p. 33).

The program directors, coordinators, and faculty who have contributed to this volume clearly agree with Stoller and see themselves as successful change agents. Their chapters document long-term initiatives, albeit with much angst and myriad setbacks along the way, to introduce new procedures, curricula, and methods that meet the needs of their students. Some chapters, such as Byleen's (chapter 11) description of a long-term curriculum documentation project at the Applied English Center at the University of Kansas, Bonfanti and Watkin's (chapter 3) work on developing a new curriculum along with marketing and expansion efforts at the English as a Second Language Center at Mississippi State University, and Beuster and Graupensperger's chapter on the challenge of a teamwork approach to curriculum reform, narrate internal IEP projects that affect only their programs' curricula or procedures. Others, such as the contributions by Royal, White, and McIntosh (chapter 4), Kırkgöz (chapter 8), Altman (chapter 9), and Potts and Park (chapter 10), draw connections between the needs of university academic departments and those who prepare students for a wide variety of undergraduate majors or graduate programs. Still other contributors, such as Rawley and Roemer (chapter 5) and Petro (chapter 7), consider how credit-bearing ESL courses should fit into the overall university curriculum. Their chapters document the extraordinarily complex process of introducing and managing innovative curricula and procedures.

Because most change occurs under pressure, it is easy to get caught up in the immediate demands of the process and not take time to consult research. In fact, one particularly important tip from many of the contributors to this volume is to know what researchers have to say before embarking on an ambitious project. The following section highlights some of the major findings in the introduction, management, and evaluation of educational innovation and diffusion, research done primarily in the 1980s–1990s (other than that related to technology). I hope that this brief survey and its accompanying bibliographic references, along with the very pragmatic information in this volume, proves beneficial (or precautionary) as you face the challenges of revitalizing your established program for adults.

A Framework for Successful Educational Innovation

Within the English language classroom, teachers may start with *yes-no* questions but quickly introduce those beginning with *wh-*: *who, what, where, when,* and *why.* These words are equally important in looking at how the literature of educational innovation attempts to answer these complex questions:

- Why do English language programs decide to innovate?
- Who should be involved?
- What factors stimulate or hinder implementation of a new curriculum or new procedures?
- How do you start a significant innovative project?
- How do you manage the actual process?
- How do you evaluate long-term results?
- What are the keys to successful management of the process?

This section addresses each of these questions.

WHY DO ENGLISH LANGUAGE PROGRAMS DECIDE TO INNOVATE?

If, as Markee (1997) reports, the majority of attempted innovations eventually fail, why should administrators and faculty in English language programs make a huge commitment in time, energy, and budget to the implementation of innovative projects? Like it or not, White (1987) says, ELT "is a service industry, supplying people with a service—English language teaching—and a commodity—the English language" (p. 211). English language programs, like other service industries, are subject to internal and external stresses that compel them to change. Competition, supply of qualified faculty, changes in student enrollment figures related to world political and economic climates, different educational preparation of new generations of students, demands of stakeholders, and so on are forces that act against comfortable, status-quo complacency and inertia. If that is the case, then it makes sense to understand what contributes to successful change before setting off on a journey fraught with potential pitfalls.

According to De Lano, Riley, and Crookes (1994, p. 491) and Stoller (1995, 1997), a decision to implement innovation may stem from, or be initiated by, multiple sources:

1. dissatisfaction with program management practices (e.g., placement, testing, recruitment)
2. dissatisfaction with current teaching methodology (skills or function based) or an awareness of new and supposedly better teaching practices, curriculum, or materials gained through attendance at conferences or exposure to research in language acquisition and teaching
3. change agents (who may be administrators, faculty, students, outside consultants, or evaluators) whose "task is often to encourage, persuade or push people to change, to adopt an innovation and use it in an appropriate context" (De Lano et al., 1994, p. 491)
4. student needs and desires, expressed formally through mechanisms such as program evaluations and surveys or informally through vocal suggestions or complaints to teachers or coordinators
5. faculty interests, often driven by new hires who have taught different types of courses in previous jobs
6. the need to respond to mandates for change from parent institutions, government regulations, market demands, and so on

Although all of these reasons are to some extent reflected in the chapters in this volume, perceived student needs and demands for change from academic departments in home institutions are paramount. The authors of the chapters clearly served as change agents: Their dedicated service was instrumental in the success of their projects.

WHO SHOULD BE INVOLVED?

As faculty and administrative workloads can increase exponentially when programs are overhauled in the name of progress, it is vital for change agents to develop strategies that encourage broad acceptance and willingness to implement long-term projects. Collaboration, communication, and cooperation are key. Teachers, naturally, are on the front line, and they, along with other stakeholders (including students, heads of departments, sponsors, curriculum developers, and others) play complex roles in ultimately deciding to adopt or resist innovation.

The most important factor researchers point out is that lasting innovation cannot be imposed by higher authority. Bottom-up participation in the change process of all stakeholders, especially faculty and students, is of vital importance. In fact, every contributor to this volume states that involving faculty in developing curricular goals is of utmost importance. Byleen talks of tapping into "the collective experience and wisdom" (p. 214) of the faculty stakeholders, as does Altman. Rawley and Roemer welcome multiple faculty perspectives and differing expertise; Bonfanti and Watkins made satisfying instructor needs part of the curriculum renewal process. Markee (1997), citing Brindley and Hood (1991), says that "teachers must experience innovations firsthand if they are to adopt and incorporate these changes into their pedagogical practice" (p. 43).

White (1987, 1991) stresses the need for a collegial school culture that nurtures staff initiatives and the building of team participation, open communication, and personal investment in curriculum decision making. This claim is supported by De Lano et al. (1994), who state that participants who see a direct benefit from an innovation outweighing personal cost are more apt to support change. They suggest that increased motivation can result from creating incentives "which promote cooperation, as teachers may quickly become disillusioned without evidence that any tangible rewards will be forthcoming for their time and effort" (p. 491). Several rewards discussed in this volume include significant professional development opportunities for faculty (see the chapters by Kırkgöz and by Royal et al.); the development of a communal bank of teaching materials resulting in less pressure on faculty (see Belchamber's chapter); confidence and personal satisfaction gained by presenting work at TESOL (see Rawley and Roemer's chapter); and, in general, program growth leading to greater job security and opportunities to develop and teach elective or content-based courses of particular interest to individual teachers (see Bonfanti and Watkins' chapter). Unfortunately, increased faculty salaries do not appear to be a common result of increased voluntary workload.

Also vital, and often overlooked, is support from higher administration.

Kennedy (1988), mentioned in De Lano et al. (1994), states, "If the head of an educational culture is committed to a change, chances of success can be increased" (p. 491). This often translates into budgetary help and increased support services, plus pressure on the larger academic community to cooperate with a department (e.g., a noncredit IEP) that has lower academic status. Bonfanti and Watkins' chapter details work done in response to the dean of continuing education's desire for their program to grow.

WHAT FACTORS STIMULATE ACCEPTANCE AND IMPLEMENTATION OF A NEW CURRICULUM OR NEW PROCEDURES?

Stoynoff (1991) and Stoller (1997) discuss a 1971 analysis by Rogers and Shoemaker of 1,500 studies of innovation from which they extracted five attributes of innovation that affect whether or not a new idea is successfully adopted:

1. relative advantage: How much better is the new approach than the one it is replacing?
2. compatibility: Is the new practice a consistent outgrowth from past practices, or is it radically different?
3. complexity: Is the innovation easy for faculty or staff to understand and use?
4. trialability: Can the innovation be experimented with for a limited time before the need for widespread adoption?
5. observability: Can others outside the department see the results of the innovation?

Stoller (1997) also speaks of a balanced divergence factor made up of six attributes that help or hinder innovation diffusion. This factor includes two of the above attributes (compatibility with past practice and complexity) along with explicitness, flexibility, originality, and visibility. In her advice to program directors, she looks at all of the above attributes and suggests that a Goldilocks syndrome affects acceptance or rejection of an innovation. When attributes are "sufficiently present—'not too much, not too little, but just right'—and fall comfortably within a perceived zone of innovation, adoption rates are likely to increase" (pp. 43–44). Stoller adds that program administrators should keep in mind two additional factors that help lead to positive results: dissatisfaction with the status quo and viability between the proposed innovation, institutional resources, and student needs. Her trenchant advice: *Practical* and *useful* are key words to keep in mind when trying to persuade faculty to embrace change.

Kennedy (1988, p. 338) speaks of more personal criteria. For an innovation to have the likelihood of establishing itself and thus a chance to achieve long-term impact, participants must feel that the innovation belongs to them. The change agents described in Altman's chapter certainly felt this sense of ownership of the innovation—an updated program to prepare students for the University of Michigan's demanding master of business administration program—and were motivated to provide the best program possible for their clients.

Equally important is the gain/loss calculation, which "assumes that a positive decision to involve oneself actively in any innovation will only be taken if gains accrued as a result of participation outweigh losses" (Kennedy, 1988, p. 340). These gains may include increased job security, better relations with higher administration, improved service to students, or the teacher's desire for increased professional skills or training or for an intellectual challenge. However, not surprisingly, a tangible economic reward is the most important motivation. Losses, which may be significant, include extra hours of voluntary work, the need to learn new skills, and the potential loss of job security if the innovation reveals teacher inadequacies. These, in turn, lead to resistance. "That won't work in my classroom," according to Hutchinson (1992), has the subtext, "I'm scared of trying that in my classroom" (p. 21). The key to dealing with resistance, he says, is to make the first concern getting the process of change right rather than focusing on the ultimate product. Among his guidelines for doing so, he stresses encouraging participants to vocalize their feelings. "So long as resistance remains hidden," he states, "it remains a problem and a potential threat to the success of the change" (p. 21). In their chapter, Beuster and Graupensperger speak tellingly of problems encountered when faculty buy-in was missing, to some extent because faculty were unable to express their concerns and fears when facing a major reorganization of their department.

Sometimes support comes after the work is completed, an unexpected but greatly appreciated reward. For example, Petro's revised English Language Studies Program created such great enthusiasm on campus that the vice provost for graduate studies arranged a commitment for its entire following year's budget.

HOW DO YOU START A SIGNIFICANT INNOVATIVE PROJECT?

As most educators are aware, preparation is the key. White (1987) stresses the importance of allotting time for significant planning and information gathering before jumping into a major innovative project. He suggests starting the process by creating two lists, the first headed *What We Already Know* and the second headed *What We Need to Know*. The former, no small task, obtains information through examination of "existing syllabuses, teaching materials, examination results and test scores, comments from students and other interested parties, ministry reports and proposals, etc." (p. 215). Equally vital in the discovery process is mining unwritten institutional knowledge. White emphasizes the centrality of faculty and administrative participation in the needs assessment stage, both as researchers and as sources of information: Their skills and expertise are "an important resource and, to ensure their involvement and commitment, should be drawn upon" (p. 215).

Many of the contributors to this volume have followed this advice, beginning their projects by conducting a significant needs assessment in order to provide solid evidence that their programs' future health demanded purposeful change. In doing so, they wanted to learn how their standard practices differed from what their stakeholders actually wanted or felt was lacking in current offerings. De Lano et al. (1994), citing Brown (unpublished manuscript) points out the twofold value of data collected during the diagnostic phase:

1. to provide convincing evidence of the need for a change
2. to provide baseline information against which changed program elements, such as goals, methods, or materials, can later be evaluated for effectiveness

Three chapters in this volume illustrate the discovery process. Altman describes a triangulation approach to obtain data from all stakeholders (students, instructors, and content-area faculty and staff). Petro, responding to the University of Rhode Island's newly instituted universitywide writing requirements, consulted extensively with faculty in the Writing Department before adapting an existing course for native speakers to ESL students. And Kırkgöz, whose discovery process survey targeted 1,000 current and former students along with three higher education departments offering English-medium instruction in Çukurova University, reaped an additional benefit: Being involved in data gathering helped faculty members become aware of the extent of existing problems and realize that they could play a role in making change decisions. Kırkgöz encouraged her faculty to review and rewrite the departmental mission statement based on the needs analysis findings. She further encouraged faculty participation in designing course goals and intended outcomes, based on their classroom experience of what progress students could reasonably achieve in a 1-year period.

In their report on recent work in the Philippines, Waters and Vilches (2005) highlight the efficacy of taking an additional step in the preparation process. They created a short in-service training course for senior change agents working on an educational reform initiative. Designed to raise awareness of the issues presented above, the course helped participants gain insight into theoretical and practical aspects of educational change management, along with a greater understanding of the interpersonal skills needed to help teachers and learners move from a skills-based to a content-based curriculum. Although most TESOL educators are not fortunate enough to experience live training, it is clear that the more insights they have from the literature, the more successful they can be in their role as change agents.

HOW DO YOU MANAGE THE ACTUAL PROCESS?

Once a commitment is made to go ahead with a major innovative project, it is important to be as specific as possible about what has to be done, who is going to do it, and when work has to be completed. White (1987, p. 215) cites Everard and Morris's Characteristics of an Effective Plan of Action. The amount of planning and supervisory work assumed in Everard and Morris' short list is, in fact, daunting, and may not be realistic for all projects.

Yet each chapter in this volume provides models and invaluable insights touching each of the list points. Belchamber stresses that her faculty wanted the curriculum to be dynamic and actively used. To this end, faculty engaged in very specific tasks that led to setting weekly course goals and timetables, with accompanying communally written materials. Royal et al. detail a four-phase working plan that stresses a purposeful action plan, target dates, and continuous review and revision. Beuster and Graupensperger provide a reality check on time and task management, and the need for strong leadership in establishing cooperative teamwork.

HOW DO YOU EVALUATE LONG-TERM RESULTS?

Most educators are so happy to finish a major project, such as introducing a new curriculum, that they conveniently forget that, just as preparation was

---

Characteristics of an Effective Plan of Action

(Everard & Morris, 1985, pp. 204–205)

1. It is **purposeful**—the activities are clearly linked to the change goals and priorities.
2. It is **task-specific**—the types of activities involved are clearly identified rather than broadly generalized and responsibility for carrying them out is unambiguously assigned.
3. It is **temporal**—target dates are specified and achievement is monitored.
4. It is **integrated**—the discrete activities are linked to show interdependencies and sequencing networks.
5. It is **adaptable**—there are contingency plans and ways of adapting to unexpected problems, such as time slippage and unforeseen resistance.
6. It is **cost-effective**—in terms of the investment of both time and people.

important before they started, analysis of the result is equally vital. White (1987, p. 216) is adamant: Evaluation, through collection of data, is not simply a final chore—did we succeed or not?—but an ongoing process to be included at every stage of the curriculum redesign (and, by extension, to other aspects of program management). Even before starting, he says, educators need to decide on times and techniques to determine whether interim goals are being met and whether stakeholders' needs are satisfied. In this volume, Byleen presents a 15-year process of curriculum change and refinement that kept the needs of graduate teaching assistants in mind at all times. Experience with the first project helped shape the second, and the second shaped the third.

White (1991) also notes that many people, especially those responsible for developing and implementing a new curriculum, find evaluation threatening. He calls for impartial, confidential, inclusive evaluation, perhaps led by outside evaluators, focusing "on issues and not individuals" (p. 177). Kennedy (1988) further suggests that not only the outcome of the project (such as a new curriculum or improved teacher behavior) be assessed,

> *but the process of innovation itself, the way in which an innovation is introduced to a system through a project, and the stages it passes through, from the identification of a problem to the selection of the innovation and its final incorporation, acceptance, and diffusion. (p. 330)*

In this volume, Kırkgöz discusses a summative evaluation that looked at teachers' and students' perceptions of new curriculum materials and assessment methods, and teachers' evaluation of their professional growth through participation in the project and of the administrative support they had received.

Most educators are familiar with two forms of evaluation: formative (ongoing feedback influences where to go next) and summative (outcomes are checked against original goals to determine success or failure). White (1987, p. 216) points out a third function of evaluation: illuminative. This means educators observe, and then try to explain, unexpected and unintended consequences of the innovations they introduce into their programs. He quotes Parlett and Hamilton (1977):

> *The introduction of an innovation sets off a chain of repercussions throughout the learning milieu. In turn, these unintended consequences are likely to affect the innovation itself, changing its form and moderating its impact. Connecting changes in the learning milieu with the intellectual experience of students is one of the chief concerns for illuminative evaluation. (p. 12)*

Potts and Park's chapter detailing use of Korean graduate students to conduct research presents wonderful examples of surprising, unplanned-for outcomes and powerful results: Formerly shy students ultimately submitted a conference paper on the impact of their focus group participation to the Korean Association of Teachers of English International Conference.

Finally, returning again to White (1991, p. 177), remember that everyone involved in an innovation shares responsibility: administrators who provide funding and support as well as faculty who implement new curricula and methods. All should be credited for effort and hard work, whether or not the effort achieves clear success.

WHAT ARE THE KEYS TO SUCCESSFUL MANAGEMENT OF THE PROCESS?

Stoynoff (1991, pp. 12–13) summarizes best practice by laying out the Ten-Step Formula for Successful Change shown here. This outline of best practices describes the ideal process. Unfortunately, it puts a heavy burden on potential change agents. However, the chapters in this volume make clear that even if change agents get only some steps on this list right and have trouble with others, they can ultimately succeed. Keep these steps in mind as you read the chapters in this volume.

Ten-Step Formula for Successful Change

(Stoynoff, 1991, pp. 12–13)

1. Foster an atmosphere that promotes change.
2. Build consensus by compromising with and co-opting those who resist and reassuring those who are anxious.
3. Instill confidence by demonstrating that you have mastered the details and specifics related to the proposed change.
4. Appreciate the importance of timing—consolidate gains before moving to the next stage of the change process.
5. Adapt proposed changes or innovations to your own particular setting.
6. Adequately communicate with and disseminate information regarding change to all affected individuals and units.
7. Ensure that key administrators and gatekeepers are behind the innovation, if possible, before attempting to broaden support for the proposed change.
8. Then, expand support to like-minded individuals and begin to build coalitions.
9. Build in rewards and incentives to promote cooperation among other units and outside individuals.
10. Finally, prepare for the postadoption period. Ongoing evaluation will facilitate periodic refinements and modifications to the institutionalized change or innovation.

Reasons for Optimism

The revitalization efforts described in this volume belie the data cited earlier that most attempted innovations ultimately fail through inertia, backsliding, or lack of institutional support. They provide evidence that programs can successfully grow and develop. Markee (1997) entreats language teaching professionals "to develop their own critically informed tradition of innovation research and practice" (p. 7). This entails becoming aware of potential problems by studying the literature in educational change management while experiencing and solving problems firsthand. It is the hope of the contributors to this volume that their experience, trials, tribulations, and ultimately successes will encourage programs around the world to achieve their desired goals more easily.

A Collaborative Curriculum Change: Teaming With Challenges

2

VIVETTE BEUSTER AND JENNIFER GRAUPENSPERGER

As teachers, we use group work extensively in our classes because we believe the benefits far outweigh the disadvantages. We tell students to participate, communicate, negotiate, and cooperate. We explain how students can learn from each other, how they need to develop interpersonal skills to have better relationships with others, and how they can share the workload. We explain that two heads are better than one and that the whole is more than the sum of its parts. And we teach students that they sometimes have to sacrifice individual goals for the good of the group. Indeed, we believe students should work productively in groups.

But what happens when teachers decide to transform their curriculum as a team? Do they practice what they preach to their students? Do things work out as planned when the shoe is on the other foot?

In this chapter, we explore a teamwork approach to curriculum renewal in an intensive ESL environment. We focus on the challenges, failures, disappointments, and successes of a team of teachers as they planned and executed the practical tasks and dealt with the interpersonal dynamics related to curriculum change. Finally, we explain what worked and what we would approach differently if we were to undertake a change process again.

Context

THE PROGRAM, INSTRUCTORS, AND STUDENTS

Green River Community College (GRCC), situated in a tranquil rural area surrounded by natural forest, is located in Auburn, Washington, in the United States, south of Seattle near Mount Rainier. This 2-year college provides degrees, technical diplomas, and certificates for local and international students. The Intensive English as a Second Language (IESL) department has offices and classrooms on campus but is a separate financial entity and determines its own standards, goals, and policies.

The IESL department is part of International Programs (IP), headed by the executive director, who is also responsible for overseas marketing and recruitment and for international student advising and housing. The IESL department has a director; two administrative assistants; five nontenured, full-time instructors; several part-time instructors (determined by enrollment); and tutors (depending on student needs). Both female and male instructors teach in the program. They have master's degrees, speak several languages, and have many years' teaching experience in the United States and elsewhere.

A large percentage of IESL students take academic classes at GRCC after completing the IESL program. The number of students in the IESL department ranges from 50 to 170, with high student enrollments in the fall tapering off in the summer. Female and male students come primarily from Southeast Asia, and a few come from Europe, South America, and the Middle East. The majority of students are young (18–22), but a few as old as 70 have attended classes. Most students are community college or university bound, some come to finish high school, and others want to attend a U.S. institution for a few months to improve their English. The students often have advanced-level knowledge of grammar rules and can read well, but they struggle with listening comprehension, have limited vocabulary, and experience problems applying grammar knowledge appropriately when writing and speaking. They prefer being in classes that have fewer than 20 students.

NEW EMPLOYEE STRUCTURE

In 2000, the IESL program director, hired a few months before we became full-time instructors, proposed an innovative employee structure for the department. The planned reorganization involved creating a three-tiered system. The director, the sole occupant of the first tier, would manage the teachers and administrative staff. The second tier would consist of a team of five full-time employees. Each would receive, in addition to a full teaching load, a specialized portfolio of responsibilities related to an important component of the program. The director designed this structure specifically to develop leadership, promote teamwork, and encourage innovation. The portfolio areas were Course Standards and Exit Criteria, Campus Liaison, Student Placement and Assessment, Electives and Academic Bridge Courses, and Technology. The third tier would consist of part-time faculty who, in addition to teaching, would help the full-time instructors fulfill various curriculum-related duties.

When the new structure was in place, several teachers were bursting with creative ideas and ready for change. One of us (Beuster), the employee responsible for course standards and exit criteria, initiated a curriculum change process that would take several months to complete and quickly found an ally in the other (Graupensperger), the employee charged with the campus liaison portfolio.

The Need for Change

When the director created the new portfolio structure, the department was growing steadily. Nevertheless, there was constant pressure from the college to recruit more overseas students because IP provides much-needed supplemental income when the state's ever-dwindling funds are not enough to make ends meet. Because recruiting more students required different and innovative products to offer in a highly competitive market, some members of the department realized it was time for change.

To start the process of questioning the status quo, the IESL director conducted a meeting during which instructors jointly sketched out a new direction for the department. They studied other college program offerings, evaluated the existing IESL program, and made proposals for change. From the notes, it became clear that a curriculum overhaul was a priority and that all teachers thought the program required improvement. In particular, teachers felt the program needed diverse and exciting offerings to distinguish it from competitors. In addition, some felt academic standards had to be raised. Students' low college placement scores confirmed reports from IESL graduates and college faculty that students were not especially well prepared for academic course work or class participation. By the end of the meeting, the teachers were convinced that they had to scrutinize curriculum content and examine current teaching approaches in order to develop a more effective academic preparation program.

Planning the Change

The planning process involved several important phases (see Phases in Planning the Change) and laid a solid foundation for further progress. The department completed all planning steps in a relatively short time, initially helping keep motivation high and maintain momentum.

PHASE 1: DEVELOPING A MISSION STATEMENT

The department wrote an initial new mission statement describing the learning environment and methods of serving the students. The director displayed it prominently in the office—a vital first step in keeping teachers focused.

PHASE 2: CONDUCTING A COMPREHENSIVE NEEDS ASSESSMENT

The next step involved a thorough needs assessment involving international students, academic instructors, the marketing department, and IESL teachers. Because customer satisfaction drives enrollments, a logical place to start was the students. IESL teachers contributed ideas to the needs assessment questionnaire, and all current IESL students completed the survey. The questionnaire was comprehensive and elicited information about instructional techniques, course content, placement and assessment, and personal learning goals. For example, it asked students what instructional methods

	Phases in Planning the Change	
Phase	**Major Tasks**	**Subtasks**
1	Develop a mission statement	Write an initial mission statement
2	Conduct a comprehensive needs assessment	Survey current students Interview alumni Survey academic and IESL faculty Interview the marketing department
3	Analyze the needs assessment data	Analyze and interpret the data Specify priorities
4	Revise the mission statement	Update the mission statement after analysis of needs assessment results
5	Address fundamental teaching issues	Identify underlying issues that might become roadblocks later in the process Start the process of resolving issues through discussion and negotiation
6	Develop a curriculum action plan	Set departmental aims Develop and agree on an action plan

were helpful or not, what curriculum assignments helped them learn, what skills they felt were most important, and what their personal goals were.

In addition, select teachers conducted several focus-group sessions with IESL alumni. The focus groups elicited information about what students found useful and not useful in the program, what they wished they had learned, how many hours they would have liked to have studied English per day, and what changes they would propose.

Academic instructors completed an e-mail survey. They commented on whether international students were able to meet the instructional standards in their classes, listed the three most important English or learning skills students lacked, and explained to what extent international students were able to interact with U.S. students.

In a focus group, the marketing department responded to four questions:

1. What courses or programs not currently offered do existing and potential students request?
2. What specific language-related services not currently offered do students request?
3. What do advisers learn from students that might have implications for the new curriculum?
4. Which current curriculum aspects satisfy students?

At this stage, the department clearly had a lot of information to digest, and it was time to get together to analyze the needs assessment results and plan the curriculum change process. One of us (Beuster) designed and executed a series of 2-hour work sessions over 1 week. During these planning sessions, the department made several crucial decisions and compiled a curriculum action plan that was to guide the department for many months.

PHASE 3: ANALYZING THE NEEDS ASSESSMENT DATA

Before the weeklong planning sessions, the IESL teachers analyzed the feedback. They listed significant findings in three categories: the IESL curriculum (oral skills, grammar, reading, and writing); a potentially expanded curriculum (elective and bridge courses); and teaching methodology. They also looked at the needs assessment from a teacher's perspective and added several items not mentioned by the students. During the weeklong planning sessions, the department discussed the teachers' analyses and reached a number of conclusions that would direct the change process.

The current student survey determined that more than 80% of the students were taking English for academic purposes. Furthermore, it provided useful information about students' needs. After careful analysis of all data collected, the department cam to the following conclusions:

1. Students wanted academic preparation for college. They did not specifically want to develop business English or English for everyday purposes or life skills.
2. Academic standards needed to be higher to prepare students more for the challenges in academic college classes (e.g., the last level would serve as a bridge into 100-level and higher level college courses).
3. Whole language development and integration of language skills were a more productive way to study language.
4. The program needed to focus more on developing productive skills, such as oral skills and writing, while not neglecting reading, listening, and grammar.
5. There needed to be core classes to develop core skills and electives to give students more choices.
6. There needed to be more variety in course offerings.
7. Classes needed to be longer to get more work done. More time would allow the teachers to cover more material in greater depth.
8. When there was more than one section of a class per subject in a level, the exit criteria, course textbooks, and course content needed to be the same for all students to provide them with a common experience.
9. A student would be placed in only one level at a time. For example, a student would not be in Grammar Level 1, Listening/Speaking Level 2, and Reading/Writing Level 3. A placement test aligned with the level exit criteria and teachers passing or failing students uniformly based on exit criteria would ensure greater uniformity of ability among students in the same level.

In addition, through discussions and e-mail, college academic instructors indicated that they would (a) welcome an improved IESL program, (b) continue to communicate their needs to the IESL department, and (c) support the IESL department in developing an improved product.

PHASE 4: REVISING THE MISSION STATEMENT

During the weeklong planning sessions, the department updated its initial mission statement to reflect student requests and teacher intent more accurately. In keeping with the needs analysis findings, the final version specified greater focus on academic preparation for students and promised to hold them to higher standards.

PHASE 5: ADDRESSING FUNDAMENTAL TEACHING ISSUES

Before the IESL teachers could start making changes to curriculum content and teaching approaches, they had to discuss three fundamental but thorny issues that had surfaced long before the need for change had been identified. Initial debates centered on the process and speed of the development of student language skills, student placement and promotion, and teacher autonomy. During the weeklong planning sessions, the department once again engaged in discussions in an attempt to resolve these issues. Although the teachers did not fully settle disputes at this stage, they made some preliminary decisions and continued thinking about and working toward better solutions.

Development of Language Skills

A pressing problem facing the IESL department was how to develop complex language skills to college proficiency levels in a short time (one to five quarters). This was not a new problem and was certainly not unique to the IESL department. Intensive English programs know that students often come to the United States with unrealistic perceptions about their language skills and see attempts to improve them as a waste of time and money. Some teachers knew the key would be to make students aware of the skills they needed to succeed in academic classes, to show them how much they did and did not know, and to provide a more strenuous and challenging program. Others suggested that it was an impossible task and that maintaining the status quo was best. Yet another group proposed consulting the literature to search for different approaches to language learning.

Teachers asked many questions about effective language teaching. For example, how could teachers integrate grammar more with writing, speaking, and reading activities? Some teachers started thinking about how to recycle vocabulary across skill areas to ensure deeper learning. Others thought about integrating all language skills, and a few tried to provide an appropriate content base for language development for academic-program-bound adults.

Student Placement and Promotion

Lack of uniformity of student ability in the same class is often problematic. It is a predicament for students as well as teachers. In extreme cases, teachers have to make decisions about whether to teach to the lowest level student at the expense of the most advanced-level students or whether to teach to the most proficient and hope the others will follow. Often teachers try to help each group equally. When there is a great disparity in ability, more advanced-level students frequently complain that weaker students drag the class down.

Disparity in student ability in the same IESL class often raised a number of difficult questions: Should teachers promote students based on ability or effort? Should there be exit tests? How can teachers set exit criteria for each level? What is the intermediate or advanced level? Should a student be in one level, or should teachers place the student in different levels in different skill areas? How can teachers challenge students but still have fair expectations?

Analyzing the problems, some teachers felt the most important was the lack of a matched set of exit criteria for each level, often resulting in teachers either over- or underpreparing students for the next level. There was no unified and organized way to promote students because of the lack of teacher coordination. Teachers often observed that the placement test was a more reliable method of identifying students' correct level than promotion from the previous level—a sure sign that something was wrong.

Teacher Autonomy

Some teachers felt a unified approach to teaching within and between levels would benefit students; however, they understood that it required teachers to give up some autonomy and be more responsible to the program and each other. Others felt that they did not want fixed sets of learning objectives that might cramp their teaching styles. They also feared that a unified approach would require more time in the office to discuss student progress and to coordinate lessons with colleagues teaching the same level. In addition, some agreed that greater cooperation would introduce additional challenges of persuasion, negotiation, and cooperation among peers. Some saw this as an opportunity to grow whereas others felt uncomfortable with the potential increase in work and emotional stress.

These three issues were difficult to resolve and led to a series of discussions and compromises over time. Although the department discussed them openly during the weeklong planning sessions, some individuals were so entrenched in their positions that final solutions emerged only later, after a long and difficult process. For example, when teachers sought a new curriculum model, they first attempted to resolve the language development controversy by choosing an integrated curriculum that would develop all language skills simultaneously. In this instance, the department made a decision through a majority vote. Later, however, facing a crucial deadline and the possibility of a key player throwing the change process into disarray, the full-time instructors compromised and adopted a partially integrated model (see the section Selecting a Decision-Making Process later in the chapter).

The second issue, placing and promoting students, was resolved only after vigorous debate over whether teachers should promote students because they could do the work or because they had tried hard. In the end, the majority chose the use of a set of coordinated and clearly defined exit criteria over exit tests and agreed that the criteria would be a more flexible and meaningful option. Teacher autonomy, the final issue, was the most difficult to deal with. After emotional discussions over many months, the department finally settled on the idea that they could coordinate teaching efforts by agreeing on broad but fixed teaching and learning aims for each course. In concept, teachers felt they could support these goals; however, it was only long after implementation that most teachers saw the value of teaching coordination.

PHASE 6: DEVELOPING A CURRICULUM ACTION PLAN

During the weeklong planning sessions, the teachers tackled the final phase in the planning process. After interpreting the needs assessment results and battling with the three thorny issues described above, the department used its mission statement as a starting point and formulated general departmental aims that focused on real and not presumed needs. The aims addressed (a) what the department was preparing the students for, (b) what it wanted them to be proficient in, and (c) how they would best learn English.

Guided by the needs assessment information and department goals, IESL teachers then considered various curriculum models. After much deliberation, the department compiled a new curriculum, borrowing from various models and adapting them to incorporate suggestions from the student needs assessment, IESL and academic teachers, and marketers (see the section Implementing the Change below for more details on the structure). Finally, the whole department developed a barebones action plan (see Curriculum Action Plan, page 24). With this important phase complete, the team was ready to start the change process.

Implementing the Change

Instructors who carry full teaching loads have little extra time to make major curriculum changes. This was true for the IESL department, and, as a result, the department decided to spread the work out over one academic year. The amount of time used to develop the new curriculum turned out to be a double-edged sword. On the one hand, individuals needed time to put careful thought into their different activities, but on the other hand, the department lost momentum. Even though there were frequent meetings, people often forgot the context and details of decisions made months or weeks earlier. Individuals changed their minds without considering previously discussed and agreed-on rationales. Some people lost interest. However, more time also meant that those who were resistant to change could get familiar with new ideas and try them out.

Curriculum Action Plan

Program Element and Activities	Responsible Committees	Milestones
By End of Spring		
1. Reading/Writing and Listening/Speaking: Build multilevel matrices • Course goals • Exit criteria • Content outline	Reading/Writing and Listening/Speaking	Goals by Week 3 Exit criteria by Week 8 Outline by Week 11
2. Support/elective courses • Investigate other programs' offerings • Compile list of potential course offerings	Support/Elective	Report on other programs by Week 5 List of offerings compiled by Week 11
3. Placement and diagnostic tests: Investigate different placement methods	Placement/Diagnostics	Report on different methods by Week 11
By End of Summer		
1. Reading/Writing and Listening/Speaking • Develop content, instructional methods, and learning activities • Investigate teaching materials and textbooks	Reading/Writing and Listening/Speaking	Content, methods, and activities by Week 8 Materials and texts by Week 11
2. Support/elective courses: Build multilevel matrices • Course goals • Exit criteria • Content outline	Support/Elective	Goals by Week 3 Exit criteria by Week 8 Outline by Week 11
3. Placement and diagnostic tests: Start developing placement tests and diagnostic tests that are in line with exit criteria for Reading/Writing and Listening/Speaking	Placement/Diagnostics	Proposals by Week 5 Prototypes by Week 11
By End of Fall		
1. Reading/Writing and Listening/ Speaking • Refine content, instructional methods, and learning activities • Select teaching materials and textbooks	Reading/Writing and Listening/Speaking	Content, methods, and activities by Week 8 Materials and texts by Week 11

continued on p. 25

Curriculum Action Plan (cont.)		
Program Element and Activities	**Responsible Committees**	**Milestones**
2. Support/elective courses • Develop content, instructional methods, and learning activities • Select teaching materials and textbooks	Support/Elective	Content, methods, and activities by Week 8 Materials and texts by Week 11
3. Placement and diagnostic tests: Finalize tests that are in line with exit criteria for Reading/Writing and Listening/Speaking	Placement/Diagnostics	First review by Week 5 Second review by Week 11
By End of Winter		
1. Try out all materials and tests	All committees	First review by Week 5 Second review by Week 11
2. Implement new curriculum	All committees	First review by Week 5 Second review by Week 11

Over time, new courses took shape as course goals, exit criteria, and course-grade weightings were developed. IESL instructors met with academic faculty to determine appropriate program exit levels. They investigated and selected possibilities for new textbooks, developed new schedules, created booklists, and renamed courses. To keep the momentum going, key individuals held meetings to encourage instructor participation and to deliver training sessions to prepare instructors for the changes. At the same time, team members communicated with key stakeholders such as marketing personnel, advisers, campus administration, and students. Before implementing the curriculum, designated individuals briefed students on the changes and implications. They also held advising sessions for students with special needs.

The mission statement, program goals, and thorough needs assessment guided the curriculum change process. Whenever there was confusion or dissention about direction or the need for specific tasks, it was useful to remind department members of the source of the information. The department based changes, such as putting more curriculum time and teaching effort toward developing language production skills like speaking and writing, on specific information from students and academic instructors.

The action plan with specific tasks and deadlines provided focus and direction throughout the process. Although the department adjusted time-lines and tasks, the original plan stayed mostly intact. Team leaders worked tirelessly to keep people informed, motivated, and on track. They wanted the new program to be successful and achieved the goal in spite of huge challenges. With the help of an action plan and the determination of a few teachers, the curriculum work was completed and implemented on time—a great feat given the workload and difficulties encountered along the way.

STANDARDIZING EXIT CRITERIA AND COURSES

The department overhauled the entire curriculum. Three committees (Reading/Writing, Listening/Speaking, and Support/Elective) carefully planned exit criteria for each level starting with the highest (academic preparation) and cascading down to the lowest (basic). Committee members considered language skills for each level and determined the order in which students should learn them. Consulting with academic staff to establish entry requirements for their courses and then working from the highest IESL level backward ensured a smoother transition for students from the IESL program to academic classes. The resulting learning objectives also challenged students more at lower levels. Having a committee work on all course levels within each integrated skills area minimized the possibility of underpreparing students for the next level.

A few key individuals served on all three committees to ensure that skill areas would complement each other. Thus, the exit criteria and learning objectives were not only coordinated from one level to the next but also matched to other skill areas within the same level. The final product was a curriculum guide folder for each instructor providing a complete set of exit criteria with course goals, learning objectives, textbook recommendations, and assignment-grade weightings for each skill area within each level.

CHANGING THE CURRICULUM STRUCTURE

The initial plan was to move away from a curriculum that developed four discrete skills separately to one that integrated all language skills. As instructors started thinking about the implications of such an approach, some got cold feet. A fully integrated curriculum would have required teachers to coordinate teaching efforts weekly and spend more time with the same students. Many instructors felt naturally drawn to this approach whereas some vehemently opposed it.

As a compromise, the team settled for a partially integrated curriculum. Instead of having classes with special focuses that integrated all skills simultaneously, the curriculum now had three classes: Grammar, Listening/Speaking, and Reading/Writing (see Progression From the Old to the Final

Progression From the Old to the Final Curriculum		
Old Curriculum: Separate and Discrete Skill Development	**Planned Curriculum: Fully Integrated Skill Development**	**Final Curriculum: Partially Integrated Skill Development**
One 50-minute class per day, 5 days a week, for each of the following: • Grammar • Listening/Speaking • Reading • Writing	All skills fully integrated every day (3½ hours) but with a special focus on • Listening/Speaking (3 days per week: Mon., Wed., Fri.) • Reading/Writing (2 days per week: Tues., Thurs.)	Partial integration of skills through three courses: • Grammar—oral and writing (50 minutes) • Listening/Speaking—includes writing and reading (75 minutes) • Reading/Writing—includes listening and speaking (75 minutes)
No uniform or coordinated integration of skills; grammar and writing voluntarily integrated by individual teachers	Skills integrated through • Uniform exit criteria • Vocabulary and grammar • Common course content • Teacher coordination	Skills integrated through • Uniform exit criteria • Vocabulary and grammar • Common course content (voluntary) • Teacher coordination (voluntary)

Curriculum). Teachers who taught Reading/Writing would integrate reading and writing skills in the same class. When possible, the Reading/Writing teacher or the Listening/Speaking teacher would also teach the grammar support class at the same level to ensure integration of grammar skills into a core skill area. Teachers were encouraged but not forced to coordinate learning activities for students in the same level for different skill areas.

Although this compromise was not ideal, the committees who worked on exit criteria and learning objectives kept the integration goals in mind and designed exit criteria and objectives so that vocabulary, grammar patterns, and language skills could be reiterated in the same level and reviewed in the next one. These exit criteria and learning objectives succeeded in giving individual teachers the freedom to choose methods they wanted without weakening the careful construction of student learning and coordination of teaching efforts. All could live with this compromise.

PREPARING THE STUDENTS FOR THE CHANGE

Due to careful planning and execution of essential tasks, students made a smooth transition from the old to the new curriculum. Teachers conducted information sessions with students at various stages. They identified students who would be most affected by the changes and explored solutions with them. They constantly provided information and sought commitment from IP marketers to ensure effective advertising of the new product and accurate student advising.

Results and Lessons Learned

Feedback, systematically obtained over the 2 years after implementation, was very positive. Academic instructors reported that students completing the IESL program before starting their academic classes were better prepared than international and U.S. students who did not go through the IESL program. According to them, IESL graduates demonstrated mature study skills, delivered professional presentations, knew how to conduct research and write successful papers, coped with the demands of group work and class participation, and focused on their academic goals. International students testified to teachers and students how much they benefited from the new program. Most importantly, students exiting the IESL program took the college proficiency test and consistently placed in higher levels than their counterparts had done before the curriculum overhaul took place.

The old saying "When the plan hits reality, reality wins" was true for the IESL department. What we originally planned to do and what we ended up doing were different in many respects. Some instructors felt we had revised and compromised too much whereas others felt we should have been more flexible. Some were disappointed with the amount of work we accomplished whereas others realized that change takes time and that *No* sometimes means *Not now*. The discussion here gives a sense of the lessons learned through the successes, compromises, and missteps and setbacks the department experienced during the process. We caution future change agents to examine their own beliefs and assumptions and invite them to consider whether a team approach is the best way to proceed. We then list potential problems and recommended solutions.

IDENTIFYING AND EXAMINING PERSONAL BELIEFS AND ASSUMPTIONS

Curriculum change involves a number of unforeseen challenges. By identifying and examining potential roadblocks preemptively, departments can reduce the number of challenges significantly. As team leaders, we operated with a definite set of beliefs and assumptions about teamwork and management's role, but at the time we were so involved with processes and tasks that we did not stop to question them. We know now that when beliefs and assumptions are not brought to the surface and considered carefully, a large number of unexpected problems can result, some so serious that they can easily derail even the best plans and intentions.

Not all our assumptions led to challenges of equal proportion, but all generated difficulties. Although it may be easy for you to look at the list below and predict problems, keep in mind that we did not foresee the need to question our basic principles, nor did we have a list at the time. Inexperience led us to believe or assume (mistakenly, in most instances) the following:

1. The department as a whole would develop the curriculum (a consensus-driven democratic process) with change leaders to steer the course.
2. All IESL teachers really wanted change and would be willing to work toward a better product.
3. All coworkers wanted to be involved at all times, were willing to put in extra effort, and would participate productively in decision making.
4. The department would make curriculum changes based on what was good for the students and program as a whole. Individual teacher needs and preferences would be of secondary importance.
5. The department would make changes based on a clear assessment of needs and not for the sake of change alone.
6. The marketing department would provide guidance about requests and requirements for courses from potential students, would support an improved product, and would be committed to selling the new product with confidence.
7. Top management would hand over authority; hold people accountable for responsibilities; stay involved with the team; and provide direction, advice, and resources.

One of our biggest assumptions related to teamwork. We assumed that the entire department had to work and make decisions together all the time. With hindsight, we now know that it was important to involve various people at important stages, but in our case, it was too time-consuming and complicated at times to change the entire curriculum by using one big team. Before embarking on the change process, change agents would do well to examine whether involving the entire department is the best way to proceed or even whether to use a team approach at all. A prerequisite of adopting a team approach is careful consideration of coworkers' abilities and levels of willingness. Before jumping to the conclusion that teamwork is the best way to proceed, future leaders might want to ask if potential team members are willing to

1. work constructively and productively with others
2. discuss ideas and work fully and openly

3. listen to others sincerely
4. find solutions to shared problems
5. accept compromise when it is in the interest of the group
6. share the workload and deliver on promises
7. try out new methods and give the outcome a fair chance
8. assume roles of leaders, followers, or peers depending on the circumstances

If we had used this checklist, we might have avoided some unnecessary complications along the way and saved a lot of time and energy.

MAKING VALUABLE DISCOVERIES THROUGH MISSTEPS AND SETBACKS

In addition to questioning underlying assumptions and beliefs, and before successful change can take place, change agents should (a) take the time to think about and plan how to allocate responsibilities carefully; (b) commit personally to a systematic team-building process; and (c) research, select, install, and use a uniform way of making group decisions.

Allocating Responsibility

Allocating team member responsibility for various tasks requires an astute assessment of others' abilities and priorities and a keen appreciation of the aims and outcomes of the project. It also requires an understanding of how individual contributions may affect the whole group and the project. Therefore, it is important to think not only about talents and experience but also about the context in which potential team members will have to function. For example, someone might be particularly skilled in a crucial task area but be incapable of working with others. On the other hand, a capable manager may be young or have few years' service at the institution. When such an individual has to lead a project, it might disrupt the power dynamics of the existing structure. Team members with longer work records may overtly or covertly question or test the new leader's abilities, wasting valuable work time. Consequently, the director must make a plan to prepare the department for the changed structure and sincerely attempt to help members deal with the reality of the change.

An example from our own change process illustrates the danger of not allocating responsibilities carefully. The three-tiered structure in the IESL department produced complications for the curriculum change team. During normal working hours, individuals knew their roles and spheres of influence, but when all department members had to work as a curriculum change team under new leaders, problems emerged. For example, as a working member of the team, the director sometimes had to be a follower and not the leader. Adjunct faculty members had to follow the lead of full-time instructors, not the director, and new full-time instructors sometimes had to lead other full-time instructors who had more seniority. A few individuals felt uncomfortable with these temporary roles, and the resulting feelings of insecurity and resentment led to acts that undermined the process and produced counterproductive competition.

To avoid these kinds of problems, we suggest that before program directors delegate the curriculum change process to a new team with new leaders, thereby disturbing existing formal and informal relationships and hierarchies, they think very carefully about allocation of responsibilities and authority within the department. Reallocation of duties and roles can cause major conflicts among members within existing power structures, and directors have to foresee and deal with them. For instance, directors have to examine their own insecurities, consider whether they are willing to hand over decision-making powers with authority, and decide what new roles they will play. Furthermore, they should think about potential rivalries among employees and ways to minimize them. Only then should they decide how much authority to give new leaders with new responsibilities. Directors have to define these responsibilities and limits of authority clearly (in writing if possible), announce them publicly in the department, and adhere to them. Most importantly, they have to support the leaders and not undermine or interfere with the teamwork process.

When making work assignments, leaders should also consider team member skills, interests, and needs. Furthermore, regular review of team leaders' and members' individual and team performance is vital because all need to reflect on successes and learn from mistakes. Finally, leaders should make every effort to work out problems with each team member, but if things do not improve, leaders should not hesitate to remove destructive individuals who deliberately and repeatedly undermine team cohesion and work progress.

Building a Team

Individuals need to learn how to function in a team. Just putting people into a group does not instantly create trust, mutual respect, cooperation, and open discussion. Cooperating, discussing difficult issues openly, and showing respect for others' ideas are all skills that team members can develop. Trust emerges only once these skills are fully functioning and individuals learn that they can rely on each other for support and constructive criticism.

We learned useful lessons about working with other people. In Sartre's powerful play *No Exit* (1955), he writes that "Hell is—other people" (p. 47), and the implication is that as much as others cause us frustration and pain, we create confusion and despair for them. We discovered that working closely with others demanded a level of self-awareness and team process responsiveness that members sometimes had to develop deliberately and systematically. For example, a few individuals in the department had needs and held opinions that they did not disclose. They wanted to maintain individual teacher authority for class curricula, liked the old curriculum but were not willing to say so in light of opposition, were not interested in working as a team, and resented extra work. Instead of discussing these issues openly, they relied on avoidance strategies such as false buy-in, delay tactics, unconstructive criticism, and unrealistic demands that frustrated and slowed the team down. It took some of their colleagues a long time to figure out what was going on and even longer to find appropriate ways to deal with their behavior.

We would advise team leaders to try to understand that team building takes time and that they should set the tone for cooperation and respect within the team. They can set the stage by creating a common goal, establishing ground rules for teamwork, and allocating work according to skills and interests. In addition, leaders should build in time at the beginning to help members learn how to function as a team. They should ensure full discussion of concerns, encourage everyone to listen carefully to each other, be willing to help people explore alternative solutions fully, and give all participants an opportunity to participate equally and perform well. People fear change and the unknown; therefore, leaders should encourage members to express those fears openly and share expectations often. Leaders should also seek real buy-in at every stage. Finally, it is important to review progress and celebrate successes regularly. Over time, these actions create trust, which in turn speeds up the work process later.

Selecting a Decision-Making Process

The importance of installing a decision-making process before any change process takes place should not be underestimated. Sometimes program directors and team leaders are naïve enough to think that if adults are able to discuss ideas rationally, the best ones will prevail. Unfortunately, this is not always true, especially when decisions involve changing deeply held beliefs and ways of operating. A decision-making process should be flexible enough to deal with minor and major decisions and, above all, provide a tool to help all people involved arrive at a decision they feel comfortable with. Of course, if the team can make its first major decision—that is, decide what method to use to make future decisions—there will be fewer roadblocks ahead.

We learned that a team has to develop a decision-making model at the beginning and use it. By default, the department selected a form of majority rule that entailed making decisions without full discussion of issues, resulting in disenfranchisement of individuals at key stages. When people felt left out or sensed others were not listening to them, some started acting as if they had no stake in the outcome. Feelings of resentment and anger took over, and potentially productive players became actively resistant, causing dynamic members to slow down in order to deal with unpleasant situations.

With the benefit of hindsight, we realize that not everybody in the department wants to be or has to be involved in the curriculum change process all the time. It may be more effective to nominate a smaller team to do most of the work. The team members can allocate and coordinate work with others and consult colleagues when making key decisions. Unanimous decisions are not always achievable, but people need to feel others have consulted and sincerely listened to them. To aid decision making, leaders need to provide alternatives and discuss their advantages and disadvantages. When people can consider different options, they become pragmatic about what the team can realistically achieve and how to minimize problems. Leaders should document all decisions because records become the collective memory that keeps the process on track.

Final Thoughts on Using Teamwork in Program Revitalization

Curriculum renewal through teamwork is fraught with risk; however, we do not want to leave the impression that departments should avoid teamwork. Changing the curriculum as a team can be destructive, or it can be the best thing your department has ever done. The outcome depends on the extent to which you are willing to ask hard questions and deal with difficult situations directly, openly, and promptly.

In our case, the department successfully achieved its main goal through teamwork, something one or two individuals could not have done alone. Teamwork also had a number of unexpected advantages. Those who stayed engaged developed professionally in ways they could not have imagined at the outset. In addition to learning from each other about teaching and curriculum design, they learned about leadership, project management, and human relationships—all vital skills for the continued growth of the department. Moreover, when fully engaged, team members produced superior work in record time. During these moments, they discovered camaraderie that motivated and spurred them on to greater things, reminding them of the reasons they so strongly believe in teaching their students how to work in groups.

Revitalizing and Strengthening an ESL Program: Meeting the Needs of Students and the Host Institution

3

PHIL BONFANTI AND MOLLY WATKINS

The ESL Center at Mississippi State University (MSU), in the United States, is a self-supporting academic unit within the Division of Academic Outreach and Continuing Education. It offers four academic programs:

1. the intensive English language program (IELP) for nonadmitted (noncredit) MSU students
2. the credit English language program for admitted (credit) MSU students
3. specialized (noncredit) group programs created for universities or other organizations in other countries
4. the (noncredit) eGrammar Series of online distance grammar courses

To complement the academic programming, the ESL Center offers a comprehensive culture program to serve the needs of all ESL students. Currently, the Center has a conversation partner program, an alumni connections program, a community connections program, and weekly cultural event programming. In addition to active participation by international students, the number of U.S. students who want to be involved in these programs is rising.

Ten percent of the IELP students have the goal of applying to a degree program at MSU. The other students are primarily interested in learning English to be more successful in their home countries. Student retention is high, as students typically stay an average of three 8-week sessions (not including short-term group students), with many staying more than 1 year. Although several students have transferred to degree programs since 2005, few students have transferred to another intensive English language program.

Although now strong, the ESL Center was not always so. Beginning operation in 1991, it experienced only modest growth through its first 8 years, so that by the summer of 1999 it still had an enrollment of fewer than 20 students. Since then, the Center has more than doubled its student population to an average enrollment of more than 50 and has become an important academic support unit to the host institution. How were we, the two administrators who have managed the Center since 1999, along with the faculty, able to revitalize the program? We began by looking at the Center's situation to determine the direction it would take based on the needs of the host institution. Every decision that molded the current form of the Center was based on the following questions:

- Why does MSU want or need an ESL Center?
- What do the current and potential students want and need?
- How can the ESL Center meet these needs?

To determine the answer to these questions, we held discussions with university administrators, academic deans, and faculty as well as formal and informal interviews and discussions with students, past and present. Based on the information gathered, we determined that MSU needed an ESL Center to support the other academic departments on campus and to provide cultural diversity. The response of the ESL Center at MSU was to (a) create a strong academic program and (b) build strong ties to the university.

Revitalizing the Program, Pre–September 11, 2001

EARLY EFFORTS

By the spring semester of 1999, the ESL Center had grown modestly. Two managers had guided the Center's growth over this 8-year period. Under the first manager, the Center was known as the American Language and Culture Program (ALCP). Housed in the Division of Continuing Education, the program was designed to teach U.S. language and culture to foreign business executives. During this period, the program enrolled small numbers of students. In 1993, a new manager took over the program, and in the fall of that year, he developed a plan of action that included three major initiatives: (a) development of a new curriculum, (b) marketing and expansion efforts, and (c) professional development of the ALCP staff.

Sample Class Schedule From Redesigned Curriculum, 1993			
	Level		
	Beginning	Intermediate	Advanced
10:00–11:50 a.m.	Literacy	Literacy	Literacy
Noon–12:50 p.m.	Lunch		
1:00–2:50 p.m.	Oral/Aural Skills	Oral/Aural Skills	Oral/Aural Skills

Curriculum Development

The manager developed the new curriculum in coordination with the TESL program in the university's Department of English. This program offers students the opportunity to take 12 hours of TESL courses at the undergraduate or graduate level, culminating in a certificate attached most often to an undergraduate degree in education or a graduate degree in English. The new ESL curriculum consisted of two courses, approximately 2 hours in length, at three levels each (see Sample Class Schedule From Redesigned Curriculum, 1993). The morning course focused on literacy skills, and the afternoon course focused on oral/aural skills. The literacy skills course contained writing, reading, and grammar components. The oral/aural communications skills course contained listening, speaking, and pronunciation components. Each level had competencies that needed to be met before a student could move to the next level. Proficiency exams were given in approximately 8-week intervals, five times a year.

Marketing and Expansion

While revising the curriculum in early 1993, the manager also undertook an overhaul of his marketing efforts. The new marketing and expansion efforts focused on three major areas: (a) revising application papers and processes, (b) getting the ALCP's name into overseas advisory offices around the world, and (c) generating a stronger identity for the ALCP on campus.

These efforts involved revising the application form to make it easier to apply to the program, mailing ALCP promotional material to overseas advisory offices, and informing university advisers about the existence of the ALCP as well as the conditional admission policy. This policy allows graduate students with Test of English as a Foreign Language (TOEFL) scores lower than those required for admission to be admitted to a program with the understanding that they would complete ALCP courses. The noncredit ALCP courses were offered concurrently through the English Department as credit-bearing, pass/fail courses for conditionally admitted students. The policy did not extend to undergraduates because the state Institution of Higher Learning Board set undergraduate admission requirements for all state institutions whereas individual institutions set graduate admissions requirements.

Professional Development Initiatives

The third set of initiatives taken in 1993, which focused on professional development, included requiring ALCP instructors to have an appropriate educational background (a bachelor's in English or foreign language instruction and preferably a master's) and to be active in professional associations such as TESOL.

These three initiatives helped grow the program over the next 5 years (1993–1998) from a handful of students to an average of 18–20 students per 8-week session. During this period, the ALCP moved from a building housing other units in the Division of Continuing Education to its own building, which included three classrooms, offices, and a computer lab. The name was also eventually changed from the ALCP to the ESL Center.

By fall 1998, it had become apparent that the program had reached a plateau, and the dean of continuing education had a desire to see the program grow beyond its current size. He was concerned that enrollment had leveled off at around 20 students, while the enrollment at the English Language Institute at another institution in the state regularly surpassed 100. The Center also suffered from low student retention and low teacher motivation. The instructors seemed unexcited about the curriculum, which, after 5 years, appeared to be falling out of date. The resignation of the current manager to pursue other interests and the hiring of one of us (Bonfanti) as the new manager in spring 1999 presented the dean with the opportunity to push the Center beyond its current level.

REVITALIZING MARKETING AND CURRICULUM

Needs Analysis

Charged by the dean to revitalize and expand the program, Bonfanti began by analyzing the Center's marketing strategy and its curriculum. The marketing efforts had not changed much over the past 6 years and still consisted of a single large mail-out of promotional material in the spring to overseas advisory offices and other types of government agencies and universities sponsoring study-abroad advising offices. The Center also purchased limited print and Web advertising from organizations such as Study in the USA and had a Web site within the university's Division of Continuing Education site. The curriculum was still based on the integrative approach as described above: three levels, two components (oral and literacy), and five 8-week sessions per year. Finally, the faculty comprised two full-time and two part-time instructors, some with master's and some with bachelor's degrees.

Beyond this initial analysis, Bonfanti and the faculty began collecting data over the next several months from several different sources. First, Bonfanti began tracking how many inquiries he received from prospective students versus how many students applied as well as how many students were accepted into the program versus the number of students who actually arrived. He also began tracking the average number of 8-week sessions in which students enrolled and their academic progress based on proficiency exam scores. In addition to gathering this quantitative data, he and the faculty began collecting qualitative information, surveying students on cultural and programming needs and gearing the questions in the oral interview portions of the proficiency exams to collect information on student perceptions of the curriculum and the program in general. They also researched current TESOL methodology, including content-based instruction and authentic oral/aural instruction, and attended conferences, getting ideas from other program administrators and teachers. Finally, Bonfanti spent several hours a day surfing the Web, examining what other ESL programs were doing in curriculum and programming as well as marketing.

A New, Two-Part Strategy

From the data gathered, Bonfanti learned that the problems of low enrollment and low retention were caused by two factors: poor recruitment and marketing and a curriculum that failed to meet the needs of the Center's students. Specifically, the data gathered revealed the following important issues:

1. The ESL Center Web site was buried too deeply in the hierarchy of the university's Web site, and difficult access to the site caused many students to overlook the ESL Center.
2. The promotional information was confusing to prospective students, especially the listing of sessions within the U.S. academic year rather than the calendar year.
3. Quick responses to questions from prospective students encouraged those students who contacted the Center to enroll.
4. Previous relationships, or some connection with the university through family and friends, were the primary reasons students chose to enroll.
5. The students who did enroll were academically focused; they had not chosen MSU for its location.
6. The student body was roughly split between those attending for language study and those attending to gain admission to MSU.

7. Retention was lowest among those wanting to gain admission to MSU.
8. The average length of stay at the Center was two sessions.

Based on these data, Bonfanti developed a revitalization strategy that would focus on marketing and curriculum revision. The two primary goals of the strategy would be (a) to recruit students who had a connection to MSU by targeting current and former international MSU students' relatives and friends and (b) to retain students through an academically strong curriculum and close program ties to the host institution.

Marketing

As a self-supporting unit on the campus of MSU, the ESL Center depends on high student numbers for its survival. Therefore, marketing is crucial to attracting the right students and growing a successful program. After determining that the majority of students who attended the Center had a prior connection to MSU, Bonfanti developed a marketing strategy to increase awareness of the program. This strategy included

- developing a comprehensive Web site
- using e-mail effectively
- selectively using print and Web-based advertising
- creating a biannual newsletter
- strengthening ties with the host institution

Web Site Development

The Web site was revised to match the print promotional material. A counter was installed to track usage. Data collected included the day and time students viewed the site, how they arrived at the site (e.g., directly, or via another link or a search engine), from which countries they were accessing the site, and what types of computers they were using.

Bonfanti was also successful in having the Web site moved up the hierarchy within the MSU site to a second-level rather than a fourth- or fifth-level page. He also obtained multiple points of entry. For example, links to the ESL Center from the Office of Admissions, the Office of International Services, and various international student association Web sites were created. The Web address was also added to every document that left the Center and registered on every free site and search engine available.

E-Mail Rapid-Response System

To make better use of e-mail, the Center developed a rapid-response system that provided a same-day response to every inquiry and at least two follow-up responses. Students received an immediate response from the ESL Center secretary, followed a few days later with a response from the manager.

Student communication was tracked, and those students failing to respond to either of the two initial responses within a 3-week period were sent a third, follow-up response.

Print and Web-Based Advertising

With one exception, the Center decided not to focus heavily on paid print advertising. If another Mississippi institution was advertising in a print publication, then the Center purchased an advertisement. This was done to provide a presence for MSU and to increase the overall presence of Mississippi in the publication.

Newsletter Development

In lieu of paid advertising, an alumni newsletter was created. Published twice a year, the newsletter always contained three articles: one on an academic theme, another highlighting a student alumni success story, and the third showcasing a cultural event. The newsletter was mailed to all international alumni of the ESL Center and their host universities. In addition, the newsletter was mailed to all faculty and administrators at MSU to help increase awareness of the ESL Center.

Ties to the Host Institution

Finally, Bonfanti worked with the Office of Admissions to rewrite letters of denied admission sent to international students with low TOEFL scores to include mention of the ESL Center. Copies of the letter were provided to the ESL Center, which mailed a follow-up letter encouraging students to enroll in the ESL Center program, get to know the university and its faculty, retake the TOEFL, and reapply for admission with the Center's assistance.

Curriculum Revision Phase 1:
The Nonconsecutive Two-Part Curriculum

The first step in revising the curriculum was determining students' motivational and academic needs. As noted above, students enrolling in the ESL program at MSU were academically focused and desired either language instruction or admission to MSU. In addition, most students

- stayed an average of two 8-week sessions
- wanted a strong academic program with plenty of homework
- insisted on having grammar lessons (no matter what current theory stated about teaching grammar out of context)
- wanted to see measurable progress

For those students with the goal of learning English, progress meant improvement in communication skills. For those with the objective of admission to MSU, progress meant marked improvement in TOEFL scores. Moreover, the data revealed that the students found the current schedule of two 2-hour sessions per day boring. Due to faculty limitations, the current schedule also meant that some students even had the same instructor all day, every day. To address these issues, the current 2-hour, two-session, integrative curriculum was revised into what Bonfanti dubbed the *nonconsecutive two-part curriculum.*

With that curriculum, students could enter the English language program at any given 8-week session. As before, a student had to complete two sessions in order to complete a level. However, the old sessions were consecutive. In other words, a level might begin with the August-September session and continue through the October-November session. This meant that a student entering the program in October was essentially thrown into a class in the middle of the semester. In addition, because there were an odd number of sessions per year (five), the start of a new level did not always coincide with the traditional start of the fall or spring semester.

To correct this, the Center developed competencies for a two-part nonconsecutive curriculum (see Sample Two-Part Nonconsecutive Curriculum for the Beginning Level). For example, in the beginning-level writing class, one session focused on sentence construction (i.e., simple, compound, complex), and the other focused on paragraph construction (i.e., form, unity, cohesion). In the old curriculum, a student might have learned simple and compound sentences in the first session along with paragraph form and unity whereas a student new to the second session would have jumped right into complex sentences and paragraph cohesion, going back to pick up the prior material in the next session. The two sessions in the nonconsecutive

Sample Two-Part Nonconsecutive Curriculum for the Beginning Level		
Class	**Magnolia Session**	**Dogwood Session**
Reading	Skimming/scanning Vocabulary Finding details	Main idea Themes General concepts
Pronunciation	Intonation Rhythm Linking	Consonant sounds Vowel sounds
Listening/Speaking	Conversation skills	Presentations
Grammar	Verb tenses	Nouns Adjectives Adverbs Modals
Writing	Sentence construction	Paragraph construction

two-part curriculum were called the Magnolia and Dogwood sessions to avoid any idea that they were consecutive (i.e., Session 1, Session 2 or Session A, Session B).

Other changes added more variety to the curriculum. The literacy and oral skills classes were divided into four 50-minute classes: Writing, Grammar, Reading and Pronunciation, and Listening and Speaking (see Sample Schedule From Summer 1999). The class schedule was revised so that students met for three classes each day in the morning and one class after lunch.

The goal of these changes was to give students the perception of a faster pace by switching topics and instructors within the maximum length of the average student's attention span as well as offering students the separate grammar class that they demanded. Although the classes were now divided by subject matter, the instructors continued to use a whole-language approach in each course, simply using the skill emphasis as the content around which the approach was developed. This organization satisfied the instructors' desire to teach using a holistic approach and, especially for students working to improve their TOEFL scores, the students' need to have a traditional, skills-based curriculum. Specific objectives developed for each course at each level allowed a student to complete a level within two sessions, the average amount of time students were enrolled in the program.

Results

The first phase of marketing and curriculum changes took place during the summer and fall semesters of 1999. The results in terms of enrollment and retention were better than expected. By fall 1999, the Center's enrollment

Sample Schedule From Summer 1999			
	Level and Class		
	Beginning	Intermediate	Advanced
8:30–9:20 a.m.	Writing	Writing	Reading and Pronunciation
9:30–10:20 a.m.	Reading and Pronunciation	Grammar	Writing
10:30–11:20 a.m.	Grammar	Reading and Pronunciation	Listening and Speaking
11:30 a.m.–12:20 p.m.	Lunch		
12:30–1:20 p.m.	Listening and Speaking	Listening and Speaking	Grammar

had more than doubled to its highest number ever, 45 students. The growth allowed the ESL Center to expand its offerings from three to four levels in spring 2000.

Unfortunately, adding the fourth level was a tactical error. The ESL Center operated an English immersion program, and Bonfanti felt that the beginning level was not really that but rather a high-beginning level. Therefore, while the students were demanding a more rigorous curriculum, Bonfanti split the intermediate level into a low and a high group. He then moved much of the material from the beginning-level class to the low-intermediate-level class and developed a true beginning level. The error that would reveal itself in a few months was that the ESL Center was not attracting true beginning-level students but rather, as the data had revealed, academically focused students who generally had some training in the English language before arriving at the center. A wiser decision would have been to develop a higher advanced level, which, in fact, Bonfanti later did.

REVITALIZING CONNECTIONS WITH THE HOST INSTITUTION

The next step was to develop the program by strengthening the program's base—its ties with the host institution and the curriculum. Overall, Bonfanti and the faculty felt that in developing the nonconsecutive two-part curriculum, they had made some progress in revitalizing the program by better serving the needs of the students, but they were not quite finished. Input from the students showed that they wanted an even stronger academic program. They wanted clearer demonstrations of progress and some cultural programming. In addition, the instructors were dissatisfied with the current placement exam, and the Center's class schedule did not coincide with the MSU schedule, which made it difficult for conditionally admitted students to take ESL and non-ESL classes in the same semester.

In order to build a broader and stronger foundation for the program, Bonfanti developed a plan to strengthen the connection of the ESL program with the host institution. He promoted the Center as an academic support unit by revitalizing the admission policy for students who were conditionally admitted to graduate programs and developing and promoting a university bridge program for noncredit ESL students wanting to gain admission to academic programs at MSU.

Conditional Admission Policy

In fall 1999, the conditional admission program was not heavily used. The graduate school required a TOEFL score of 550 for full admission (see Conditional Admission Policy). Students could be conditionally admitted with a score as low as 475. Students with scores lower than 475

Conditional Admission Policy		
TOEFL Score Range		**Admission Status and English Placement**
Paper	**Computer-Based**	
550 and above	213 and above	Full admission
525–549	193–210	English 1103, 1003, or 1113 (special sections of freshman English)
500–524	173–190	ESL 5120
475–499	170–153	ESL 5110
Below 475	Below 153	Noncredit ESL classes

were denied admission and encouraged to study in the noncredit English language program at the ESL Center. A student admitted with a score between 475 and 499 was required to take the two highest levels offered by the ESL Center as well a freshman composition course for international students offered through the English Department. A student admitted with a score between 500 and 524 had to enroll in the highest level of the ESL program and the freshman composition course, and a student admitted with a score between 525 and 549 was required to take only the freshman composition course.

Most students and faculty, however, were unaware that the program existed. Moreover, the program was not always user-friendly. MSU is a doctorate-granting research institution, and almost all graduate studies are research focused. The students, and the professors who admitted them, were anxious to get into the classrooms and labs. They did not extend much legitimacy to the ESL program and felt that the ESL courses were a waste of valuable time. These students and professors were often successful in getting permission from the Office of Graduate Studies for the students to enroll in at least one non-ESL course; however, these courses often conflicted with ESL Center courses, which did not follow the same schedule as the university. Building stronger ties to the university through conditionally admitted students therefore required matching the ESL course schedule with the main campus course schedule and building legitimacy for the program in the eyes of the faculty.

Matching the course times was the easy part. In order to establish legitimacy, Bonfanti took two initiatives. First, all ESL courses offered for credit, although taught by ESL faculty, were approved and listed as English Department courses. Bonfanti proposed and gained approval for official ESL credit-bearing courses to replace the English courses, which were essentially the same. This change had the effect of making the ESL Center a legitimate academic department. He then had the conditional admission policy rewritten to require the successful passage of university-approved ESL, rather than English, courses. The second initiative was to obtain faculty status for ESL instructors by requiring them to meet university qualifications for faculty at the instructor level. This change helped gain a tremendous amount of legitimacy for the program in the eyes of the university faculty and administration.

Curriculum Revision Phase 2: University Bridge Program
In addition to successfully gaining university approval for pass/fail credit courses for the Center's two highest levels, Bonfanti along with the faculty developed and gained university approval for a new, fifth-level set of courses called the University Bridge Program. The plan was that the fifth-level writing course would eventually replace the required freshman composition course in the conditional admission policy.

Planned for the fall 2000 semester, the University Bridge Program was originally designed to facilitate the transfer of nonadmitted ESL students into academic programs. It consisted of the following four courses: Academic Lectures and Note Taking, Academic Readings and Assignments, Academic Research and Writing, and Academic Communication and Presentations (see Five Levels, Including the University Bridge Program). The level was marketed to students attempting to earn admission into MSU, as was a new, elective TOEFL preparation course offered in the evenings. In addition, the faculty revised the Center's placement exam and attempted to calibrate it to the TOEFL. Bonfanti's plan was to lay the groundwork for eventually developing and gaining approval for the admission of gradu-

Five Levels, Including the University Bridge Program				
High Beginning	**Low Intermediate**	**High Intermediate**	**Advanced**	**University Bridge**
Grammar	Grammar	Grammar	Grammar	Academic Lectures and Note Taking
Reading	Reading	Reading	Reading	Academic Readings and Assignments
Writing	Writing	Writing	Writing	Academic Research and Writing
Speaking and Listening	Speaking and Listening	Speaking and Listening	Speaking and Listening	Academic Communication and Presentations

ates from the ESL program directly into MSU without the submission of a TOEFL score.

The final curriculum change was a small modification to the courses in the first four levels. The pronunciation component was removed from the reading and pronunciation classes, and a separate elective pronunciation class was developed. This class was open to all students at all levels and foreshadowed the major changes to come to the curriculum in the next phase. Cultural programming was also introduced during this phase, including a conversation partners program and biweekly cultural events.

Results

Like the first round of changes, these changes helped increase enrollment and retention. By the fall semester 2000, enrollment at the ESL Center had reached 60 students and climbed to a high of 80 students in the spring 2001 semester. However, there were still some issues facing the Center, and there were new ones on the horizon that no one could have predicted. The majority of students were still staying for an average of two sessions and were still demanding tougher academic challenges. More important, it was becoming obvious to Bonfanti that although the Center had more students, they were not evenly spread across all levels and that sustaining the five levels was going to be too difficult.

REVITALIZING THE PROGRAM THROUGH A MARKETING AND CURRICULUM MARRIAGE

By summer 2001, the ESL program had been consolidated into four levels. In order to make the curriculum more challenging, Bonfanti consolidated three levels (high beginning, low intermediate, and high intermediate) into two more challenging levels called the Foundations of English Program and the Basic Mastery of English Program. The advanced level became a challenging, higher intermediate level called the General Mastery of English Program, and the University Bridge class became the advanced level, or the Professional Mastery of English Program. Conditionally admitted students now enrolled in the middle two levels, still making possible the goal of the highest level one day serving as the third and final courses referred to in the conditional admission policy. Moreover, because the highest level did not contain a separate grammar course, the grammar material that had previously been covered over four levels was condensed into the first three levels.

These changes, especially the condensing of grammar, finally allowed the curriculum to reach the academic rigor that the students had been demanding. Bonfanti also began scheduling the three courses that became known as the *core curriculum* (Reading, Writing, and Grammar) into the three morning slots. In a bit of irony, he also began scheduling the Grammar courses, which had always been the most important to the students, at the 8:00 a.m. slot; this helped improve early morning attendance.

Curriculum Revision Phase 3: Certificate Programs

That summer, however, Bonfanti and the faculty took on the final and most significant revision of the curriculum when they addressed the issue of length of enrollment. As mentioned earlier, the average length of stay for students was two 8-week sessions. The Center's English language program, however, was built and marketed on a progression through four levels that could take up to eight 8-week sessions, something the majority of the students simply were never going to do. Bonfanti had also become aware that the earning of certificates was very important to most of the students.

With this in mind, he challenged the Center's faculty to develop four certificate programs rather than four levels. Each program would have specific goals and a statement of what each student earning the certificate would be able to complete. A student would be expected to complete a certificate program in two 8-week sessions. Students would be tested and placed into an appropriate program. After completing 16 weeks, they would be tested on the skills taught in each program and, if successful, awarded a certificate of completion. Students choosing to stay longer would simply be placed in the next certificate program.

What the faculty developed turned out to be almost perfect for the ESL Center and its students. The four certificate programs were called the Foundations Program, the Basic Mastery Program, the General Mastery Program, and the Professional Mastery Program. Each was built around the core curriculum noted above. Each had clearly stated goals and competencies (see Certificate Program Descriptors).

In addition to the core curriculum, the faculty developed elective courses that would be offered in the afternoon. Each would meet 3 days per week for a slightly extended amount of time, and like the earlier pronunciation course, each would be open to students at any level. These courses were designed to replace the former Listening and Speaking courses. The faculty felt that the students were getting significant practice in listening and speaking in the core courses as well as in their daily activities outside class. What they preferred was an elective course that would truly be content based and, to be honest, more fun for the faculty to teach.

There were several reasons behind allowing the levels to mix in these courses. Because the Center did not have enough students to offer multiple courses at each level, the only way to provide choice was to open the electives to all levels. More important, the academically focused students had always complained that they were placed at a level too low for their skills. The faculty felt that one way to stop the complaining was to put students in

Certificate Program Descriptors

The Foundations Program

Students in the Foundations Program will achieve an introductory understanding of the English language. Through the core curriculum, they will gain an understanding of elementary English vocabulary and grammar and be taught the skills of reading, understanding, and writing sentences. Students completing the Foundations Program should be able to communicate in English in simple, everyday social situations.

The Basic Mastery Program

Students in the Basic Mastery Program will achieve a practical understanding of the English language. Through the core curriculum, they will gain an understanding of the fundamentals of English grammar. They will be taught the skills of reading, understanding, and writing paragraphs. Students achieving basic mastery of the English language should be able to communicate in English in extended, informal social situations.

The General Mastery Program

Students in the General Mastery Program will achieve a broad understanding of the English language. Through the core curriculum, they will gain an extensive understanding of the use of English grammar. They will be taught the skills of reading, understanding, and writing extended discourse. Students achieving general mastery of the English language should be able to communicate in English in more complex, formal and informal social situations.

The Professional Mastery Program

Students in the Professional Mastery Program will achieve an advanced understanding of the English language. Through the core curriculum, they will learn the skills of reading, writing, and speaking at an academic/professional level. Students achieving professional mastery of the English language should be able to communicate in English in professional, academic, and business situations.

a mixed-level course, the idea being that lower level students would in fact realize that their skills were not equal to those in higher levels while being challenged to improve their skills. Finally, the faculty felt that mixed levels more closely mimicked real-life situations: When students go to parties, restaurants, or other social gatherings, the levels of conversational ability are indeed mixed (see Sample Class Schedule With Certificate Programs, page 50).

Results

Although the development of the multilevel elective courses has had its problems, the development of the core curriculum allowed the Center to strengthen its ties to the host university even further. With the three core classes offered in the morning, the conditional admission policy was revised

Sample Class Schedule With Certificate Programs				
	Program			
	Foundations	**Basic Mastery**	**General Mastery**	**Professional Mastery**
8:00–8:50 a.m.	Grammar	Grammar	Grammar	—
9:00–9:50 a.m.	Writing	Writing	—	Communication
10:00–10:50 a.m.	Vocabulary	—	Writing	Writing
11:00–11:50 a.m.	—	Reading	Reading	Reading
12:00–12:50 p.m.	Lunch			
1:00–2:40 p.m.	Elective course 3 days per week			

to require conditionally admitted students to register only for these three courses instead of for an entire level of four courses. Conditionally admitted students were required to take the core courses Monday through Friday. However, the faculty developed syllabi for the Professional Mastery Program core courses that provided for the introduction of new material on Monday, Wednesday, and Friday and reserved the class time on Tuesday and Thursday for reinforcement exercises. This meant that MSU students choosing to take classes in the higher levels could attend classes only on Monday, Wednesday, and Friday if they chose to register for non-ESL classes in the afternoons and on Tuesday and Thursday.

An unintended consequence of this change was the attraction of regularly admitted international students to ESL courses. As a result of these changes, the academic department enrolling the largest number of international students at MSU required, for the first time, that its international students complete the Oral Communication course in the core curriculum of the Professional Mastery Program.

In creating the certificate programs, the ESL Center had, after 2 years of work, nearly achieved the goals Bonfanti had set out in fall 1999. The Center had been expanded and revitalized through a new marketing strategy and an extensive revision of the curriculum to meet the specific needs of the center's students. Above all, the relationship between the Center and MSU had been renewed and strengthened. This new relationship would prove to be crucial in fall 2001 as the center moved into the post–September 11 world. That same semester, many changes would take place at the local level for the Center, including an invitation to Bonfanti to serve as the interim director of the Division of Continuing Education. Although he still maintained responsibility for the ESL Center (the Center being one of several units reporting to him), the responsibility for the day-to-day operation went to the interim manager (Watkins). A faculty member, she took responsibility for the Center in a much different world than the prior manager had.

September 11 and Beyond

The effects of the terrorist attacks of September 11, 2001, did not hit the ESL Center immediately; in fact, they did not significantly affect enrollment until fall 2003. However, Watkins built on the programs already in place in order to adapt to the changing world. Apprehensive that enrollment could begin dropping at any time, she focused on three main goals to survive:

1. continuing to improve the quality of the program to increase retention
2. marketing to universities and organizations to bring in groups of students for short- or long-term study
3. strengthening the ties with MSU to make the ESL Center a strong academic support unit for the academic departments on campus

IMPROVING PROGRAM QUALITY

The least complicated of these goals was to improve the program's quality. The program had been significantly strengthened, and all of the changes could be made internally. The certificate programs worked well for the ESL Center, but they constantly needed fine-tuning.

Improving Individual Courses

Changes were made at the course level instead of at the program level during this time. First, the faculty quickly realized that students did not perceive the elective courses as challenging. Grades, homework, and tests were few, and students did not see as much value in simply using the language as they did in studying the language—a distinction they made. Therefore, the Center developed clear, academic objectives and gave them to the students. Students became motivated when they clearly understood why they were doing different tasks. Finally, the faculty was instructed to require more academic work—tests, homework, projects—from the students. Although students complained about the work, they responded more favorably to the courses as a whole.

In spring 2005, the elective courses became integrated skills courses, meaning that grammar, reading, writing, listening, and speaking were incorporated into each class. The frequency and length of the courses were also changed from 3 days per week for 90 minutes each day to 5 days a week for 50 minutes each day. For the students, the skill focus and the time change to match the other courses added legitimacy to the courses. Changing the name from elective courses to integrated skills courses also helped the students view the courses as less of an option and more of an academic core course.

The reading courses were another concern. They were essentially the same ones taught at the beginning of the nonconsecutive two-part curriculum development. The concepts were good, but the courses were weak. They were strengthened by having the faculty approve and select outside readings for each certificate program. In the past, each faculty member had discretion over his or her reading choices. The leveling and selecting of novels for each certificate program enabled the reading courses to become more consistent and reliable, and some of the pressure was taken off the faculty to choose readings.

Developing Online Grammar Courses

A post–September 11 concern was that students would have increasing difficulty getting a visa to study in the United States. Because of this concern, Watkins decided to take the English courses to students through online course development. Because the grammar courses had always been the ones most in demand by the Center's students, it was decided to begin with them. The faculty was challenged with adapting the three grammar courses to an online interface so students who were unable to travel to the United States could still take ESL courses. The eGrammar Series, as the online courses were named, consisted of three independent grammar courses and a placement test. Students registered for a course, took the placement test, and were placed into one of the three classes without the need for a visa.

Unfortunately, the Center has had little success with this program to date. Students are interested in the program, but the Center is unable to offer the courses at a rate that the students are willing to pay. At the time of writing, the online course initiative was under revision.

Developing the Culture Program

The culture programs were also strengthened. Watkins developed a Connections program to tie the cultural programming together. The conversation partner program was renamed Conversation Partner Connections but was not changed further, as it was successful. An Alumni Connections component was added to support students before they entered the program, when they were in the program, and as they left. This program mainly entailed creating a Web site where alumni could register and keep in touch with each other and the ESL Center. Prospective students could also log in and join the community. Because the ESL Center's main marketing target remained people who already had a connection with the program or the university, supporting the alumni was a logical step in attracting more referrals.

Another program developed was Community Connections. Similar to Conversation Partner Connections, Community Connections paired students with families in the community. Host families included students in small parts of their lives so that students could have a more realistic U.S. experience. The family might help a student set up a bank account and get to the grocery store, then take the student to a child's baseball game. The Connections program proved successful in increasing student retention.

DEVELOPING SHORT-TERM GROUP PROGRAMS

The second goal Watkins set was to develop short-term group programs. The ESL Center had been working with a few universities that sent groups to MSU for many years, and this focus increased after September 11, 2001. One of the difficulties caused by legislation after the attacks was increased delays in F-1 visa issuance. These delays caused a perception among students that getting a visa was extremely difficult and perhaps not worth the effort. However, group programs seemed not to have this perception.

Watkins tried to capitalize on these programs by catering to university groups. She contacted any non-U.S. school that MSU had had relationships with previously. Four-week sessions were advertised to hit various university breaks in other countries. As a result, the ESL Center developed consistent relationships with several universities that sent large groups of students each year, two of these sending two groups a year. Students in these programs were funneled into the regular courses offered by the Center, so costs were low. Commonly, some of the students from the groups elected to continue studying at the Center after the group program, increasing student numbers. These large numbers of students helped support the Center during lean sessions.

BECOMING A FULL-FLEDGED ACADEMIC SUPPORT UNIT

The final, and perhaps most crucial, goal was to strengthen the ESL Center's ties to the host institution. As alluded to earlier, one of the larger departments on campus had approached the Center regarding problems with international students' writing and editing skills. In response to this, Watkins developed the Professional Mastery Program writing course to meet the needs of these students. Data gathered by this department revealed that graduate students who took the ESL writing course fared much better in writing skills than students who did not take the course. As a result, the department required all international teaching assistants (ITAs) to take the ESL Academic Writing and Research course. This added about 20 students to these classes each semester. These students were mixed with the noncredit Professional Mastery Program students, and sections were added as needed. Watkins then began approaching other departments on campus, encouraging them to send their students to these classes.

Watkins also worked with the Office of Graduate Studies (OGS) to find ways for the Center to support the ITA workshop, a 1-week course developed by the OGS that all international students who had been offered teaching assistantships had to take and pass before they could begin teaching at MSU. The workshop was offered once a year, and if a student failed, he or she had to wait until the following year to attempt to pass the workshop. Watkins, however, was able to reach an agreement with the OGS that allowed students who were unsuccessful in the 1-week summer workshop to be given the option of taking the ESL Classroom Communications and Presentations course in the fall or spring. Watkins created a special evening class to accommodate these students. These courses, which had been the original University Bridge Program and were now the Professional Mastery Program courses, became support courses for the university as a whole. Students took the courses for pass/fail credit and, eventually, were able to register for the courses online, similar to any other course on campus.

Another initiative the MSU administration developed in coordination with the ESL Center addressed two parts of the conditional admissions policy. First, a pilot program for undergraduate conditional admission was developed. Previously, only graduate students had the option of being conditionally admitted to the university. In 2005, undergraduate students from Japan were given this option, under the condition that the students take one or two semesters of ESL courses. Second, and most important, the dream of making the University Bridge Program writing class, now the Professional Mastery Academic Research and Writing class, the final stage of conditional admission for graduate students came true in 2004. In fall 2004, students who were previously required to take the English Department's English composition class to complete the conditional requirements were now required to take the approved ESL research and writing course. This increased student numbers in the 2004–2005 academic year. Currently, every conditionally admitted international student must take classes at the ESL Center.

Conclusion

Although the effects of the terrorist attacks of September 11, 2001, were slow to come, come they did, and enrollment at the ESL Center began to suffer, as it did at many programs across the United States. However, because of the close ties that had been developed with the host institution, the Center has never been in any real danger. By fall 2003, the number of students at the ESL Center had only dropped from an average of 56 students to 45 students.

It is important to note, though, that the type of student taking classes at the ESL Center has changed dramatically. In the past, almost all of the students were noncredit students taking a full load of classes, 20 hours per week. Only a few students were taking one or two classes for credit. In fall

2003, however, only 27 of the students were full-time noncredit students, whereas the other 18 were graduate students taking individual courses for credit. In fall 2004, the number of credit students had grown to 29, with full-time noncredit students growing only to 28. In fall 2006, 51 credit students and 31 noncredit students enrolled in classes.

This change in student composition reflects the marketing of the conditional admission program for graduate students, the collaboration with the graduate school on the evening ITA course, and the development of the advanced-level credit courses for academic departments on campus. Special groups in the summer and the spring have also added to student numbers. By the end of the 2005–2006 academic year, the ESL Center had maintained its self-supporting status, and fall 2006 numbers seemed to be on the rise.

A very recent addition to the program that developed out of the relationships fostered with other departments at MSU was the Fulbright Preacademic Program sponsored by the Institute for International Education in the U.S. Department of State. MSU was named as one of six U.S. schools to host international Fulbright students as they prepared for their graduate studies in the United States in fall 2006. The program was supported by a collaboration of six different offices at MSU. Thirty-five Fulbright students from more than 20 countries attended a special 3-week program, centered around the ESL Center's Professional Mastery Program courses. We hope this program will continue in the coming years.

A Look Ahead

The ESL Center has been able to revitalize and strengthen itself by paying close attention to the needs of its students and the host institution. The quality of the curriculum is high, but revisions are always necessary to keep the material and techniques fresh and effective. At the time of writing, the faculty was examining ways to provide the students with more feedback on their performance and to further challenge the students in meeting their goals. The Professional Mastery Program courses were also being revised to find a seamless way of incorporating the noncredit and credit students into the same class comfortably. Integrated skills courses were constantly under revision, and scheduling changes to make these courses seem less different were being discussed. Finally, the eGrammar Series was financially stable but ultimately unsuccessful, as few students chose to take the course. Efforts were under way to make this program more viable.

The culture program is a strong aspect of the ESL Center and has expanded to serve the needs of all international students. A pilot program called Conversation Connections was developed in summer 2005, was fully implemented in fall 2005, and continued through 2006. This program began as a weekly meeting in a campus coffee shop for ESL students, U.S. students, faculty members, community members, and other international students to gather for informal conversation. This program was immediately successful because the MSU student association and the honors program decided to sponsor it with the ESL Center. Each week, about 25 people attend to engage in information conversation on themes related to cultural aspects of the United States, specifically Mississippi and the university. Finally, more varied cultural activities for ESL students are always under development.

Relationships between the ESL Center and universities in other countries are also developing. In 2006, Watkins visited seven universities in South Korea. As a result, relationships with three universities have developed, which has led to new short-term programs. Also, Watkins heard the universities' concerns about visa issuance problems, housing issues, and curriculum and used this information to improve the short-term group program. One idea under development is the specialized group concept, where students take ESL courses in the morning and have lectures or training in their academic or professional fields in the afternoons. We traveled to Japan and Taiwan in May 2006 and established connections with nine universities. Packaging all of MSU's international programs, including the ESL Center programs, exchange programs, and study abroad, has been an effective way to develop relationships with schools and attract more students to the university.

Finally, the Center is looking to meet the needs of immigrants throughout the state, whose numbers have grown in the past few years. Watkins is currently exploring the possibility of offering ESL courses throughout the state to serve these students. As a land-grant institution, MSU considers outreach a major element of its mission. Extension Services is working to develop the financial support to offer free ESL conversation courses to immigrants in other counties. Although this program was not fully developed at the time of writing, a pilot program was being planned for the upcoming year.

The programs at the ESL Center have changed dramatically over the past several years. However, it remains dynamic. All of the revitalization efforts described in this chapter were developed as a result of a focus on the needs of the students and the host institution. Through this focus, we were able to identify MSU's specific needs and, with the help of the faculty, develop targeted marketing strategies and academic programs. These strategies and programs are continuously being analyzed and reinvented and have enabled the Center to remain stable in difficult times. By continuing to focus on the needs of its students and the host institution, the Center should be able to continue to grow and succeed in the coming years.

Revitalizing a Curriculum: The Long and Winding Road

4

WENDY ROYAL, M. JOYCE WHITE, AND HEATHER MCINTOSH

A curriculum is a moving form. That is why we have trouble capturing it, fixing it in language, lodging it in our matrix. (Grumet, 1988, as cited in Davis & Sumara, 2000, p. 840)

This chapter describes a curriculum revitalization project in the Intensive English Program (IEP) at the English Language Institute (ELI), University of British Columbia (UBC), in Canada. We discuss the problems that generated the renewal process; explain the mandate of the project leaders; give a brief overview of the literature, which provided the framework for the project; and explain the strategies used in collecting relevant data. We also describe the four phases of the renewal process, from design to implementation. Finally, we discuss the resulting changes and innovations, and reflect on the complex issues involved in revitalizing a curriculum.

Historical Context

The ELI began in 1969 with federally sponsored programs supporting bilingualism in Canada. Since that time, the ELI has expanded rapidly, and by 1996 it had developed three program areas: year-round intensive English for individual enrollment (IEP), specialized courses for specific user groups (University and Professional Programs), and a program designed to meet the needs of college and high school students.

At the start of the curriculum revitalization project, the IEP had

IEP Curriculum		
Skills-Based Courses		
Beginner	**Intermediate**	**Advanced**
Academic Stream		

	Reading A & B
	Writing A & B
	Grammar, Listening,
	  Speaking A & B
		Reading C
		Writing C
		Grammar, Listening,
		  Speaking C
		Reading & Writing

General Stream		

Effective
  Communication I
Basic Pronunciation &
  Listening
Basic Writing &
  Grammar
Basic Vocabulary
Conversation
	Effective
	  Communication II
	Listening, Speaking, &
	  Pronunciation
	Sound & Structure
	Basic Vocabulary
	English Through
	  Discussion
		Effective Communication III
		Fluency & Pronunciation
		More Sound & Structure
		Vocabulary Development
		Creative Writing

Content-Based Courses: General Stream		
Beginner	**Intermediate**	**Advanced**

Introduction to the News	Introduction to the News
	Introduction to Business
	English Through Business
	Stories Around the World
	Intercultural Learning
	Social Issues
	Public Speaking &
	  Debating
	Canada Studies
	Drama
		English Through the News
		Crime
		English Through Business
		History of English
		Short Stories
		Critical Reading &
		  Thinking
		Public Speaking &
		  Debating
		Men & Women
		Drama
		Critical Thinking

30 teachers and 300 students. It offered 12-week semesters in spring, fall, and winter and a 6-week semester in summer. Students studied in class from Monday through Thursday with directed independent study on Friday mornings. There were three 2-hour course blocks per day. Students usually took two to three courses for a weekly load of 18–26 hours (see IEP Curriculum). Language lab sessions were incorporated into most classes.

Results of a 1996 student survey, which had 210 respondents, showed that students were primarily from Asian countries (75%), followed by Mexico; Switzerland; Quebec, Canada; South America; and Europe. The majority of the students (88%) were aged 18–30. Most (77%) had studied English in their home countries for more than 6 years. Fifty percent had some college or university education, 35% had been working before enrollment, and two small groups had come directly from high school or other language institutes.

The IEP consisted of three proficiency levels—beginner, intermediate, and advanced—with students placed into these levels after an initial placement test. There were two streams, General and Academic, with the Academic Stream differentiated into A, B, and C levels (corresponding to upper intermediate, lower advanced, and advanced levels). Three academic courses were offered: Reading; Writing; and Grammar, Listening, Speaking (GLS). Students who wished to take academic courses could do so only if they scored higher than 400 on the Test of English as a Foreign Language (TOEFL). Students often took a combination of Academic and General courses. Placement in the Academic or General Stream was relative to intake and not according to absolute performance criteria. Hence, in terms of language skills mastered, an Academic Reading B student in one semester, for example, might not have resembled an Academic Reading B student in another.

Students could choose from five skills-based courses, such as Pronunciation, Effective Communication, and Basic Writing and Grammar, at each level in the General Stream. In addition, a wide variety of content-based courses, such as Introduction to the News, Intercultural Learning, and Drama, were offered: 1 at the beginner level, 9 at the intermediate level, and 10 at the advanced levels. Some of these courses rotated, depending on student interest.

A curriculum guide was available for the Academic Stream, but it was not used consistently. There was no curriculum guide for the General Stream, but extensive course development existed for some courses. Students chose their courses based on course descriptions and teacher input. Students, on average, spent 3–6 months at the ELI and left after completing a variety of language skills–based and content-based courses. Students received a certificate of attendance, but there was no exit test reflecting their progress during their study at the ELI.

The Mandate

The Faculty of Continuing Studies was reviewed in 1995 in compliance with the Office of the President, which requires regular evaluation of every UBC department. As part of the restructuring of Continuing Studies, and in accordance with the recommendations of the ELI's Program for Renewal Report (Vertesi, 1995), we were asked to revise the IEP curriculum.

Our mandate was to develop a curriculum that would accommodate the following:

- a course format for intensive English study that included goals, objectives, and evaluation criteria appropriate to a university setting
- an internationally recognizable system of levels of language competency
- a program that was easily adaptable for conditional admission to UBC and other postsecondary institutions
- a program that would meet the requirements for certificates and diplomas as determined by the UBC senate
- a program that built on the strength of current course offerings and that included many of the distinctive pedagogies developed by ELI teachers
- a program structure that would meet students' differing educational goals

Framework for the Renewal

We found the following questions posed by Tyler (1949), still one of the most influential thinkers in the field, to be the most appropriate to our situation:

- What educational purposes should the institution address? (objectives)
- What educational experiences can be provided to attain these purposes? (design)
- How can these educational experiences be effectively organized? (sequence)
- How can we determine if these objectives are being met? (evaluation)

We decided to adopt Brown's (1995) model (see A Systematic Approach to Designing and Maintaining Language Curriculum) to inform the process of revisions because it offered a systematic approach to designing and maintaining a language curriculum. We analyzed the traditional, structural definition of curriculum, which consists of a description of how courses are organized by a school, department, or academic institution. In the traditional curriculum, learning takes place in a linear, sequential, and developmental progression toward prescribed goals and objectives, often devoid of human relevance. We contrasted this with a postmodern definition, which includes all learning opportunities provided by the institution and the student's wider learning environment (Freeman & Richards, 1996; Pinar, 1995).

Our challenge as curriculum developers was to acknowledge both definitions—the importance of students' and teachers' formal knowledge (language skills) and informal knowledge (background knowledge, personal

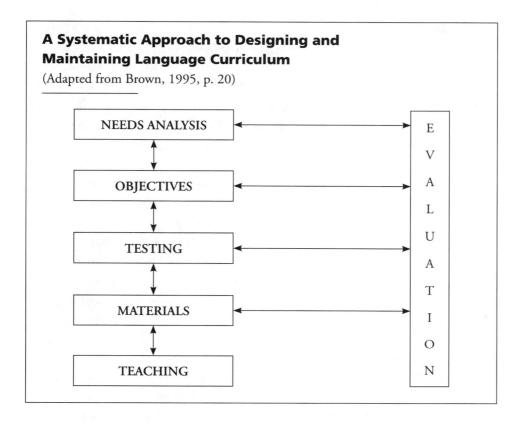

A Systematic Approach to Designing and Maintaining Language Curriculum

(Adapted from Brown, 1995, p. 20)

NEEDS ANALYSIS

OBJECTIVES

TESTING

MATERIALS

TEACHING

EVALUATION

experience, cultural conditions)—and incorporate them into the new curriculum. With this in mind, we believed that the curriculum had to be practical and structured in order to guide teachers and students effectively, yet fluid and flexible enough to allow for continued interpretations and the shifting of identities and boundaries. The curriculum not only should be a vehicle for educational theories, issues, and practice but should also present possibilities for educational experiences, experiments, and critical pedagogy, utilizing critical thinking skills to question the status quo.

Many researchers (Benesch, 2001; Cummins, 1996; Pennycook, 2001) have criticized traditional English language programs for being too mechanistic, that is, focusing predominantly on teaching decontextualized linguistic skills. However, one of the distinctive attributes of the ELI was teachers' freedom to develop in-depth course content, drawing on their personal academic backgrounds in political science (e.g., Social Issues), anthropology (e.g., Men and Women), English literature (e.g., History of English), and fine arts (e.g., Drama). On the other hand, teachers and students were understandably irritated by content overlap in some courses and confused by the lack of information regarding the explicit language skills to be covered in those courses.

Similarly, although researchers (Benesch, 2001; Cummins, 1996; Oakes, 1985; Pennycook, 2001) rightly argue that standardized testing and over-testing can be detrimental to ESL learners and cause teachers to focus on test taking rather than student learning, the ELI had little, if any, testing. Consequently, although teachers and students appreciated the flexibility and creativity this gave them, it was difficult to chart student progress and mastery. As curriculum developers, we faced the task of retaining the flexibility and creativity within the curriculum while bringing it into line with the cognitive and linguistic demands of more rigorous and academic situations.

Sumara (1996) and Sumara, Davis, and Kapler (2000) explain that a written curriculum does not adequately convey the complexity of the reconceptualized, dynamic curriculum. A curriculum must allow not only for change, defined as an "alteration in the status quo," but also for innovation, defined as "deliberate and conscious efforts to bring about new and improved practices" (Stoller, 2001, p. 214). According to Stoller, although change is inevitable in university-based IEPs, innovations are desirable. Consequently, we wanted to ensure that our revitalized curriculum included innovation as well as change. With this in mind, we sought to integrate linguistic and critical thinking skills into innovative content courses and explore a range of creative evaluation criteria such as portfolios and group projects, which would better reflect students' abilities than traditional testing would.

In determining what should be included in curriculum design, developers draw from all sources: textbooks, resource books, conferences, professional interactions, collegial discussions, course outlines, and course descriptions. Ideas and interpretations become integrated; the familiar is rearranged so that it is understood differently. A balance is struck between maintaining what is valuable and transforming what calls for reinterpretation. Sumara (1996) contends that this process highlights the fallacy of individual ownership of thoughts, ideas, and language and the impossibility of a truly authentic product. Consequently, we came to understand that the curriculum would become not our invention but the product of all the contributors, the focal point around which the individual and the collective become inextricably entwined in an ever-changing, ongoing relationship, embedded in real experiences.

Likewise, Sumara (1996) contends that it is not so much the written text that is significant as it is the spaces and action for movement that such texts occasion. When teachers implement the curriculum in their classes, they bring to the written text their own interpretation, creativity, expertise, style, and personality. We understood from these interpretations that the collective curriculum becomes individualized and unique each time it is used.

Renewal Process

After several weeks of reading the relevant literature, discussing approaches, and finally establishing a plan of action, we started the curriculum revitalization project. Our main goals were to update teaching methods, revise and standardize course content, integrate linguistic and critical thinking skills into content courses, and introduce effective assessment mechanisms. This process consisted of four overlapping phases. Each of the first three phases took approximately one semester (3 months) to complete, and the fourth involved piloting the new curriculum.

PHASE 1: NEEDS ANALYSIS

Conducting the needs analysis involved these steps:

- development of an action plan with administration
- a literature review
- institutional visits and conferences
- a needs analysis involving students, teachers, administrators, and marketing personnel
- consultations with the department curriculum committee
- a presentation to the department of Draft 1 of the curriculum model

This phase involved extensive consultations with administration in order to unpack the official mandate and develop an action plan. In addition, we examined previous in-house curriculum development work and contacted other Canadian and U.S. colleges and universities to identify curricula currently in use, changes that had been made over the past few years, and procedures that had been followed in making these changes.

We also conducted an extensive needs analysis with students, teachers, administrators, and marketing personnel, through surveys, focus groups, and individual interviews (see Elements of the Needs Analysis, page 64). Based on their responses, we identified the most important issues and needs:

- more academic support and preparation
- clearly defined language proficiency levels
- clear descriptions of each course
- elimination of overlapping courses
- clearly defined objectives for each course, with suggestions for books and materials
- more accurate placement testing
- assessment at each level
- more well-developed courses with core texts to avoid reinventing the wheel

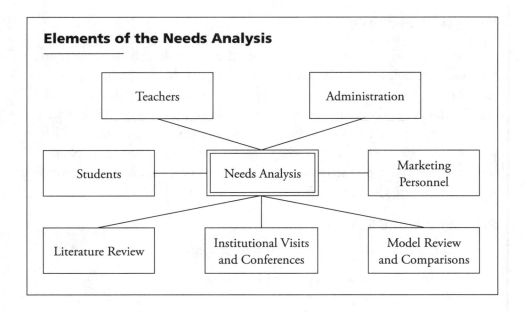

Elements of the Needs Analysis

Teachers   Administration

Students → Needs Analysis → Marketing Personnel

Literature Review   Institutional Visits and Conferences   Model Review and Comparisons

- a continuation of specialized courses to meet student needs and interests
- a continuation of the opportunity for flexibility and creativity in the classroom
- more counseling of students in course selection

At the end of Phase 1, we presented the first draft of the curriculum model to the ELI faculty. We also explained the design process and the results of the needs analysis, and encouraged input through small-group discussions and written feedback

PHASE 2: DESIGN OF THE MODEL

Designing the curriculum model involved these steps:

- examining placement tests and evaluation measures
- writing a first draft of objectives for academic courses
- examining objectives, course descriptions, course materials, and textbooks used in other courses
- presenting Draft 2 of the curriculum model to the department
- giving a presentation at a local conference
- rewriting objectives to include sample tasks and themes as well as suggestions for field trips and final projects
- drawing up guidelines for criterion-referenced tests for each level
- examining textbooks, attending publishers' displays, and consulting with publishers' representatives
- assigning core texts and suggesting supplementary texts and materials

- drawing up Drafts 3 and 4 and presenting them to the department
- drawing up Draft 5 to reflect feedback from presentations

Phase 2 involved the specific design of the model, incorporating faculty's feedback (see Designing the Curriculum Model). The old curriculum had a plethora of content and skill-based courses, which we wanted to use more efficiently and effectively. Consequently, we arranged them into a model that included six levels of proficiency. We then organized the skill-based courses into separate skill areas (speaking/listening, reading, and writing) and integrated them with content-based courses, which thus provided a context in which the skills were taught. For example, we integrated the skill-based General Stream course Listening, Speaking, and Pronunciation offered at the intermediate level with the content-based course Social Issues at the same level. Similarly, we believed the advanced-level course Critical Thinking should be integrated across the curriculum. In this way, we were able to balance some of the conflicting needs identified in the needs analysis: streamlining the curriculum and eliminating overlap while retaining specialized content courses and opportunities for flexibility, creativity, and critical thinking.

Once we had established the overall framework, we began articulating

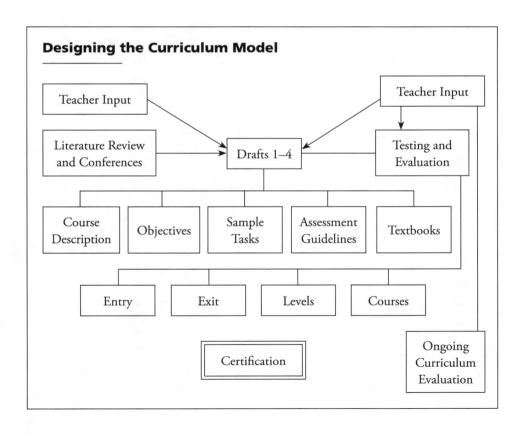

Designing the Curriculum Model

specific objectives for each course at each level, ensuring a progression of complexity from one level to the next. We developed an outline for each course that included the following:

- a course description consisting of a general overview
- (skills-based) objectives to be covered
- sample tasks
- possible field trips, contact assignments, and guest speakers
- a final project to be presented to students in the level below
- recommended core texts to alternate from session to session
- supplementary texts and other materials (e.g., audiovisual)
- assessment guidelines and suggestions, such as quizzes, portfolios, and a final project

We continued to elicit teacher input through committee work, pilot testing of core texts, and a series of professional development workshops on classroom-based assessment. These workshops focused on such issues as teacher-referenced assessment, alternative assessment practices, and use of portfolios. The workshops were particularly critical because assessment had not previously been carried out systematically and had been identified as one of the weaknesses of the old IEP curriculum. In addition to assessment at the course level, we compared existing placement tests, met with testing experts, and examined different exit-testing strategies. This met another crucial requirement of the mandate, namely, to establish evaluation criteria appropriate to a university setting, which could lead to conditional admission into UBC and to the development of a UBC Certificate in English Language.

PHASE 3: FINAL REVISIONS TO THE MODEL

Revising the curriculum model involved these steps:

- a presentation at a NAFSA: Association of International Educators conference
- further consultations with the department in the form of written feedback, open discussions at staff meetings, lunch-hour and afternoon focus groups, and working groups
- amendments based on feedback
- presentation of the most recent model to the department

In this phase, we introduced the most recent curriculum model to the department and invited teachers to give input through written feedback, open discussion, focus groups, and working groups (see Designing the Curriculum Model above). Many tensions surfaced during this phase. Feedback sometimes became vitriolic, and personal divisions between management and faculty emerged.

As both curriculum developers and teachers, we found ourselves in a vulnerable position, caught between our colleagues' concerns and demands and our responsibility to implement the university's mandate. For example, in our efforts to streamline the curriculum and prevent duplication, we dropped or integrated some courses, which resulted in fierce resistance from some instructors. In often making difficult decisions, we had to respond sensitively to teachers' concerns while still maintaining our vision of the overall framework and long-term goals of the curriculum. At the same time, we had to be responsive to, and independent of, managerial constraints in order to retain our integrity and credibility. It was a painful and stressful time that necessitated much discussion, reflection, and soul-searching in order for us to make decisions that satisfied the widest group of stakeholders—students, faculty, and management. We made further amendments and revisions, and the curriculum model was finally ready for implementation in the upcoming session. In total, it had taken 1 year from the initial design to the implementation of the curriculum, including several drafts of the model.

PHASE 4: IMPLEMENTATION

Phase 4 consisted of these steps:

- piloting the revised curriculum
- setting up committees to provide ongoing evaluation and amendments in response to students' and teachers' feedback
- holding departmental meetings devoted to professional development and ongoing support
- designing a student evaluation form

In Phase 4 (see Making Final Revisions to the Model, page 68), discussed more fully below, we implemented the new curriculum and encouraged feedback through weekly feedback forms and weekly course and level meetings, at midterm, and more extensively at the end of the semester. At this point, we handed over the curriculum work to a series of new revision teams because we felt that this would result in more buy-in by instructors, especially those who had resisted the changes. In this way, we hoped the curriculum would become not our creation but the product of all the contributors. The first postimplementation team reviewed feedback from the teachers and students that had emerged from the piloting phase. In response to this, they adjusted course objectives and content options, renamed some courses to make the content more explicit, and added courses.

By the time the teachers had worked with the curriculum for 1 year

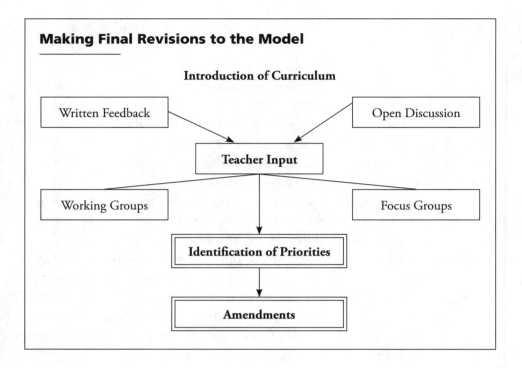

Making Final Revisions to the Model

Introduction of Curriculum

Written Feedback → Teacher Input ← Open Discussion

Working Groups → Teacher Input → Focus Groups

Teacher Input → Identification of Priorities → Amendments

(three sessions), a number of issues had been identified, most notably the place of grammar. In the original model, grammar was taught explicitly in the reading course and was dealt with as it arose in the writing and speaking/listening courses. However, teachers felt that grammar needed to be integrated more across the curriculum. The new revision team interviewed teachers to determine the best way to accomplish this, and other teams were brought on to integrate grammar first into the lower levels and later into the higher levels. Other teams evaluated the core texts that had been suggested for each course and compiled a list of texts that would alternate from semester to semester.

Changes and Innovations

Change, often identified as one of the most stable features of organizational life, results in an alteration in the status quo, but not necessarily in improvements. Innovation, on the other hand, results from deliberate and conscious efforts that are intended to bring about new and improved practices. (Stoller, 2001, p. 214)

We hoped that the introduction of the new curriculum at the ELI in September 1997 would provide the impetus for not just change but also innovation. At the time of writing, 9 years have gone by since the revised

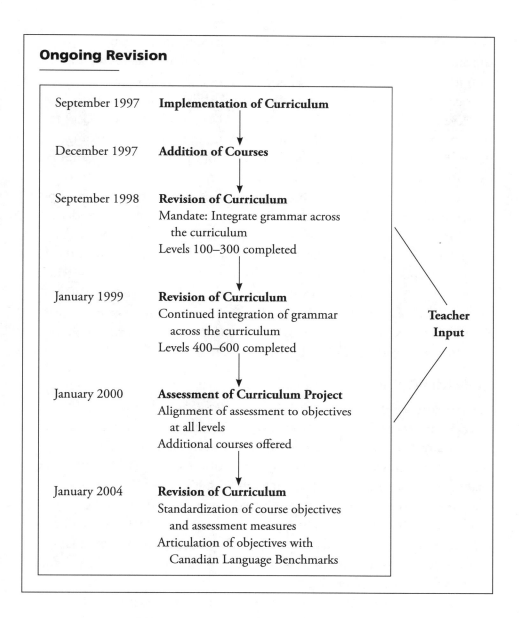

Ongoing Revision

September 1997	**Implementation of Curriculum**
December 1997	**Addition of Courses**
September 1998	**Revision of Curriculum** Mandate: Integrate grammar across the curriculum Levels 100–300 completed
January 1999	**Revision of Curriculum** Continued integration of grammar across the curriculum Levels 400–600 completed
January 2000	**Assessment of Curriculum Project** Alignment of assessment to objectives at all levels Additional courses offered
January 2004	**Revision of Curriculum** Standardization of course objectives and assessment measures Articulation of objectives with Canadian Language Benchmarks

Teacher Input

curriculum was first implemented (see Ongoing Revision). Here we discuss the changes and innovations as well as the benefits and drawbacks that have resulted from the new curriculum.

The implementation of the new curriculum coincided with the ELI moving from its former building at UBC, which had inadequate classroom space, into a newly constructed building on campus and with a large increase in enrollment for the fall term. These significant changes had short-term and long-term impacts on instructors, staff, and program delivery.

In the short term, the large enrollment allowed the new curriculum to be offered in full; that is, all the courses developed for the curriculum ran, and instructors could begin working with the curriculum in its entirety.

During the first term, a process of curriculum evaluation began; this process continues today. The new building, with well-equipped classrooms and new computer labs as well as a shared, open-area work space for teachers, provided an excellent venue for working as a team and utilizing the new curriculum. However, to begin with, teachers were in two camps: those who welcomed the opportunity to work with the new curriculum in the new building, and those who resisted the new curriculum and mourned the loss of the old facility, particularly the more traditional, closed office space for instructors.

In the long term, the new building with its open office space has supported instructor collegiality. In addition, in fall 2001 increased student enrollment necessitated moving from a three-course to a five-course daily timetable, which makes better use of classrooms and facilities. After initial anxiety, teachers and students have welcomed this change. Teachers, who previously prepared separately, now frequently work in teams on course materials and assessment. Resistance to the curriculum has decreased over time and is now virtually nonexistent. As one instructor commented, "Change is difficult, but there have been some rewards."

COMMITTEE WORK

The structure of the ELI, which includes an academic director and head teachers to handle administrative work, includes mandatory participation in committees made up of interested instructors. These committees act as vehicles through which instructors can contribute to decision making and change in the institution. Along with fulfilling his or her teaching duties, every teacher is a member of a committee. These committees, ranging from Professional Development to Safety, meet several times each term and make recommendations to the administration. They have been instrumental in redirecting resentment about changes and in involving instructors in adaptations to the curriculum and related issues.

Two of the most active committees have been the Assessment Committee and the Curriculum Committee. They took on important roles in evaluating the new curriculum and addressing instructor and student concerns. Based in part on recommendations from these committees, since 1999 the administration has offered teachers half-time and full-time positions in some terms (conditional on enrollment and budget) to work on assessment and course development projects.

USE OF TEXTBOOKS

Teachers at first bitterly resisted using textbooks, preferring to use their own materials, arguing, correctly, that they were more authentic, were contextualized, and could be adapted more easily and appropriately to students' needs, interests, and desires. However, the lack of textbooks had a negative side: It necessitated an unwieldy amount of preparation; rather than being adapted to new situations and classes, some teacher-developed materials became entrenched and stale; it was one of the main reasons for content overlap because teachers often drew from the same sources; and it was a possible site of copyright infringement.

Although choosing textbooks is always a contentious issue, teachers have since become quite comfortable working with them. Teachers have retained creativity by adapting textbooks, using them in innovative ways, and supplementing them with teacher-developed materials. In addition, two ELI teachers wrote *The World Around Us: Canadian Social Issues for ESL Students* (Hoppenrath & Royal, 1997), which was used for many years as a core text in the advanced listening and speaking course Social Issues. Because this text encouraged students to question the status quo and dealt explicitly with controversial issues such as racism, sexism, discrimination, and medical ethics, it was on the cutting edge of critical pedagogy, providing practical content and activities for implementing critical language theory.

CURRICULUM CHANGES

As previously documented, initially feedback procedures were built into curriculum implementation. The curriculum has been augmented and revised several times since it was introduced, and the latest revisions were ongoing at the time of writing. However, the core framework of the curriculum remains unchanged.

Some of the main changes and additions to the curriculum have involved placement testing, classroom assessment, and exit testing. Our faculty now includes a full-time assessment head teacher position and a full-time student adviser. Also, textbooks have been introduced in almost all courses, old courses have been revised, and new courses have been developed and offered. Administrative staff has also improved and streamlined procedures for tracking students for transcript and certificate purposes.

Another ongoing concern has been the straddling of levels by students whose placement test scores result in their being at three different levels of the curriculum (e.g., Reading Level 3, Writing Level 2, and Speaking and Listening Level 4). After several terms, we decided that, despite raw scores after testing, students may straddle two levels but not more, with the understanding they may sometimes need to spend more than one term at each level. Most of these changes have been made through the work of committees and in-house instructors, that is, through internal, bottom-up responses rather than as a top-down reaction by administration to the curriculum.

Faculty professional development sessions, which are held two or three times a term, are part of an instructor's paid working hours and are organized by the Professional Development Committee. The sessions have often been devoted to further discussion and direction of course and assessment development. In particular, the place of grammar in the curriculum has been contentious. The curriculum, which is skills based, has seen the addition of courses directed at teaching grammar; these new grammar courses are part of the speaking and listening stream and provide an option for students who need to focus on grammar. Courses have also been added to prepare students for the TOEFL. For a 2-year period, students were encouraged to write an institutional TOEFL each term; data were collected and analyzed to articulate the appropriate range of TOEFL scores for each of our levels. We also used University of Cambridge ESOL Examinations materials as a resource for assessment materials and as a means to articulate comparative scoring.

ASSESSMENT PROCEDURES

Teachers have developed and used a variety of testing measures. Rather than using external tests, the curriculum developers initially chose to promote the use of midterm and final in-class exams and a variety of other performance-based assessment measures, including projects, portfolios, and quizzes. After consultation with an outside expert, Lindsay Brooks, in 2001, the assessment committee phased in the use of exit tests. The need for exit tests as a measure of language proficiency became evident early on, particularly for movement of students to the advanced levels (500 and 600) and for students exiting the program with a UBC certificate. Students had to pass course work and the exit test to complete the course successfully and progress to the next level. Exit tests were introduced and piloted at the upper intermediate level (Level 400) in 2002. At the 100–300 levels, instructors used in-class assessment only. In 2004, exit tests were integrated with course assessment, so that they are now administered as course final exams. We made this change because we found that the exit tests were onerous for students and teachers and that, rather than continue to the 600 level, many students were exiting from the 500 level after gaining admission through TOEFL scores to local colleges and some universities.

Standardization of in-class assessment has been another key part of the changes and revisions to the curriculum. Instructors are encouraged to utilize past tests and work with others teaching the same course to develop new testing instruments. However, over time, assessment measures have altered and in some cases have shifted from what was initially described in the curriculum. In January 2004, an instructor interviewed other instructors, met with the entire teaching staff and the Curriculum and Assessment committees, and revised course descriptions and assessment with the goal of standardizing course objectives and assessment measures across the curriculum. Along similar lines, these course objectives were brought in line with the Canadian Language Benchmarks, which required adding and altering some course objectives.

Placement testing also benefited from the advice of the outside expert. Since 2002, speaking proficiency levels have been assessed using a group oral-interview procedure. This procedure requires less time and fewer teachers than individual interviews, thus reducing the time required to process and place new students.

Benefits

TO FACULTY AND ADMINISTRATION

A new curriculum can be regarded as successful if it has helped the institute meet most of its initial goals for the curriculum. Some of these goals can easily be measured; others are less tangible.

The original goals of the new curriculum included the need to increase enrollment and retention of students. In fact, this goal has been achieved. Enrollment has fluctuated in keeping with trends at other IEPs at universities in North America, due in no small part to the effects of world events such as an economic crisis in Asia, SARS, avian flu, and the terrorist attacks of September 11, 2001. Overall enrollment in ELI programs increased steadily from 1997 to 2005 but has leveled off and stabilized since then. Despite short but significant dips in 1998, 2003, and 2004, the trend is encouraging. Also, the number of students who continue from one term to the next is usually more than one third of the total student population.

Student satisfaction can be measured in part by student retention and through end-of-term course evaluations, which are reviewed by instructors and the program director. In general, these evaluations reveal satisfaction with the courses and course delivery.

Another key goal of the curriculum was to ensure a closer relationship between UBC and the ELI. Again, although the ELI's profile needs to be raised even further, this is being achieved in a variety of ways. For example, the expertise of the ELI is being used to assist other departments in the evaluation of the language proficiency of prospective international students, particularly for specialized programs (e.g., the dentistry program and the international MBA program at the Sauder Business School). Also, the profile of the ELI has been raised as a number of ELI students enter programs in other faculties. Recently, some ELI instructors have also participated in programs with other departments.

As previously stated, the program offers certificates granted both by UBC at the proficiency (600) and advanced (500) levels, and by the ELI at

Levels 100–400. These certificates meet another of the initial goals, namely, closer ties to the university and recognizable outcomes for students.

Our courses have been articulated with the Canadian Language Benchmarks, and data are being collected to support articulation with the TOEFL and the Cambridge exams. Thus we have also met another of our stated goals, which was to offer a program with internationally recognizable levels. We feel we have also been able to meet students' differing needs and build on the strengths of previous courses and teachers' distinctive pedagogical practices. Clearly, the stated goals of reducing overlap of course content and of encouraging instructors to teach new courses have also been met. In particular, it has been rewarding for teachers to develop in-house assessment tools and course materials. Of course, innovations and changes in response to student and teacher requests will be ongoing.

The increase in enrollment, although it has not been consistent (but is higher than precurriculum days), has resulted in more permanent teaching positions and in the hiring of new, younger teachers. Management has been able to require a higher level of skills and experience when hiring; job stability and increased remuneration for instructors have been beneficial to all. New teachers bring fresh ideas, and the pool of new instructors is a boon to the institution.

When enrollment has increased, the ELI has been able to offer and run more courses each term, new courses have been piloted, and funds have been available for more teacher projects that will continue to improve the program. In addition, the ELI's support structures (administrative staff, support staff, resources, and technology) have been enhanced where necessary.

Student satisfaction is evident, and the ELI has set itself apart from many other language schools and programs in the Vancouver area through its curriculum and assessment measures; the ELI is known as a "serious" school. Teachers generally like to work with students of the caliber and attitude of those attracted to the program.

The ELI also offers a short-term program, of 3 or 4 weeks in duration, called Language and Culture (L&C). This program attracts clusters of students as well as individual registrants who wish to have a less demanding introduction to using English in Canada and learning about Canadian culture. Although this program began as separate from the 12-week IEP, the L&C levels have been articulated with those of the IEP so that students can move from one program to the other with ease.

TO STUDENTS

Within the curriculum model, students can move through the levels at the ELI and have a clear idea of their language competence. They receive a transcript at the end of each term that indicates their performance in each class as well as exit test scores. Students who complete Level 600 and have been admitted to UBC are not required to write the TOEFL. Students who pass Levels 100–600 receive both level certificates and transcripts of their grades, which can be used in their home countries and for admission to colleges and universities abroad.

A variety of courses are available to students, who can now spend more than one term at each level and not repeat courses. They continue to work on the language skills for that level but do so through different course materials. Students can also focus on particular areas, taking courses in, for example, grammar, business, media, or social issues.

TO THE UNIVERSITY

Recruitment of international students is one of the goals of all major universities nowadays, including UBC. The ELI attracts many students to UBC, some of whom would go elsewhere were an English language program not available. The UBC certificate also provides some motivation for students to remain at UBC and move from the ELI directly into regular studies. In addition, the Faculty of Continuing Studies, which houses the ELI, has benefited from the program's increased profitability.

Evaluation of the Curriculum Revision

In summary, the new curriculum has many successful elements, some of which are recognized by instructors and administration as innovations. A few elements have been problematic. We hope that the list below provides a few guidelines for other institutions that are considering, or are in the process of, curriculum change.

SUCCESSFUL ELEMENTS

Elements of the new curriculum that have worked well include

- the overall framework of the curriculum (e.g., levels, courses, assessment)
- continued enrollment and retention of students
- development of new course materials and publication of teachers' textbooks
- innovative assessment materials

- innovations in proficiency assessment (e.g., the new group oral-interview procedure, exit tests)
- use of textbooks integrated with course materials
- integration of short programs (i.e., L&C) with long programs over time
- increased expertise of teachers in curriculum and materials development
- increased expertise of teachers in assessment, including development of achievement and proficiency testing measures
- greater collegiality and teamwork among teachers
- sharing of resources and skills
- integration of computer facilities into coursework
- enhanced profile of the ELI at UBC
- increased use of ELI expertise by UBC

Instructors have identified three items from the list above as the key benefits in the long and sometimes painful process of curriculum change. First, instructors have enjoyed the professional development experienced from working on courses, materials, assessment measures, and proficiency tests. Second, and closely related to the first item, instructors have benefited from the increase in collegiality as they work collaboratively and share materials and resources. Third, instructors view their innovations in assessment, courses, and materials as beneficial. From the perspective of curriculum developers, the establishment and effective operation of committees, which ensure that teachers are at the heart of changes and modifications to the curriculum and assessment measures, have been critical to the success of this process.

Markee (1997) delineates nine general principles of curricular innovation. In the case of innovations at the ELI, these principles have proven to be true:

1. Curricular innovation is a complex phenomenon.
2. The principal job of change agents is to effect desired change.
3. Good communication among project participants is a key to successful curricular innovation.
4. The successful implementation of educational innovations is based on a strategic approach to managing change.
5. Innovation is an inherently messy, unpredictable business.
6. It always takes longer to effect change than originally anticipated.
7. There is a high likelihood that the change agents' proposals will be misunderstood.
8. It is important for implementers to have a stake in the innovations they are expected to implement.
9. It is important for change agents to work through opinion leaders, who can influence their peers.

UNSUCCESSFUL ELEMENTS

In several areas, the revised curriculum did not live up to our expectations:

- the initial backlash to the curriculum, the new building, and the schedule
- the drift back (by a few instructors) to old materials and methods under the guise of new courses
- the gradual return by a few instructors to "doing their own thing"

Although the list above is short, it is substantial. In particular, we found that the initial stages of curriculum development and implementation were fraught with emotion and difficulty. In retrospect, responses to the new curriculum initially may have been more positive had the changes occurred at a slower pace. As it was, despite department meetings, attempts to mediate between different viewpoints, and many people's best efforts, the changes were difficult and emotionally laden for instructors and administrative staff.

It took some time before instructors began to engage with the curriculum and own it. During the first year of pilot use of the curriculum, instructors were constantly suggesting changes, such as renaming courses, adjusting objectives, and changing textbooks. Although these changes did not significantly alter the basic structure of the curriculum, they did provide a significant opportunity for instructors to put their mark on the curriculum.

As we reconsider the whole process of change, we see that the more substantial development of course materials and assessment measures resulted in clearer innovations and a fleshing out of the skeleton structure of the curriculum. In particular, teachers were focused on the always problematic decision of where grammar fits into the curriculum and how best to teach grammar. This drew teachers' attention away from the overall design of the curriculum. Course development is ongoing; at present, many teachers have taught a number of different courses and can refer to well-developed binders of course materials and online folders of materials for courses they take on.

The last two items on the list—teachers' drifting back to old ways and doing their own thing—are ongoing concerns. Some senior teachers may not wish to change, but at the least, these few instructors are surrounded by changes and innovations. Perhaps despite themselves, they have in many ways adapted and changed for the better. In particular, they are accountable for assessing students and for making decisions about student language proficiency, and they often work with other instructors on course content and materials. Past practices, methods, and content may creep into their course delivery, but they do so within the framework of the curriculum.

Recommendations for Curriculum Developers

We base these suggestions on the wisdom of hindsight. Some may seem obvious; all are important considerations for anyone contemplating curriculum change.

- Undertake changes to existing curriculum or the development of a new curriculum as a project all instructors are invited to participate in and contribute to. All members of the institute should feel that they bear responsibility for the changes undertaken.
- Make sure management supports curriculum designers and does not expect them to handle all of the responsibility for changes. Collegiality and teamwork at all levels are key to success in curriculum innovation.
- Introduce other changes (e.g., in facilities or in timetable) in a planned and gradual way. A long-term timeline of changes would assist in mentally preparing people for changes.
- Allow for constant consultation between faculty and administration.
- Have clear goals for the curriculum project and a vision of what the curriculum will achieve. Ultimately, the curriculum developer should be given responsibility for the final decision making during the curriculum development process.
- Provide a variety of methods and opportunities for fellow instructors to be involved in the curriculum renewal process before, during, and after the new or revised curriculum is implemented.
- Once the job is done, relinquish ownership of the curriculum so that others, particularly instructors, can own it; however, the curriculum must have an advocate (e.g., a head teacher, a committee chair, other teachers) to ensure the continuing integrity of the new curriculum structure.
- Remember that the greater the number of instructors involved in various aspects of the development of the curriculum, the better the buy-in by instructors, and the more instructors will be able to see the whole picture of the revitalized curriculum.
- Remember that student satisfaction and program success are in part a result of instructor involvement in curriculum renewal and implementation. One way to involve teaching staff in the ongoing response to the curriculum is through participation in committees.

In conclusion, as Stoller (2001) states, "Curriculum renewal depends, in large part, on a program's ability to innovate" (p. 208). It is not an easy process; it is often messy and elusive, emotional, and stressful. As stakeholders—administrators, instructors, and the development team—none of us always did it right. However, perhaps our trials and errors will help guide others down the long and winding road of curriculum revitalization.

Reading, Writing, and Web-Page Design: Content-Based Courses Within a Skills-Based Curriculum

5

LEE ANN RAWLEY AND ANN ROEMER

Any change effort requires a healthy respect for the constraints that shape the context where the innovation will take place. The challenges we faced in changing from a skills-based curriculum to one that blends skills-based and content-based courses, and the constraints we had to work within at Utah State University (USU), in the United States, are particular to our institutional setting. At the same time, the innovation we introduced to our intensive English program may provide a new way for others to think about renewing their programs. We hope the information in this chapter will help you compare your settings and constraints with ours in deciding whether this model is suitable for your program.

We decided to reinvigorate our program through the addition of a new set of courses, courses that reflect an expansion in our philosophies on curriculum. On the surface, the changes may appear to be a mere cut-and-paste affair—the addition of a few classes to an existing program. But change does not work that way. Introducing content-based courses to the existing curriculum revived the entire program; the process of deciding what changes to make and how to proceed reframed our collective thinking about language learning and provided a formal opportunity to put our heads together in rejuvenating the courses and the program.

Making one key change refreshed the philosophical grounding of the program. In particular, we found that the addition of an element of choice for students and faculty had a noticeable influence on attitude and morale. Students felt more in control of their learning when they could select one of their six classes, and faculty appreciated opportunities to select content relevant and interesting to them in designing new courses. In the process of bringing change to our program, we also came to a new understanding of the importance of learning together—of the role each student and faculty member plays in creating and sustaining a community of learners.

Curricular Context

The Intensive English Language Institute (IELI) has been in existence at USU since 1970 and has been an autonomous program in the College of Humanities, Arts, and Social Science since 1984. As such, it has an independent budget and functions within the college much as any other academic department at the institution does, except that it does not offer a major. It is a four-level academic ESL program oriented toward the language, culture, and academic skills students need to be successful in university course work. Although academic English is the focus of the curriculum, IELI defines *academic* broadly to include social and quasi-professional uses of language for students who must live and function in a U.S. university setting—interacting with other students, office personnel, professors, administrators, and residents of the surrounding community of 50,000.

Students receive university credit for all IELI courses. Full-time students register for 18 credits each semester, and the grades they earn in their IELI courses are calculated into their USU grade-point averages. Depending on their major department, undergraduate students may apply up to 18 credits from IELI as electives toward graduation. Credits earned in IELI also qualify students for the bachelor's degree on graduation, just as foreign language credits qualify U.S. students for the same degree.

IELI students are primarily international students, though a small percentage are immigrants. Enrollment varies from approximately 50 to more than 100 students. All IELI students have been admitted to USU based on their previous academic records and are therefore USU students like any others at the institution who register for credit-bearing courses. The program also accepts nondegree students who want to study academic English for personal or professional reasons. These students are mainly visiting scholars, spouses of visiting scholars, and community members. With the exception of those who are auditing classes, all students are expected to fulfill the same course requirements as the degree-seeking students.

All IELI faculty members are highly qualified ESL professionals. The eight full-time faculty have tenure-track positions and undergo the same rigorous review process as other USU faculty. In addition, the IELI faculty includes adjunct instructors hired to teach classes as student numbers demand. All adjunct instructors are also highly competent and experienced, with master's degrees in teaching ESL.

HISTORY AND CHANGE IN THE IELI CURRICULUM

Before 1998, the IELI curriculum was composed solely of what the IELI calls *core courses* organized primarily by language skill. At each level, students took reading, writing, speaking, listening, and culture classes. The courses segregated the skills by name, though in practice most courses integrated the basic language skills. For example, in the advanced-level listening classes, students practiced listening to academic lectures and supported their growing listening skills by reading materials connected to the lecture topics. In addition, all courses had language, culture, and academic goals best described as task based and flexible; that is, the goals often evolved as a result of interaction between faculty and students in response to specific student needs and abilities. (See Appendix A for the Curriculum Statement of Philosophy and a discussion of its evolution.)

When the institution changed from a quarter to a semester calendar in 1998, all departments, including IELI, were required to revamp their curricula to fit the new scheduling guidelines. This institutional edict became the primary motivation for making more than cosmetic changes to the IELI curriculum. We began by debating how best to transform the program to benefit students. One of the options that surfaced again and again was moving to a content-based curriculum.

Throughout the decision-making process, a period of one academic year, we examined the benefits of and the impediments to making a sweeping change from a skills-based to a content-based program. We charted USU's new scheduling guidelines, government requirements for full-time international students, and overall program goals for students and faculty, and attempted to ensure that proposals for a new curriculum matched these needs. Content-based courses had much to recommend them, as discussed below; however, as faculty discussions progressed, we realized that such a major change was not realistic at IELI. The faculty was not in full agreement, and there were institutional and student concerns that we had to consider. So, although a particular curricular approach, such as content-based instruction (CBI), seemed to meet our philosophical criteria for implementing a change, it did not fully fit the context of the language program and the housing institution.

After weighing the pros and cons, we opted to add a content-based capstone course to each level of instruction while maintaining the program's overall skills-based approach. The new courses, called Topics in ESL, are multilevel, integrated-skills, content-based courses. They are taught during the last 3 weeks of a 15-week university semester. The creative scheduling encourages students to apply the language skills learned in the previous 12 weeks of regular intensive English classes to content of their choice. In addition, because Topics classes meet for a total of 45 hours, students have the opportunity to explore the content in depth.

WHAT COULD WE GAIN FROM A CONTENT-BASED APPROACH?

Faculty discussions included a focus on the elements of CBI that seemed to mesh with our overall curricular philosophies and the desires of some faculty members to explore what CBI had to offer. And although in the end we decided against a content-based curriculum, exploring what others had to say about the approach influenced our eventual innovation.

What Is CBI?

CBI, also known as sustained-content language teaching (SCLT), is the teaching of one subject, such as geography or psychology, over time in conjunction with a second language. By using this approach, the teacher creates an authentic context for using the language within the discourse community of the students, whether academic or professional. The students practice language skills as they are studying one subject area for a sustained period. They learn the skills because they need them in order to understand the content and to perform authentic academic tasks related to the particular content under study.

According to Pally (2000), the four most popular types of CBI are as follows:

1. theme-based: These language courses are structured around topics or themes. For example, if the theme is medicine, reading units, grammar lessons, and listening exercises are developed around materials that convey information about that theme: a visit to a doctor's office, the way to become a nurse, alternative medicine, or the cost of medical care.
2. sheltered: In sheltered instruction, the language used to teach the content is adapted for ESL/EFL students (Chamot & O'Malley, 1987), who receive language support in order to understand the content and complete the course assignments. A sheltered course can be taught by a language teacher or a content teacher.
3. adjunct: In this model, students enroll in a content class and a language class simultaneously. In the language class, they work on content and language. For example, college-level ESL students would register for a designated section of Biology 101 and con-

currently enroll in an ESL class that offers language support for understanding the content of the biology class.

4. task based: In this type of CBI, the teacher identifies the tasks students must accomplish in order to be successful in academic work and matches the tasks (e.g., note-taking) with content. Students become proficient at the task while learning the content. The students typically use the language to engage in academic tasks such as research, discussion, reading, and writing to demonstrate their understanding of the subject.

Why Follow a CBI Approach?

Grabe and Stoller (1997), Murphy and Stoller (2002), Pally (2000), and others promote CBI as a means for building curricular coherence and promoting the acquisition of language and content. Pally as well as Grabe and Stoller cite research in a variety of disciplines (e.g., second language acquisition and cognitive psychology) to support CBI. The points listed in Content-Based Instruction summarize the conclusions of their research. In addition to the benefits shown, Pally proposes that CBI can fill the gap between the academic skills that students need to be successful in the university and those offered in traditional skills-based ESL programs. At IELI, we further value the concept of both teachers and students as learners and think that offering content courses encourages students to see us as models for learning as we investigate new areas of knowledge and develop new courses.

Faculty Issues

Although CBI was appealing on a philosophical level, we faced a number of roadblocks in planning—notably, a lack of agreement among the faculty

Content-Based Instruction

1. Uses language that is meaningful and useful
2. Increases students' intrinsic motivation
3. Allows for flexibility and creativity
4. Lends itself to student-centered classroom activities
5. Supports approaches such as cooperative learning, apprenticeship learning, experiential learning, and project-based learning
6. Helps in memory and language acquisition by recycling vocabulary and grammar
7. Teaches critical thinking skills through acquiring content-area expertise in a natural and authentic way just as native speakers do

that the benefits of CBI outweighed the work involved in making such a major change. Not everyone thought this was a sensible direction for the curriculum. The time and energy it would require to create a completely new curriculum alone gave some faculty members pause. In addition, some anticipated a problem convincing students they would be learning English within a content-based framework. Many students come to IELI with traditional, even narrow, views of what language learning should look like. We often have trouble convincing students that they are learning grammar because we teach it embedded within other skills and in response to specific language tasks and needs, so the thought of orienting them to CBI loomed as another major task added to that of crafting a new curriculum.

Institutional Issues

Orienting students was not the only reeducation effort some faculty anticipated. We knew we faced institutional expectations as well. Colleagues across campus were accustomed to thinking they could send students to IELI for work in listening or writing, for example. Some IELI faculty thought it might prove difficult to explain to professors in chemistry or engineering that courses were now organized according to a multiskilled, content approach. Finally, we anticipated varied student interests and were reluctant to decide for them what might hold their interest and attention for 15 weeks.

The Innovation: Topics in ESL

Our debates led us to the conclusion that, even with the problems we anticipated, CBI would offer many benefits to learners and instructors. However, for the reasons enumerated above, we could also see that it simply was not practical for IELI to make the major changes to the curriculum required to move from a skills-based to a full CBI program.

We decided instead to blend the old with the new. We worked together over an academic year to craft a curriculum that incorporated content-based courses into the existing curriculum; we maintained IELI's skills-based program while introducing theme-based capstone courses at the end of each level of skills-based instruction. The designation *capstone* indicates that these content courses provide an opportunity for students to apply the language skills they have already studied in a culminating course. The hope is that such a course allows students to feel confident that they are improving in the language as well as continuing to learn by using the language to read, write, speak, and listen to information on a topic of interest to them. Maintaining the core courses as skills based allowed us to continue to serve the needs of USU students and faculty who used IELI courses as support for students already mainstreamed into their academic majors. It also satisfied the traditional expectations of IELI students.

COPING WITH SCHEDULING CHANGES AND CHALLENGES

During the first 12 weeks of the 15-week semester, students continue to take five skills-oriented core courses. Then, during the last 3 weeks, they take one content course, as shown in IELI's Previous and New Curricula.

MEETING INSTITUTIONAL CHALLENGES

The schematic shown here makes the scheduling of courses look deceptively simple. As a program, we had to work with the university scheduling office to secure rooms to accommodate our needs, a task complicated by the fact that, because the courses offer university credit, they have to satisfy USU's requirement that the credit offered correspond to the number of hours a course meets per semester. Three-credit courses, which are what IELI offers, must meet 45 hours during the semester. Normally, a 3-credit course satisfies this requirement by meeting 3 hours a week for 15 weeks. When we changed our core courses to the 12-week format, we had to increase the number of hours classes met each week so that they totaled 45 by the end of the 12-week period. The new content courses also carry 3 hours of USU credit. To satisfy university requirements, the Topics classes meet 3 hours a day, 5 days a week, although there is some instructor discretion in scheduling. As long as courses meet a total of 45 hours over the 3-week period, the schedule can be shaped to fit the needs of courses, students, and teacher.

A second constraint that accompanies giving credit is that our institution requires departments and programs to submit course descriptions and rationales before receiving permission to offer a course for credit. Curriculum committees at the college and university level must approve any new course at USU. In keeping with this regulation, we submitted a course description, which portrays the Topics in ESL courses as similar to special-topics seminars offered by other departments at USU, and we received

IELI's Previous and New Curricula		
Previous Skills-Based Curriculum	**New Curriculum**	
15 weeks	12 weeks	3 weeks
Reading Writing Speaking Listening Culture	Reading Writing Speaking Listening Culture	Topics in ESL

approval. This designation allows us to alter the actual course content to suit our needs and wishes from semester to semester and allows students to repeat Topics courses (with different content) for credit.

SELECTING COURSE CONTENT

As a faculty, we addressed the concern over what topics to offer students by conducting a programwide survey of instructors and students. Although the results covered a broad range of topics, we began to see patterns. Students were more interested in content relating to their majors or general education requirements (e.g., business, agriculture, computer science, or math) than in U.S. history or literature.

We conducted this formal, programwide survey only once—during the term before we launched the new curriculum. However, faculty members continue to survey students informally to help determine what they are interested in studying. Faculty discussions concerning how to proceed also led us to institute the element of course choice in order to increase student engagement in the topics we would eventually decide to offer. In addition, to facilitate that choice, to ease scheduling constraints, and to focus on the contributions of all in the learning experience, we designed the Topics courses as multilevel.

Revitalizing Students and Faculty

Two principal benefits to this curricular change emerged as we implemented and lived with it: learning from one another and offering students and faculty some choice.

LEARNING TOGETHER

It is IELI's philosophy that students at all levels of English proficiency can contribute to the learning of the group. Because the Topics courses are designed to bring together students at different levels of language proficiency, as well as of different nationalities, educational backgrounds, and interests, there are always opportunities for students and professors to learn from one another.

For example, one of us (Rawley) offered the class The Earth and Us: Environmental Issues and Perspectives for students in IELI Levels 1, 2, and 3. Although the Level 3 students offered their language expertise in giving advice on how to analyze a piece of reading, we discovered that two of the Level 1 students had advanced-level science backgrounds and were eager to share their content knowledge. The class engaged in much metatalk exploring how class assignments as well as the course content required an awareness of interconnectedness—among people and the earth, and among the learners in the group, an awareness that no organism can exist in isolation (Capra, 2002). This approach embodies the IELI philosophy that learning is a social endeavor and facilitates including students of varying language proficiency levels in one class, focusing on the notion that everyone has knowledge to contribute to the group's learning. Putting forward students who have expertise and knowledge also allows the teacher to step aside and model a learning role, encouraging students to blur the boundaries of language proficiency levels and find ways to learn from and teach one another.

Another way that learning together is valued in this multilevel class is through the final project, a poster session. Each student is required to present information on an ecological topic of his or her choice by creating a poster, explaining it, and answering questions as visitors and classmates circulate through the poster display area. Students become experts on their topics and work with the teacher to select a way of presenting themselves that is most personally comfortable and suitable to their language abilities. For example, students who are less sure of their speaking abilities often provide more written text on their posters to guide them as they interact with their audience. Those who are more certain of their abilities to explain orally often use diagrams with less written text. All students are expected to turn in a written summary and a list of references. These summaries are more or less sophisticated depending on students' language abilities, but all are factual and based on information students have gathered from outside sources. This culminating activity is a real highlight of the course; students dazzle one another with their creativity and knowledge, and demonstrate that they are all learners from and contributors to the group.

One of us (Roemer) teaches English for Algebra, in which students with varied backgrounds, language proficiency, and academic abilities also learn from each other. The course is designed to have students work in pairs, using materials based on information-gap activities. Students who are more knowledgeable in mathematics tutor those who are less familiar with the content. This tutoring takes place in English, the language of instruction, and illustrates the use of meaningful language that lends itself to a student-centered classroom supporting cooperative learning—three of the reasons for including CBI in the curriculum. When learning is the focus, issues of who is a Level 3 and who is a Level 4 student fall away.

OFFERING STUDENTS AND FACULTY SOME CHOICE

Choice is a second benefit of IELI's capstone Topics courses. The core courses are all required; in order to complete the program and move into major course work at USU, students must pass all of the classes with a grade of C– or better. There are no electives, and there was no element of choice until we introduced the Topics courses.

When we began designing this new aspect of the curriculum, we reflected on the power of choosing and built it into the innovation for faculty and students. Faculty select topics they want to teach. Creating new courses of choice provides us all opportunities to develop and teach in depth a content area that we already have expertise in or in which we want to develop a new expertise. It is a stimulating change from our usual teaching fare and contributes to a feeling of engagement and freshness.

As indicated above, we have attempted to make educated choices by formally and informally surveying groups of students before offering these courses to find out what topics appeal to them. Preferences vary from semester to semester, but we now have a fairly good idea of what students do and do not want. For example, they enjoy media-related topics such as television and movies, but are not too thrilled about studying the U.S. Civil War. They prefer courses that they can see relate directly to their future major course work. One semester when we had many students who were planning to be business majors, Jim Bame designed a course called Spoken Communication for Business Managers for Level 3 and 4 students. It was so popular that the next semester he offered Written Communication for International Business Managers. Another popular class has been Jim Rogers' Web Page Design. (See the Sample Course Descriptions below and Appendix B for other Topics in ESL courses we have offered.)

Students also have a choice; they select and register for Topics courses. We have found that students respond very positively to having a say in which class they take. We know that they do not always make their selections based on the course topic, though. Sometimes they choose based on which class their friends are taking and sometimes based on who the instructor is. However, no matter what criteria students apply, they appreciate having a choice. Designing the courses for multiple levels means students in each level can have two, or sometimes more, topics to choose from. Students make their selections using materials IELI prepares detailing each course and orienting students to the concept of a 3-week content course. Students are given the print materials (see Information About Topics for ESL, which is excerpted from these materials), and instructors and program administrators meet with students to answer questions. We were especially careful to have conversations with the students when we first implemented the new courses; these conversations were part of a general orientation to the change from quarters to semesters.

We give students descriptions of the classes available each semester, including goals for language, academic, and content learning, to help them select the course they want to take. We also encourage them to talk with instructors as they make their course selections. We ask them to report

Information About Topics for ESL

- During the last 3 weeks of the semester, you will take one three-credit class called Topics for ESL. You will be able to choose one class from a list of possible classes for your level.
- All Topics classes will offer language skills (e.g., reading, writing, speaking, pronunciation, vocabulary) in addition to the study of the topic. The purpose of these classes is to give you an opportunity to use the English you have learned in your 12-week courses.
- Topics classes begin November 22 and finish December 10.
- Final testing will take place December 13 and 14; your professor will tell you exactly when your final test is scheduled or final project is due.
- Each class will meet a minimum of 15 hours a week.
- These are the classes that are available this semester at each level. You will be taking your Topics course with students from other levels in IELI.

Level 1	Level 2	Level 3	Level 4
American Television (Section 1)	American Television (Section 1)	American Television (Section 1)	
Current Events (Section 2)	Current Events (Section 2)	Current Events (Section 2)	
	Written Communication for International Business Managers (Section 3)	Written Communication for International Business Managers (Section 3)	Written Communication for International Business Managers (Section 3)
		Reading a Novel: *Tuesdays With Morrie* (Section 4)	Reading a Novel: *Tuesdays With Morrie* (Section 4)
		Academic Literacy (Section 5)	Academic Literacy (Section 5)

their first and second choices to the office; scheduling priority is given to advanced-level students, and when a course reaches an optimal number of students, we place the remaining students in their second-choice courses. The materials students receive emphasize that they will continue to study and learn language in their content classes. The course descriptions students receive (see Sample Course Descriptions, page 90) are essential to the

Sample Course Descriptions

Course Title: The Earth and Us: Environmental Issues and Perspectives

Levels: 2, 3
Instructor: Lee Rawley

Course Description: In this course, we will begin by deciding what environmental issues are most interesting to the group. Some possible topics include air and water pollution, recycling, alternative sources of energy, whether environmentally protective ("green") practices can make good sense in business, how culture influences views of how to live on this planet, and how consumerism (buying lots of things) affects environmental attitudes and practices. Then we will explore those issues, gathering information from videos, the Internet, the media (magazines and newspapers), and books.

Materials: No textbook. The teacher will provide some materials, and students will find others at the library and on the Internet.

Language Skills: Listening, speaking, reading, writing.

Academic Skills: Using conflict resolution skills in group discussions; listening and taking notes; reading and summarizing information from the media, the Internet, and books; interviewing people and synthesizing information in writing; presenting information orally in a poster session and panel discussion.

Evaluation: You will do basic research searches and reading and write one-page reports, do listening and vocabulary exercises, prepare a poster session (a picture of what you have learned that you present to the class), and participate in group discussions.

Course Title: English for Algebra

Levels: 3, 4
Instructor: Ann Roemer

Course Description: This course will focus on the English needed for algebra. Students will learn the vocabulary and other language skills to move between mathematical symbols and the words used in English. Working in pairs, they will practice listening to, reading, writing, and solving equations in addition to discussing basic algebraic concepts.

An example is the concept of $\sqrt{}$. For most international students, the equation $\sqrt{3} = 1.73$ is easy to understand, but how many of them can read it aloud in English? English for Algebra is designed to provide these students with the specialized language that they need for mathematics and algebra.

Language Skills: Listening, speaking, reading, writing.

Academic Skills and Content: Participating in daily pair work and class discussions; identifying and using numerical symbols, numbers, measurements, and operations in English; using terminology and formulas from geometry; participating in class

continued on p. 91

discussions; reading and explaining algebraic expressions, equations, and inequalities; solving word problems and talking about the processes involved.

Textbook: *English Skills for Algebra* (availability TBA)

Course Title: Written Communication for International Business Managers

Levels: 3, 4
Instructor: Jim Bame

Course Description: In this course, students will take on the role of an international manager (either advertising, sales, product, country, or financial) in a product development team. These teams will form an imaginary international company; decide on a logo; choose an imaginary product; and do market research for the product, product research for the product, and country research.

Language Skills: Development of discipline-specific vocabulary, reporting information, writing for common business genre, reading for information.

Academic Skills: Library and Internet search skills, synthesizing information, self-regulation, group (team) work, e-mail use.

Content: Content will be business oriented. Students will learn about various aspects of advertising, sales, and marketing; culture and its effect on product development; and marketing and financing a product. Content will be from ESL business English books, the Internet, books, and magazines. Business ethics, company formation, and logo making will also be investigated.

Evaluation: Students will write memos, letters, short reports (e.g., on advertising, competitors, packaging), progress reports, and a product feasibility study. They will be evaluated on their writing, either individually, as a subcommittee, or as a team. Students will also evaluate each other's contributions and participation in the subcommittees and teams.

innovation because they encourage students to make informed choices as they play their role in our learning community. (For descriptions of other Topics courses, see Appendix C.)

Evaluating the Innovation

A REVITALIZED CURRICULUM

Faculty and students have informally reported approval of this curricular innovation. Regular curriculum discussions at weekly faculty meetings indicate that professors enjoy teaching the courses and having the opportunity to create new ones. Student responses on the USU Teacher/Course

Evaluations are equivalent for the core and Topics courses. Students completing the program have also expressed satisfaction with the Topics courses on the program exit survey they fill out.

In addition, anecdotal evidence points to success, especially as it relates to the practical application of the new subject matter. For instance, two IELI students from Taiwan who had just completed Jilda Yap's course, Western Medicine and You, were put to the test one afternoon when the program director received a call from a local doctor's office, where a Chinese-speaking patient was unable to speak English well enough to inform the doctor of her medical symptoms. The IELI students, armed with their new knowledge of medical terminology and the U.S. health care system, succeeded in communicating the information to the doctor. And Roemer's former English for Algebra students often visit her office to tell her how pleased they are to hear familiar language when they attend the College Algebra course that is part of USU's general education offerings. "The professor uses the same words we learned in your class!" they marvel.

CAVEATS: NOTHING IS PERFECT

Though we viewed the Topics courses favorably, we did not anticipate certain problems that arose as we proceeded with the new curriculum. The biggest drawback was scheduling, both from the perspective of the university and from that of a few students. The problem with the university was that all other departments on campus followed the 15-week semester schedule and conformed to a Monday-Wednesday-Friday or Tuesday-Thursday timeframe. IELI did not fit into that mold: We were fitting the five three-credit courses into a 12-week semester, and then adding the three-credit Topics courses into the last 3 weeks.

The problem with the students also related to scheduling. Although the scheduling scheme suited the needs of full-time IELI students, it did not work for part-time students—advanced-level students who had only one or two IELI classes remaining and were taking them in conjunction with classes in their major-field departments. It was also unsuitable for (mainly graduate) students whose major departments had requested that they take one or two language courses to support their other studies. We found we had to assign these students' classes only from the set of core courses and reserve the Topics courses for full-time IELI students.

In our enthusiasm to add a new set of courses to our curriculum, we also found that we had inadvertently increased our own teaching workload—and one of the objectives of moving from quarters to semesters was to do just the opposite. This meant that in order to offer the new curriculum, the full-time faculty had to teach four classes in the fall semester, three in the spring semester, and two in the summer.

Consequently, we have had to make some compromises from the original curricular change—a testimony to the ongoing nature of curriculum innovation and implementation. We no longer follow the 12-week-plus-3-week configuration. All of the classes in the curriculum are now part of the 15-week semester. Unfortunately, that means the Topics courses are no longer considered capstone courses. This change is probably our biggest disappointment.

As for the workload issue, as faculty we agreed that the number of class preparations constituted more work than the number of teaching hours. In other words, most of us thought that it was more of a burden to teach four 3-credit courses, say, Reading, Writing, Speaking, and Topics, than to teach three 4-credit courses, for example, Reading, Writing, and Topics in ESL. As a result, we revisited the issue of workload and decided to keep the total number of credits (18) the same but to change the number of classes the students are required to take from six to five and change the number of credits for each of those classes. That meant reducing the course offerings from six 3-credit classes to five 3- and 4-credit classes (see Current IELI Curriculum). In discussions on which classes to change, we agreed that reading and writing classes required more class time and should carry 4 credits; because of our enthusiasm for the content classes, we also made Topics a 4-credit course. We concurred that because of the nature of many Topics

Current IELI Curriculum			
Level 1	**Level 2**	**Level 3**	**Level 4**
Writing I (4 credits)	Writing From Sources (4 credits)	Writing From Authentic Texts (4 credits)	Writing From Academic Sources (4 credits)
Reading I (4 credits)	Reading II (4 credits)	Reading Authentic Texts (4 credits)	Reading From Academic Sources (4 credits)
Integrated Skills (3 credits)	Integrated Skills (3 credits)	Comprehending Academic Discourse (3 credits)	Comprehending Lecture Discourse (3 credits)
Cross-Culture Talk (3 credits)	Cross-Culture Talk (3 credits)	Spoken Discourse and Cross-Cultural Communication (3 credits)	Academic Discourse (3 credits)
Topics in ESL I and II (4 credits)	Topics in ESL I and II (4 credits)	Topics in ESL III (4 credits)	Cross-Cultural Perspectives (4 credits)

courses, that is, the fact that they are task based and sometimes experiential, we needed to schedule those courses at the end of the day. That made it easier for the teachers of the content courses to schedule off-campus activities and assignments.

A final change that we made to the Topics courses was related to our consensus that communication is not just language; a crucial part of successful communication in a second language is related to cultural knowledge. The IELI faculty agree that students need to be aware of their own individual cultures and values; U.S. culture in general; the local culture of Logan, Utah; and the academic culture of the university. Therefore, we decided to offer Level 4 students a Cross-Cultural Perspectives course to give them a grounding in understanding what culture is and how it shapes people.

Conclusion

In the curricular change from a completely skills-based curriculum to the addition of a content-based course, the disadvantages we have encountered have been logistical, not pedagogical. Pedagogically, we feel that, by incorporating theme- and task-based instruction into our academic intensive English program, we have enhanced its quality. Incorporating this innovation into our curriculum has underscored for us that as teachers we are also learners. As faculty, we have been revitalized by continually investigating new topics and creating new courses. Four teachers have developed Topics courses into academic papers, which they have presented at TESOL conferences. Other professors have seen the Topics course as an opportunity to establish new interdisciplinary relationships on our campus. One has consulted with the education curator of the art museum to assist in planning an art appreciation course. Another has met with a professor in the Drama Department to discuss a possible collaboration on a student play.

The students also see the Topics courses as a welcome change from their routine language classes. In addition to delving into a new subject each term, they often get the chance to work outside the classroom, visiting new places on campus and off. Expanding the curriculum philosophy to include content-based courses, recognizing the importance of giving choices to faculty and students, and bringing to life the notion that we are all learners within a community have brought a sense of renewal and energy to the program.

Appendix A: Curriculum Statement of Philosophy

At IELI, we revisit the Curriculum Statement of Philosophy from time to time to ensure that it reflects our current thinking. Each member of the faculty has knowledge, perspectives, attitudes, and interests that influence the crafting of this statement. We work together to write the statement in a process of shared meaning making, so that the final product reflects our collective beliefs, priorities, and desires for IELI.

The statement shown here came about through a series of discussions and collaborative writing activities conducted in faculty meetings; outside meetings, everyone is too busy to respond to requests for input. We initiated a discussion of the then-current statement, focusing on the elements we wished to see remain. Following the faculty meeting, the assistant director wrote her understanding of the discussion as a draft statement and returned it to the faculty at the next meeting for further input. This time, each person wrote statements he or she wanted to see in the document and shared them with the group. Together we questioned, commented, reworded, added, and deleted until we had the basis for a second draft. This sometimes involved making sure the document included a statement for an element of the program that we thought was working. For example, we use an exam that places students in one level and a process that allows students to move up or down a level in individual classes. We crafted this philosophy statement: *Learners' abilities develop differentially in the various language skills. Therefore, in administering the curriculum we want students to be able to progress through the IELI program according to their individual needs and performances.*

Following the second round of discussions, the assistant director again wrote a draft and returned it to the faculty for final approval or refinement. We hammered out problems, and people raised questions we had not anticipated in the previous discussion before words were committed to paper. The result, shown here, involved the entire faculty in constructing collective beliefs about curriculum. Further, the process resulted in an extension of the prior understanding any one of us had about curriculum.

Curriculum Statement of Philosophy
The Intensive English Language Institute
Utah State University

A curriculum is always in process.

Knowledge is socially constructed. The role of faculty is to facilitate students' construction of knowledge of language and its use. The role of the curriculum is to guide this construction by providing tasks and opportunities relevant to students' academic goals that will allow them to continually test and verify their knowledge.

We take a holistic, integrative view that recognizes the interplay of viewpoints often labeled as cognitive, humanistic, and sociocultural.

We aim for a curriculum focused on learning and believe that all members of a classroom community learn from one another.

We strive for an open, supportive learning environment where students can explore individual interests, learn to make decisions, negotiate issues and take responsibility for their own learning.

Broad Faculty Ownership

We value the contributions of a professionally active faculty, and seek to integrate the multiple perspectives and collective expertise of the faculty through regular curriculum discussion.

A Cross-Cultural Perspective

Having an informed cross-cultural perspective will help our students interact with IELI classmates from diverse cultures, and all members of the university community.

We value materials and tasks oriented toward university success, and recognize that such success requires knowledge of the American university culture and academic genres as well as linguistic competence.

Meeting Students' Needs

Students are more than language learners; they are whole people with lives, preferences, and individual goals.

Students at all levels of language proficiency can engage in scholarship, critical thinking, and problem solving.

Learners' abilities develop differentially in the various language skills. Therefore, in administering the curriculum we want students to be able to progress through the lELI program according to their individual needs and performances.

We can serve students well by helping them become independent, autonomous learners capable of functioning on their own in a university environment.

Appendix B: Topics in ESL Courses

- Academic Literacy (Susan Carkin)
- American Television (Lee Rawley)
- Current Events (Ann Roemer)
- The Earth and Us: Environmental Issues and Perspectives (Lee Rawley)
- English for Algebra (Ann Roemer)
- The Environment and Logan Canyon (Tom Schroeder)
- An Introduction to Film Studies (Ann Roemer)
- Spoken Communication for Business Managers (Jim Bame)
- *Tuesdays With Morrie* : Language and Service Learning (Gabrielle Goodwin)
- Using Field Experiences to Promote American Cultural Understanding (Beth Kozbial)
- Web Page Design (Jim Rogers)
- Western Medicine and You (Jilda Yap)
- Writing My Story: An Experience With Autobiographical Writing (Glenda Cole)
- Written Communication for International Business Managers (Jim Bame)

Appendix C: Additional Course Descriptions for Topics in ESL

COURSE TITLE: AMERICAN TELEVISION

Levels: 1, 2, 3
Instructor: Lee Rawley

Course Description: In this course students will watch American television programs (which they will help select). They will analyze the programs and the advertising to see how American TV portrays men and women, people from different cultures, and people from different American ethnic groups. Students will also write and conduct surveys to learn such things as what Americans think about television and how often they watch it.

Language Skills: Listening, understanding fast speech, speaking (in class and out of class to Americans), writing, speaking.

Academic Skills: Strategies for understanding authentic material; critical thinking skills (predicting, summarizing, analyzing, synthesizing); note taking; working collaboratively with others; presenting information orally to a group.

Content: The specific content of the course will be decided by the students and teacher together. Possible content includes news programs, comedies, mysteries, drama, sports, and music.

Evaluation: Will be based on in-class listening activities, journal writing, and a final project (working with a team to write and conduct a survey of Americans and present the results to the class).

COURSE TITLE: READING A NOVEL: *TUESDAYS WITH MORRIE*: LESSONS ON LIVING

Levels: 3, 4
Instructor: Gabrielle Goodwin

Course Description: This course will focus on the true story of Morrie Schwartz, who died of Lou Gehrig's disease. Students will read the novel, watch television news programs, and listen to the story on audiocassette. Class discussions and writing assignments will revolve around students' reactions to the material. Students are also required to become involved with an appropriate member of the community.

Textbook: *Tuesdays With Morrie* by Mitch Albom (available from Barnes & Noble, http://www.bn.com/, for $10.50 plus shipping); audiotape (available from http://www.bn.com/)

Language Skills: Speaking, listening, reading, writing.

Academic Skills: Keeping a journal, interviewing, participating in group discussions, writing reflective essays, reading and listening to authentic text, summarizing.

Content: The content will include the following topics gathered from various sources: old age, death and dying, cultural norms and stereotypes, lessons learned from life, reading skills and interview techniques.

Evaluation: Students will be evaluated on their journal and essay writing, and on a service project with members of the local community.

COURSE TITLE: WEB PAGE DESIGN

Levels: 3, 4
Instructor: Jim Rogers

Course Description: This course will ostensibly focus on designing a Web page. The students will be engaged in the design and building of a personal Web page. In doing so, they will read related articles on HTML and design principles. Students will also attend lectures and workshops by the professor and other Web and graphics experts that will be focused on various aspects of design and Web-page building.

For more details, see http://cc.usu.edu/~fajimr/courses/web_design/index.htm.

Language Skills: Reading, writing, listening, speaking.

Academic Skills: Summarizing a chapter both verbally and in writing, analyzing a Web page using ideas from readings, listening to lectures, presenting a topic (a design idea or an editing process) to the class, developing metacognitive awareness of learning processes, working collaboratively.

Content: Chapters from a book on Web design, Web pages assigned by professor and found by students, lectures.

Evaluation: Will be based on written critiques of the design elements of the Web page as well as other model Web pages, written and verbal summary of a design chapter, a paper describing the process of creating a Web page (focusing on the learning involved), presenting one aspect of Web design to the class, writing a summary of two guest lectures.

COURSE TITLE: WESTERN MEDICINE AND YOU

Levels: 3, 4

Instructor: Jilda Yap

Course Description: The course will present an overview of the medical system in the United States and health care available through USU insurance. It will provide practice with vocabulary, questions, and expressions that students will encounter when they visit a doctor or go to the hospital emergency room. The course will also discuss types of Western medical treatment and medicines, and questions that students should ask when they visit the doctor or pharmacist. In addition, reliable—and unreliable—sources of self-education about medicine will be discussed and explored. When possible, field trips and invited speakers from diverse health care providers will be involved.

Language Skills: Listening to lectures, invited speakers, and explanations given during tours; speaking in class discussions and prepared interview situations; reading related articles on medicine, both hard copy and on the Internet; writing short reports.

Academic Skills: Understanding and answering questions concerned with and affecting one's health; understanding doctors' explanations and basic medical vocabulary; taking notes; forming questions, conversational skills, presentation skills, and polite expressions; Internet search skill building; preparing interviews.

Class Materials: Three-ring binder, filler paper; materials on reserve or other materials to be photocopied as needed; information found on the World Wide Web (Internet); additional materials provided by the instructor; a good dictionary, preferably *Longman Dictionary of American English* or *Longman Advanced American Dictionary.*

Making the Syllabus Relevant: Closing the Gap Between Policy and Practice

6

REBECCA BELCHAMBER

Do you have two syllabi—one to satisfy the auditors, agents, and observers of your center and another driven by students' needs and teachers' interpretation or preferences? Sometimes, what happens in the classroom is at odds with the formal program. At the La Trobe University Language Centre, in Australia, we found that this was often the case. The ideal is to have a workable syllabus, and for it to work, it must be relevant to all concerned.

I became involved in curriculum renewal through my role as a senior teacher in the General English component of the English Language Intensive Courses for Overseas Students (ELICOS) program. The academic coordinator felt that there was a need to make some changes so that the program would better meet students' and teachers' needs. As part of a small group of teachers, I became involved in determining needs in different areas, designing changes, and implementing them.

Curriculum is often considered as a broad concept encompassing all the learning opportunities created by the school: class-based lessons plus electives and activities, assessment, and excursions as well as all the decision-making processes of all the participants (Johnson, 1989b). The term *syllabus* refers to a subset of curriculum: the content of a given course (sometimes the teachers' interpretation of the curriculum; see Rodgers, 1989). A syllabus results from selecting and ordering content. I use the term *syllabus* or *program* here because the focus is on content at the classroom level and not assessment choices or learning opportunities outside the school.

Curricular Context

La Trobe University Language Centre is medium sized, with 230–320 students, 24 full-time staff members, and class sizes capped at 18. Most students are international students studying ELICOS in either the General English or the Academic English stream. Some students also study English for business or prepare for the International English Language Testing System. This chapter, however, deals only with curriculum renewal for the General English program's five 10-week stages. Each term is 5 weeks long, and students progress to the next class after achieving the objectives set for each stage. There is no set textbook. For each stage, teachers receive a collection of objectives, structures and functions, and designated resources (mostly from course books) with which to teach. Teachers use these as a framework and often create their own worksheets.

An earlier change had come about with the broadening of the Centre's focus about 10 years earlier. Originally largely a migrant education center, it had begun to develop in the area of international education. For quality assurance and accountability purposes, the curriculum documents needed to be expressed in terms of objectives, be quantifiable, and reflect a linear approach. The migrant program uses the Curriculum for Spoken and Written English, so this was adapted to reflect the five stages of the program.

At the same time, the acting director proposed a new, direct-entry English for foreign students (EFS) course (i.e., an English for academic purposes course), leading students to enrollment at La Trobe University. This affected the General English course, as students following this pathway were starting in low-level General English classes and progressing to EFS. As a result, the focus on grammar, vocabulary, and tasks related to skills development had to be tightened.

Motivation for Curriculum Renewal

In the renewal, we attempted to make the inherited curriculum more relevant to teachers and learners. As stated, the existing guidelines, models, and materials had been developed for earlier purposes. We decided to focus on reworking these areas, because we could see that they were the ones that needed the most attention. In looking at the research, we noticed that when Nunan (1988) looked at lack of curriculum continuity, he saw that a deficit of guidelines and models was a major factor leading to an unworkable curriculum.

Nunan (1988) also identified the nature of the program as a potential reason for veering from the given framework. A particular model may be a constraint on delivering the program if imposed on teachers when it does not sit comfortably with their ideas and beliefs. However, van Lier (1996) refers to the curriculum as an interplay between constraints and resources; it is a structure that sets limits on what can be done, but it also provides opportunities and can be enabling. Our objectives-based curriculum is a nonnegotiable part of the program and could have been a stumbling block for some teachers. Competency-based instruction often arises from a desire for accountability and cost-effectiveness. It results in objectives couched in behavioral terms. Detractors might argue that having objectives prevents the teacher from teaching to the moment and being spontaneous. Then there is the argument for the creative nature of language proficiency. Can it be reduced to elements, similar to the way learning a skill can?

We looked for the merits in the objective-based approach. According to Nunan (2002), it makes the learner the main focus and describes what the learner rather than the teacher is to do. As he argued,

> It has been suggested that articulating precise statements of what the learner is to be able to do at the end of a course is an essential step in the curriculum design process, because it greatly facilitates a number of other steps. (p. 2)

This approach has been adopted by the Council of Europe (2001) in designing a common approach for curriculum and syllabus for the *Common European Framework of Reference for Languages*. That framework is also used in Australia and New Zealand.

THE ROLE OF CONSULTATION

We also believe that a curriculum that invites input from everyone with a vested interest, from management to learners, will be more workable and relevant. Not heavily learner centered, neither is the curriculum specialist directed. It does acknowledge that decisions made at different stages should be made by those best qualified.

The essential element is consultation. We made sure to survey staff and students, invite comments, and discuss ideas. Burton (1998) stresses the role teachers can play as curriculum developers. They can be given a degree of ownership, the encouragement to be creative within the curriculum framework, and the responsibility for tailoring their program to meet learners' needs.

One reason to have an explicit syllabus is to make language learning more manageable. However, a syllabus should not be followed without critical evaluation of the elements. This is why we invited comments and contributions from those involved at both ends of the process. Their beliefs about a usable syllabus, transparent and adequate models, the objective-based approach, and the valuing of teacher contributions informed our curriculum development effort.

SPECIFIC CURRICULAR CONCERNS

For some time, at end-of-term reviews and staff meetings, teachers had been identifying problematic issues with the curriculum. These included

- too many objectives for each stage
- the fact that listening and speaking objectives were combined.
- the lack of a clear division between the two parts of each stage (Ten-week stages were divided into two parts, A and B. Within a stage, the teacher for the first term might select certain objectives, which could then be repeated in the next 5-week term.)
- too many grammar or function items to deal with in 5-week terms
- lack of challenge in the themes, activities, and objectives for Stages 4 and 5
- the fact that much of the material was dated or British in content

Adapting and Evaluating the Program

A curriculum team of two teachers, of which I was one, worked with the academic coordinator 1 day a week. We asked staff for input and suggestions via a survey and then began making changes based on agreed directions in five areas: objectives, grammar and functions, materials development, listening and speaking, and assessment.

OBJECTIVES

We first tackled the area of objectives, because the most immediate need was felt to be in this area. Teachers had been working with a set of objectives, such as those shown in Combined Stage 3 Objectives. Our faculty survey indicated that teachers had encountered these problems:

1. The number of objectives was too high for a 5-week term, leaving little time for building skills in four reading or writing genres.
2. The combining of listening and speaking was too imprecise; teachers were unsure how to apportion classroom activities.
3. Some objectives achieved in the A stage might be repeated in the B stage, whereas others might not be addressed at all, leading students and teachers to be confused about assessment and promotion.

As a result of extensive discussions, the curriculum team decided to reduce the number of objectives and revise some of the terminology. We

Combined Stage 3 Objectives

By the end of the course, learners will be able to do the following:

3LS	Listening and Speaking
3LS1	Understand extended spoken information texts
3LS2	Understand extended spoken exchanges
3LS3	Understand extended spoken narratives
3LS4	Give short presentations on familiar topics
3LS5	Negotiate extended spoken exchanges
3LS6	Participate in extended casual conversations

3R	Reading
3R1	Understand extended written information texts
3R2	Understand short persuasive texts
3R3	Understand short critiques
3R4	Understand texts outlining problematic situations

3W	Writing
3W1	Write short persuasive texts
3W2	Write short reports
3W3	Write extended narratives
3W4	Write short responses to problematic situations

3IL	Independent Learning Strategies
3IL1	Fulfill attendance and punctuality requirements
3IL2	Participate effectively in class activities
3IL3	Follow unmodified teacher instructions
3IL4	Participate effectively in goal setting, feedback, and evaluation processes
3IL5	Revise class work at home and complete homework tasks
3IL6	Organize notes in a folder and maintain a vocabulary book
3IL7	Use an English-only dictionary with teacher guidance
3IL8	Apply linguistic rules and patterns with teacher guidance
3IL9	Independently access the Independent Learning Centre and outside resources to enhance language learning
3IL10	Use Microsoft Word proficiently; access computer-assisted language learning programs; access e-mail and Internet

Assessment is continuous through the course and is based on achievement of the course objectives. For promotion to the next stage, you need to achieve as follows:
- listening and speaking: at least five objectives
- reading: at least three objectives
- writing: at least three objectives
- independent learning strategies: all objectives

decided on eight objectives per stage, two for each macroskill. We separated the listening and speaking objectives, each focusing on interactive, goal-oriented situations as well as the traditional recounts (see, e.g., Objectives for Stages 3A and 3B). Thus the first 5 weeks of each stage were quite distinct from the second.

Terminology was also an issue. The original objectives referred to

---

Objectives for Stages 3A and 3B

Stage 3A Course Outline

By the end of the course, you should have achieved the following objectives:

Listening (22.5%)	
3AL1	Understand extended spoken interactions (goal-oriented and interpersonal)
3AL2	Understand extended spoken narratives
Speaking (22.5%)	
3AS1	Participate effectively in casual conversations
3AS2	Give presentations on topics related to course themes (5–7 minutes)
Reading (15%)	
3AR1	Understand extended written text describing an issue
3AR2	Understand extended written narratives
Writing (15%)	
3AW1	Write about past and recent events and situations
3AW2	Write a response to an issue
Grammar and Vocabulary (15%)	
3AG	Control grammatical forms and sentence structures taught at this stage
Positive Learning Strategies (10%)	
3PL1	Fulfill attendance and punctuality requirements
3PL2	Participate effectively in class activities
3PL3	Follow unmodified teacher instructions
3PL4	Participate effectively in goal-setting, feedback, and evaluation processes
3PL5	Revise class work at home and complete homework tasks
3PL6	Organize notes in a folder and maintain a vocabulary book
3PL7	Use an English-only dictionary with teacher guidance
3PL8	Apply linguistic rules and patterns with teacher guidance
3PL9	Independently access Independent Learning Centre and outside resources to enhance language learning
3PL10	Use Microsoft Word proficiently; access computer-assisted language learning programs; access e-mail and Internet

continued on p. 107

Objectives for Stages 3A and 3B (cont.)

Stage 3B Course Outline

By the end of the course, you should have achieved the following objectives:

	Listening (22.5%)
3BL1	Understand extended spoken exchanges (goal-oriented and interpersonal)
3BL2	Understand extended spoken information texts
	Speaking (22.5%)
3BS1	Negotiate extended goal-oriented spoken exchanges
3BS2	Give oral presentations on topics related to course themes (7–10 minutes)
	Reading (15%)
3BR1	Understand extended written passages of descriptive text
3BR2	Understand extended persuasive text
	Writing (15%)
3BW1	Write short persuasive text
3BW2	Write structured report of at least 250 words on a course theme
	Grammar and Vocabulary (15%)
3BG	Grammar points and vocabulary taught at this stage
	Positive Learning Strategies (10%)
3PL1	Fulfill attendance and punctuality requirements
3PL2	Participate effectively in class activities
3PL3	Follow unmodified teacher instructions
3PL4	Participate effectively in goal-setting, feedback, and evaluation processes
3PL5	Revise class work at home and complete homework tasks
3PL6	Organize notes in a folder and maintain a vocabulary book
3PL7	Use an English-only dictionary with teacher guidance
3PL8	Apply linguistic rules and patterns with teacher guidance
3PL9	Independently access Independent Learning Centre and outside resources to enhance language learning
3PL10	Use Microsoft Word proficiently, access computer-assisted language learning programs, access e-mail and Internet

information text, which implied that we wanted students to comprehend and write or speak connected chunks of information, with long turns. This expectation seemed to be a rather blunt instrument for our purposes, particularly in speaking and listening. To solve this problem, we introduced two terms: *spoken exchange* (often referred to as *goal-oriented* exchange) and *spoken interaction.* We identified the former as interaction in which participants have a specific purpose that calls for the use of functional language (e.g., making arrangements, suggestions, apologies, or requests; asking permission; using various discussion functions). The latter, more descriptive term characterized mainly interpersonal interaction, such as casual conversations.

GRAMMAR AND FUNCTIONS

We reviewed the grammar and functions documents to achieve better articulation between the stages. Teachers had a variety of opportunities to discuss these documents, such as during professional development days and end-of-term curriculum reviews.

An Outline of Work for Stage3A shows an example of the revised grammar and functions for one stage. Before the functions reached this point, we had produced a more ambitious version, but we decided to scale it down for two reasons. First, we wanted a version that teachers could use and that could be presented to students as a map of where they were going over the 5 weeks; second, we realized we would not make much headway if we spent so much time on one set of documents.

MATERIALS DEVELOPMENT

The other arm of the curriculum work was materials development. We assessed existing materials and slotted them into the new format where suitable. Needs for additional materials were identified, and we obtained the materials from course books or developed them at the Centre. At this point, an additional teacher joined the curriculum team for one or two terms to produce materials that would fill gaps identified in the growing syllabus.

We composed a week-by-week guide as an inventory or record of all materials. Week-by-Week Guide for Stage 3A (page 110) gives an example of the resources collated for one objective. The guide, which is added to regularly, includes teacher comments and guidelines for teaching the objective.

As with the grammar and functions documents, we started by producing a much more detailed document, trying to include a range of features for each objective. We began with a table that included the headings *objective examples of text types, grammar functions, lexis discourse features/strategies,* and *pronunciation.*

We soon realized that the items could be specific to the texts selected and could change over time. Again, with more work ahead of us than already done, we realized we were being too particular. We decided that it was better to set down guidelines and establish a culture in which teachers produced their own worksheets than to be prescriptive and bewilder teachers with so much detail. After all, the discretion available to teachers is where

An Outline of Work for Stage 3A

Theme	Grammar	Functions
Personal relations	Phrasal verbs Adjective order, adverbial modifiers Present perfect for reporting family news	Giving advice/criticizing (*ought to* for obligation) Making suggestions
Work	Present perfect, simple and progressive Past simple, progressive, perfect Comparatives and superlatives (including *more/less* + adjective)	Requesting assistance Giving opinions; agreeing/disagreeing
Crime and mystery	Past simple, progressive, perfect Reported speech forms Speculation/deduction modals (e.g., *must, can, can't, could, must've, could've*) Third conditional (introduction) Subject and object questions (e.g., *Who killed JR?/ Who did JR kill?*)	Expressing concern, anxiety Expressing admission and denial Asking for and reporting information
Where people live	Present tenses Wishes and hopes Comparatives and superlatives *Very, too, not . . . enough* *So* + adjective, *such a* adjective + noun	Discussing preferences Complaining
Indigenous Australians	Passives as Stage 2 + present perfect, present progressive Past tenses and *used to* Time markers and sequencers	Expressing certainty/uncertainty Expressing strong opinion Expressing regret (*it's a shame/pity that . . .*)

many of them find satisfaction; putting their own stamp and style into a piece of work and having the flexibility to address needs as they arise—to teach to the moment even when the lesson is a set one—is the mark of proficient teachers.

Encouraging Communal Materials

Although teachers had often created and shared materials at the Centre, there had not been a central place for the collation of these materials. Teachers would keep their own collections at their individual workstations.

Week-by-Week Guide for Stage 3A

3AL2	**Understand Extended Spoken Narratives**
	Interpretation of the objective: In the final assessment, the following criteria must apply. However, teaching tasks should be seen as developmental, building skills for the final task. • Learners should identify main ideas and specific details in extended narratives of about 2–3 minutes relevant to Stage 3 themes. Can be part of a longer text. • The narrative must feature a clear, fluent speaker (not the class teacher) live or on TV, radio, or audio- or videocassette. Single listening only. • About 10 questions must be given to learners first. • Written responses need not be grammatically correct or in sentence form, but errors should not interfere with meaning.
WK 1	Language Centre (LC) video, Part 1: "Dai and Linda," interviews on marriage (located in Resource Room) LC Video, Part 2: Steve and Jenny talk about marriages
WK 2	Three different talks about jobs (*difficult—may be suitable for class of good listeners or listening lab work*) *Headway Australasia Intermediate* (Bradley, Dyer, & Hayman, 1996), Unit 7, p. 26
WK 3	Language Centre video: Centre staff interviewed about crimes; located in Resource Room *Four speakers; can be used individually. "Steve" can be used as assessment task—see assessment folder.*
WK 4	"Living With People," *Impact Listening 3* (Harschi & Wolf-Quintero, 2001)
WK 5	Videos: Stolen generation or dreamtime stories
	Assessment Tasks "Steve" as assessment task; see assessment folder.

As teachers came and went through the various stages, teaching themes and objectives that others had already completed, they had to rely on colleagues' goodwill to share what had been created or continually collect new materials and write new exercises. Also, we realized that curriculum reference documents were inconveniently located in the library, at the other end of the building.

To make materials and reference documents more accessible and more easily shared, we developed course materials folders, which are kept in cupboards in the corridor outside teachers' offices. There are five folders per stage, with a subsection for each objective as well as for grammar/functions and computer-assisted language learning activities. They contain curriculum documents as well.

The materials development initiative shifted the focus from the individual to the teaching community. Resources were developed to be shared; finding an existing lesson was no longer a case of luck or chance. Teachers were not required to use what others had developed, but the communal materials folders have certain advantages. It is easy to see where gaps exist and direct our energies to meeting those needs rather than making yet another worksheet when one is readily available. Also, when an emergency teacher has to be called in at short notice, the lessons are readily obtained. A glance at the timetable is a guide to the objectives being addressed that day; the relevant folder (according to week or theme) has a section for each objective.

Keeping a Record of Materials

Once the folders had been set up and labeled, teachers got used to looking in them for lessons and adding their own worksheets. The week-by-week guide is now more of a snapshot of the syllabus at a particular point in time. Having created it, the curriculum team will have to decide how it is to be managed. Updating it regularly can be demanding, but we need to find a way to include lessons that have been added to the folders.

Ideally, teachers would type an entry in the document as they physically add to the folder, but this is expecting a lot of staff who are already putting a great deal of creative energy into their materials and their classes. The other approach would be to have all materials pass through the curriculum team. Although this would make collation easier, it may inhibit teachers, perhaps making it seem as though a committee were screening their worksheets, and we do not want to reverse the existing willingness to create and share materials. This issue is one that we have to discuss and act on in the near future.

LISTENING AND SPEAKING

Through end-of-course evaluations and anecdotal reports, we realized that General English students wanted more speaking and listening relative to reading and writing. This was particularly apparent when short-term study groups came to the Centre. These groups come predominantly from Japan and Korea during their university summer breaks. The students are usually strong in reading and grammar and identify listening and speaking as their weaker skill areas. To make sure we were not just responding to the needs of the more outspoken students, we surveyed all the General English students during one term (see Appendix A for the survey form). Because students indicated that they would like more opportunities for listening and speaking, we made some significant changes to the curriculum and the focus of some class activities.

The responses confirmed our sense of students' needs, and we adapted the curriculum accordingly. We decided to assess only one reading and writing objective each term, with that objective to be decided by the teacher and coteacher of each class. Although letting the students decide might have been more democratic, we needed to work this out beforehand for two reasons. First, slots on the timetable refer to the objectives in language easily understood by students, and, second, the timetable indicating when they may not be in their usual classroom but in the language lab or the computer room is given out on the first day of term.

Students indicated that they wanted more listening and speaking opportunities outside the classroom. They were looking for more variety in the activities offered and requested more interaction with native speakers. We responded by utilizing the volunteer tutors already at the Centre (available for individual consultation in the Independent Learning Centre [ILC]) and inviting them to classes for discussion on stage themes or work on particular functions. We also discussed the practicalities of providing more interaction with native speakers and decided to hold a workshop on ideas at our next in-service day.

However, teachers raised the issue of the needs of some continuing students—those with the goal of attaining a tertiary qualification in English who might later shift to the Academic English stream. These students could be disadvantaged by the reduced focus on reading and writing. The concern was valid, so we decided that teachers should look at the needs of the students class by class. We decided that the second reading and writing objectives could be introduced but not taught as rigorously because they would not be assessed.

ASSESSMENT

The original course outline had listed only the objectives students needed to pass; the new version, with objectives divided between Stages A and B, gave weighting to the various areas (see Combined Stage 3 Objectives and Objectives for Stages 3A and 3B earlier in the chapter). We decided to make listening and speaking worth more (22.5% each) in the General English program. Reading, writing, and grammar/vocabulary are worth 15% each, and the list of positive learning strategies is worth 10%. Formerly called *independent learning strategies,* this group of skills was renamed to better reflect the elements grouped under that heading.

The next phase of the project was to review the assessment tasks developed by teachers. The curriculum team asked teachers to indicate what tasks were being used to determine how well the objectives had been achieved.

Several issues arose from the range of material presented, including the need to indicate assessment criteria and maximum marks per question so the process was more transparent to students, the benefit of having an answer sheet to assist with marking, and the need for samples of good and weak responses for writing assessments and for more moderation sessions for written tasks. As with previous initiatives, the issues will be brought to a workshop at a professional development session, and we will canvass opinions before setting some goals.

Evaluation of the Changes

The evaluation of the renewal involved getting staff's response to the new materials, getting feedback from students, and assessing how well the new syllabus met national standards.

Teachers are very conversant with both the new syllabus and the relevant materials. There is a strong sense of working together with a core bank of lessons and a familiarity with the assessment tasks. Nevertheless, we are not at the end of the process. Although we have a strong framework and sound matrix, we are constantly evaluating and renewing the materials. This has become easier since the awarding of more permanent and contract positions to replace some of the casual staff working at the Centre. In practical terms, this means the Centre has a core body of teachers with more preparation time and job security, which encourages them to develop materials for general use. In addition, teachers are given release time to consolidate tasks and assessments for the stage they have been working on recently. A culture of adding to the bank of materials is developing, with teachers enjoying the creativity and challenge of the process.

Students evaluate the course each term through a short survey (see Appendix B), with questions on areas such as course work, assessments, and electives they have attended. Since the Centre reduced the General English assessment tasks for reading and writing, students have been happier about the class time given to the four skill areas. However, realizing we were collecting qualitative rather than quantitative data, we altered the survey form so that students circle responses on a scale of 1 to 5.

The accreditation body to which we are accountable, National English Language Teaching Accreditation Scheme, has a set of guidelines for checking that the curriculum in place can assist and support teachers in selecting and sequencing course content. It states the following:

1. The curriculum should be set out in an accessible document.
2. The document should be available to staff.
3. Teachers should feel they can add to or amend the document.

4. The document should provide useful information, such as what and when to teach, with some flexibility to allow for teacher creativity.

5. The document should include practical considerations for teachers, such as a list of available resources and a realistic timetable. (Price & Smith, 2003)

We feel that the syllabus renewal is achieving all of the above points. In addition, we have developed a document and materials that are used daily. It is vital to have resources that can be interpreted by staff who come in for emergency teaching or for a single term as well as by the longer term staff. The aim is to have an easily understood curriculum, which translates into a deliverable syllabus.

Conclusion

We wanted our syllabus to reflect what was being taught, not just be a document on a shelf brought out for administrative purposes while teachers walked into class with teaching materials that sometimes had only a tenuous relationship to the syllabus. This was important because of our beliefs about language learning and our assessment of our learners' needs. In addition, we believed that teachers would refine the existing worksheets and develop new ones over time, with these materials becoming available communally. As such, the Centre would be using a range of materials and activities that reflected students' interests and teachers' contributions. What is evolving is a dynamic syllabus that is driven by context and that teachers and students see as an asset and a resource for offering English learning opportunities.

Appendix A: Survey Form Given to General English Students

Stage _____   Questionnaire No. _____

QUESTION 1

Rate the following in order of importance to you. Use the numbers 1–5 to fill in the boxes, where 1 is the most important to you and 5 the least important. Use each number once only.

Listening ☐
Speaking ☐
Reading ☐
Writing ☐
Grammar ☐

QUESTION 2

In the classes you have taken, what do you think of the amount of time spent on listening and speaking? (Please circle one choice.)

| Enough | Too little | Too much |

QUESTION 3

Would you like more chances to use English outside your classroom (but during class time)?

Examples (cost would be small or nil):

Yes   **No**

Surveying La Trobe University students
  on the main campus
Using the hall for role plays, drama, or short lectures
Holding discussions/conversation with students
  from other classes
Requesting information at shopping centers,
  travel agents, and so on
Visiting information centers
Visiting a local school
Visiting the La Trobe University wildlife reserve

Are there any other activities you would like to add to this list for Question 3?

QUESTION 4

In general, I would like to spend more time on: (Please circle one box.

| listening and speaking | OR | reading, writing, and grammar |

Thank you for answering these questions.

Appendix B: Student Course Evaluation

Class: _____   Term/year:_____/200__

Class Teacher:_____   Co-teacher(s):_____

DO NOT WRITE YOUR NAME ON THIS FORM.

QUESTION 1: COURSE CONTENT

What did you think of the CONTENT of the course? (e.g., topics, materials, classroom tasks). Was it interesting? Please write a comment.

Please circle a number to give your opinion about the content of the course.

Not interesting for you				Very interesting for you
1	2	3	4	5

QUESTION 2: ASSESSMENT

Every term the teachers give you tests to assess your language learning. What did you think of these tests or assessments? For example, were there enough or too many assessments? From doing the assessments, did you learn about your strong and weak language skills? Did the assessments encourage you to study and practice your language skills?

Please circle a number to give your opinion about the assessments.

Not useful for you				Very useful for you
1	2	3	4	5

QUESTION 3: WHAT WOULD YOU LIKE MORE AND LESS OF?

I would like MORE	I would like LESS

QUESTION 4: HOW WAS YOUR PROGRESS IN ENGLISH?

Please tick.

	Excellent	**Good**	**Fair**	**Poor**
Listening				
Speaking				
Pronunciation				
Reading				
Writing				
Grammar				
Vocabulary				

QUESTION 5: WHAT DID YOU THINK OF THE MORNING OR AFTERNOON ACTIVITIES?

I attended the following activity/activities:	Please comment and circle a number (1 is not good, 5 is excellent)				
	1	2	3	4	5
	1	2	3	4	5

QUESTION 6: WHAT AREAS OF ENGLISH DO YOU WANT TO IMPROVE MOST?

QUESTION 7: HOW WOULD YOU RATE THE COURSE OVERALL?

Please tick:

Excellent ☐   Very good ☐   Good ☐   Fair ☐   Poor ☐

QUESTION 8: DO YOU HAVE ANY MORE COMMENTS ABOUT THE LANGUAGE CENTRE?

Finding the Institutional Logic for Change

7

ALLISON N. PETRO

Each university has a logic and rhetoric that guides what courses and programs it offers. Curriculum changes generally need to be in line with that institutional logic—for example, one does not expect an extensive art department in an engineering school, or vice versa, though there are a few notable exceptions.

In the English Language Studies (ELS) Program at the University of Rhode Island, in the United States, the key to improving the curriculum was to analyze existing institutional constraints and keep proposals within those constraints. The key to change, therefore, was to find the institutional logic at the university and adhere to that logic in proposals to add courses.

Motivation for Revitalizing the Program

The ELS Program was less of an organized program and more of a hodge-podge of courses. Staffed initially by adjuncts, these courses were a series of attempts to address the needs of international and immigrant students on campus, but there was no central plan or means of assessing effectiveness. As long as there were students in the classes and faculty to teach them, the administration seemed satisfied. At times enrollment rose or fell, following campus or international trends, but there had been almost no opportunity to conduct a coordinated assessment of the curriculum or an analysis of whether it was meeting students' needs.

For the ELS faculty, there was a pervading sense that the program was stagnant. We had hobbled along for so long without additions or changes and with constant threats to our budget that the assumption was that nothing would ever change. In fact, we were wrong. In 2002, a key component of our offerings for undergraduates—a peer-tutoring program—was canceled by the university administration because of a worse-than-usual budget crisis. In the aftermath of that cut, the program was shrinking at a time when the number of international students was growing. Staff morale hit an all-time low.

What seemed like a setback turned out to be an opportunity. I became director of the program the year after the budget cut. Oddly, I was assigned the same teaching schedule as my predecessor, including supervising the peer-tutoring program that had been cut—even though, naturally, I could not teach a course that no longer existed. Wondering what to do with my time, I began to dream about other courses we could teach—new ones designed to meet the current needs of international students on campus. We conducted a needs assessment of the student population. In the process of talking to colleagues, gathering data from departments, and surveying students, we narrowed down several needs that were not being met.

However, the problem was not merely coming up with ideas for courses but overcoming the negative momentum of the program. I could remember countless meetings with department chairs and deans where it seemed that my colleagues or I had clearly articulated the needs of international students on campus and proposed reasonable changes, yet nothing had happened. We decided to take an entirely different tack, or else, we feared, our proposals were likely to have the same results. Rather than look at our numerous failures at expanding our program, we decided to look at our successes: the courses we did offer. What did they have in common? Why had they been added in the first place?

We searched for underlying patterns in the institutional logic for why certain courses existed in our program (e.g., we had two sections of an ESL freshman writing course but no other English courses for undergraduates). There were very real institutional constraints, with seemingly no exceptions, on what courses we could justify: We could not offer any courses that were considered remedial. We also had budget constraints, which meant that no new faculty could be added. Our courses for graduate students (international teaching assistants [ITAs]) were state mandated. If we could stay within those constraints, our proposals were more likely to be successful. The key to overcoming the negative momentum was to figure out why our program had been created in the first place—that is, to find our university's institutional logic.

Curricular Context

STUDENT POPULATION

The University of Rhode Island is the main campus of the state university system, with 14,000 students in a semirural area of the northeastern United States. The ELS Program is housed in the Department of English and serves the university's immigrant and international students. In the 2003–2004 academic year, there were 365 international students on campus; approximately 14% were undergraduates, and 86% were graduate students. No corresponding figures are available for the immigrant population because of the difficulty of identifying students who do not require visas. (In talking with colleagues who serve that population, we arrived at a rough figure of approximately 100 immigrants in the undergraduate student body.)

Despite the significant number of international and immigrant students on campus, enrollment in ELS courses remained low. In an average semester, only 15 undergraduates and 15 graduate students would be enrolled in our courses. One of the problems, we had always thought, was the limited course offerings: only two each semester—an undergraduate writing course and a graduate course for ITAs. One faculty member also worked as an ESL specialist in the Writing Center, but our limited offerings did not reach the vast majority of international students on campus.

When we realized that we could add one new course per semester, we had to think about who our students were, which of their needs were being met by existing courses, and what additional needs existed. We began by analyzing the international student populations on campus. The students who had traditionally been in ELS courses could be divided into three different groups: (a) immigrant students who had lived in the United States for a number of years but whose first language was not English, (b) exchange students who were studying on campus for a semester or a year, and (c) international graduate students who typically completed their undergraduate studies in their home countries and came to the United States for graduate school.

The immigrant students typically had better skills in informal speech but had difficulty with the expectations of formal language, both spoken and written. They may or may not have had solid literacy skills in their first language. In general, they had had more exposure to U.S. culture than the other groups, though they may not have felt completely comfortable with the cross-cultural differences between their ethnic community and the mainstream United States. They were typically graduates of inner-city high schools and often had some gaps in their academic preparation.

The exchange students usually had solid academic skills and high fluency in their native language. Their mastery of English varied greatly, though they tended to have strong skills in speaking and reading but weaker skills in listening and writing. They may have had a limited understanding of U.S. cultural patterns and tended to surround themselves with students from their own countries. Nonetheless, they were highly motivated to improve their English skills in the short amount of time they had on campus, and often it was their main purpose for seeking out the exchange program.

The graduate students were typically highly motivated and well prepared in their field of study but found that they did not have the English skills to communicate effectively as teaching assistants in U.S. classrooms. Their strongest skills were usually in reading and grammar, well suited to scoring high on standardized tests of English, such as the Test of English as a Foreign Language (TOEFL). Speaking and listening to Americans was more of a struggle. Their English preparation tended to be heavy on passive language skills that did not fit their current situation well.

THE PROGRAM

As for the place of the ELS Program within the larger university community, the program was named English Language Studies instead of English as a Second Language for several reasons. First, the students are advanced-level learners of English (as evidenced by the TOEFL score required for admission), and the ESL label does not seem to apply to them. They do not need to learn English, but they need to be able to use their English skills at such a high level that they begin to notice advanced-level language skills that are missing. Far from being beginning-level students, they are at a more advanced level than most of the foreign language learners on campus. They are also totally immersed in an English-only environment, and they need a chance to develop skills and strategies to cope with the onslaught of information.

A second reason for choosing the name ELS was to sidestep the attitude that studying advanced-level English is remedial work. The University of Rhode Island does not offer any remedial courses: All courses carry credit toward a degree. Thus, an agreement was made years ago that the campus would not have an ESL program. The ESL courses in the state university system—offered at community colleges and at Rhode Island College—are considered remedial and often do not carry degree credit. Our courses, by contrast, count for degree credit, the rationale being that they cover material that is offered elsewhere in the university. This logic is the key to justifying the fact that our courses count for credit while the ESL courses on the other campuses do not.

Thus, the name of the program reflects a fundamental difference in goals, in curriculum, and in the level of the students. At close examination, the difference is occasionally more rhetorical than factual, but this approach and vision have been both an asset and a liability over the years. When they allow students to work at an advanced level and receive credit for their efforts, the difference is helpful. When they limit the program's ability to respond to new student populations or changing needs of students, however, it becomes more of a constraint.

EXISTING COURSES

The undergraduate writing courses (ELS 112 and ELS 122) had undergone many changes in focus over the years, adjusting to the balance of immigrant versus exchange students and their preferences for more work on oral/aural or reading/writing skills. However, in a single semester it was difficult to develop all of the skills that undergraduates need for total immersion in an academic environment. Because the course was our only offering for undergraduates, the faculty had attempted to combine a reading/writing component with an oral/aural skills component. Consequently, covering the required material in sufficient depth had become impossible in the limited time available in a three-credit course. Also, because the course fulfilled the university writing requirement, it had to focus on students' knowledge of analytical reading and expository writing. A recurring problem was that this course was being asked to accomplish more than was humanly possible.

The ITA courses, designed specifically for international graduate students who worked as teaching assistants, focused on developing pronunciation skills (broadly defined), presentation skills, and intercultural awareness. We had redesigned the ITA courses various times over 10 years, so these courses did not change significantly as part of this reorganization. However, because the ITA courses were designed with a specific subgroup in mind, the goals and learning outcomes necessarily focus on a specific set of skills. Now that the curriculum could expand, we wanted to consider whether international graduate students needed skills that the ITA courses did not address.

Adapting and Evaluating the Program

Initially, the task was to identify students' unmet needs and design a curriculum to meet them. In fall 2003, we undertook a needs assessment that included a survey of departments, discussions with colleagues who regularly work with English learners, and both a survey of and discussions with English learners on campus.

To reach faculty in other departments, we sent an e-mail to department chairs, asking them to describe the difficulties they noticed among English learners (undergraduate and graduate students). We then followed up with e-mails, telephone conversations, and informal chats with colleagues who had specific ideas. We also spoke with staff members who deal with international and immigrant students (in the International Center and the Talent Development Program) to ask what courses they suggested adding. The consensus was that we did not offer enough of a variety of courses.

To reach English learners, we conducted a written survey (see the appendix) in the undergraduate writing class, which asked them to identify English skills they needed to improve—grammar, writing, reading, speaking, listening, pronunciation, and others. We followed up with informal discussions with students, asking them what kinds of skills they wanted to develop in our courses.

The goal was not just to make sure that students' needs were met; it was also to spread the word that the ELS Program was expanding and to let various interested parties on campus know that new courses were being added. On our campus, the success of curricular changes does not depend solely on how well the curriculum meets students' needs; without sufficient numbers of students actually enrolled, the courses would be in jeopardy. A secondary goal of the needs assessment, then, was to begin the steps necessary to ensure adequate enrollment in new courses.

DEVELOPING NEW COURSES

Based on discussions with colleagues and departments across the university, we identified several types of courses that were needed:

- courses to help international exchange students develop their speaking and listening skills
- courses for immigrant undergraduates (including so-called Generation 1.5 students) that would focus on academic writing and formal speaking skills
- courses to help international graduate students develop their academic writing skills, especially in scientific and technical fields

Aural/Oral Skills Courses

In order to design a new listening/speaking course for undergraduates, we needed to gather information on the target population and the skills needed. We distributed a needs assessment survey to all undergraduates enrolled in ELS courses in January 2004 (the same one previously given to the undergraduate writing class; see the appendix). Most were satisfied that they were able to develop the skills they needed in grammar, vocabulary, and writing in the existing ESL writing course for undergraduates, but many indicated that they also wanted to develop skills in public speaking and academic listening, as well as pronunciation skills in such areas as segmentals and suprasegmentals.

We discovered that one reason for the growing number of undergraduate English learners was a concerted effort on the part of the university's Office of International Education to bring more international students to campus, often on exchange programs. These exchange students typically come to the university during their fourth or fifth year of university from countries such as France, Germany, Spain, and South Korea, sometimes in direct exchange with University of Rhode Island students who are studying abroad in those countries. Many of these students live or eat at the International Engineering Program House. I decided to eat lunch there twice a week in order to get to know these students better through more informal, personal contact. In spring 2004, I also allowed a number of advanced-level undergraduates—all of them exchange students—to enroll in the graduate-level ITA course on a trial basis, which helped me learn more about their academic skills and weaknesses.

We also consulted with faculty in the Communication Department who teach the required undergraduate courses in communication studies. They gave us copies of the textbook they use as well as the syllabus for introductory oral communication courses. In designing the new courses, ELS 312 and ELS 322, we chose assignments and materials that resemble those used in the required communication course (COM 100), but redesigned them to be more appropriate to English learners. Our goal was to prepare students for their academic studies by choosing assignments that echoed those in field-specific courses.

Graduate Writing Seminar

In order to design a new course in graduate writing, we needed to consider two factors: the target population and the range of skills students needed to be successful. The ELS faculty had been teaching and testing ITAs for over 10 years, so we knew the range of English language ability among those students. We also knew something about their writing skills because we had given writing tasks in all of the ITA courses. However, the courses we had taught focused mostly on developing aural/oral skills, with only occasional writing tasks, so a writing-focused curriculum was new to us. We needed to understand more about the skills students required to be successful writers as graduate students in mostly scientific and technical fields.

We consulted faculty in the Writing Department, who have specialties in academic discourse as well as in scientific and technical writing. The director of the Writing Center had taught a writing course for international graduate students at Purdue University, and her adviser there generously shared his syllabus and assignments. A professor in the Life Sciences Department had created a graduate writing workshop, but very few international graduate students were taking the course, perhaps because of the high level of oral and written fluency required in the fast-paced workshop environment. Nevertheless, the existence of this course allowed us to design the ELS course as an equivalent—keeping in mind the issue of institutional logic. If a graduate writing workshop exists for native speakers of English, we can argue that a similar one for English learners is not remedial but a linguistic and cultural adaptation of an existing course to serve the international student population.

We also contacted colleagues at other universities who offered writing courses for international graduate students and received many suggestions for textbooks, materials, assignments, and topics. Research universities with large numbers of international students typically offer an ESL graduate writing course, and often the ITA trainers are asked to create the courses, so it was not difficult to find colleagues at comparable universities who could share their knowledge.

A common theme to the advice was this: There is no single standard for good writing in the academic world, so a graduate writing course has to include some field-specific assignments. Some tasks, such as writing a proposal for a universitywide grant, writing a résumé, or writing a cover letter for an article submission, have somewhat unified standards and expectations even though there may be some minor differences from field to field. Other writing tasks (e.g., reviewing an article, analyzing the submission requirements of a journal, writing a research article, drafting a proposal for a conference presentation) vary greatly from field to field and require more open-ended standards. For these assignments, the graduate students must investigate the expectations for effective writing in their discipline. The writing course instructor cannot be an expert on the expectations of every field, so it is preferable to involve faculty in the students' departments—either informally as consultants on assignments or more formally as departmental mentors. The course we designed, ELS 635, combines general writing tasks (e.g., writing proposals, résumés, cover letters) and field-specific writing tasks (e.g., writing article reviews, research articles, conference proposals) and encourages students to find a faculty member in their department to act as a writing consultant.

TAKING A ROLLERCOASTER RIDE

Designing the courses was just the first step. After creating a course, we had to write formal proposals for each of the courses and get them approved first by the Curriculum Committee within the School of Arts and Sciences and then by the Faculty Senate. The process was agonizingly slow at times, especially when we were trying to change the curriculum for the following semester, and we had more failures than successes. Interestingly enough, however, having gone through the needs assessment and course design, we were absolutely positive about what courses we needed and why we needed them. Without this clarity, we might have given up; it certainly helped us weather the ups and downs of having our proposals rejected, amended, and eventually approved.

In the first round, we proposed an undergraduate listening/speaking course (at the 400 level) for fall 2004. We submitted the proposal in January 2004 and received approval from the Arts and Sciences Curriculum Committee. For a time, we heard nothing. In May, we learned by chance that the Faculty Senate had rejected the proposal. When we inquired, we learned that the Faculty Senate committee did not understand why the course should be at the 400 level, so they had rejected it. Oddly enough, no one had thought to notify the ELS Program. If we could rewrite the proposal at the 300 level, they said, they were fairly sure it would be approved the next time. At that point, however, fall was approaching, and we did not have time to rewrite the proposal. Our only option for getting approval over the summer was to add the course as a temporary one. This short-term approval allows a course to be offered three times before it needs formal approval. One advantage of this temporary status, we learned, is that the track record of successful curriculum and enrollment established over 3 years of provisional status makes it easier to get a temporary course approved as a permanent course.

Our next round of proposals met with similar failure. The graduate writing seminar was approved by Arts and Sciences but got held up in the Faculty Senate. What did the Graduate Council think of the course, they wanted to know? (We did not know what the Graduate Council was, but it was clearly an important group on campus that we had overlooked.) Eventually, the proposal was rejected by the Faculty Senate, apparently because we did not have the solid backing of the Graduate Council.

We also wrote a proposal for a spring-semester undergraduate listening/speaking course (at the 300 level, very similar to the course approved the previous year as a 400-level course) and submitted it to the Arts and Sciences Curriculum Committee. This proposal was rejected. In fact, every attempt we made to add a course was unsuccessful. Rather than give up, however, we were energized by our lack of success. The committees never said, "Your program shouldn't expand" or "Those courses don't belong in our university." The reasons for our failures always seemed like minor points that required fine-tuning the curriculum rather than fixing fundamental flaws. Clearly, if we could survive the proposal process, we would eventually get the courses approved. Ironically, we eventually discovered that the existing ELS courses had initially been approved only provisionally; again, we should have looked to the institutional logic of the courses we had in place. Apparently, part of the institutional logic of our university involves provisional approval for new courses as a first step.

Initially, we were only able to get temporary approval for the two undergraduate listening/speaking courses. Getting formal, permanent approval took a little longer and required that we meet with faculty members on the Curriculum Committee to answer their questions and concerns. After rewriting our proposals several times, we finally got approval for both courses. The graduate writing seminar is on hold at the time of writing because we need to build support for it within the Graduate School and because our staff does not have time in its current schedule to offer it.

LEARNING THE ROPES

Another lesson we learned from our lack of success in course proposals was that we needed to know more about the process of curriculum assessment in the university. Faculty in other departments were deciding what courses would be approved, so we needed to improve our ability to explain curriculum to colleagues in other fields.

We decided to attend some universitywide training sessions on curriculum and assessment. Over the course of several years, I attended several workshops on the new general education curriculum as well as a series of workshops on assessment. Participating in those sessions with faculty from around the university was another step in bringing our curriculum more into the mainstream of the university. Course design is not something program staff members should do alone in their offices. It is inevitably a universitywide process, no matter what program staff dream up in the confines of their own program. If staff cannot explain their curricular goals and learning objectives to colleagues in other departments, they will not get the necessary approval. These workshops made us realize how much we were already doing right as well as how we could design courses more effectively.

In the future, one area we hope to develop is assessment. In analyzing and redesigning our courses in the past, each staff member had worked alone, so the assessment had inevitably been personal and informal. There was no program review process, and we did not answer to anyone outside our program. This solo approach to assessment is changing on our campus. Each department and program is being asked to create a mission statement and to document the learning objectives for each course and the entire curriculum. This documentation process will be an opportunity for us to take our informal assessment to a more formal, professional level.

FINE-TUNING EXISTING COURSES

In addition to adding courses, we wanted to redesign existing courses to better meet the needs of students. In the two existing ELS writing courses, we were forced to reevaluate the curriculum because of a change in the university's writing requirements. Originally, the Writing Department had offered a single course (Writing 101) that focused on expository writing. A new curriculum introduced in fall 2003 allowed students to choose from three different writing courses—one in expository writing, one with assignments appropriate to various fields (writing across the curriculum), and one with assignments using both print and electronic sources. Because the ELS writing course had always been listed as a Writing 101 equivalent, the administration wanted to know what our courses were going to be equivalent to, given the new writing requirements.

This question was a chance to reexamine the ELS writing curriculum and bring it more in line with the university's new general education requirements. Based on the needs of our students, we decided that the two most useful courses were the expository course and the writing-across-the-curriculum course. (The data and electronic sources course, though initially attractive because of the use of both print and electronic media, turned out to be geared more to the social sciences, with a focus on qualitative rather than quantitative data. Such a course is not as useful to our target population.)

We wrote a course-change proposal with new syllabi and course descriptions that more closely resemble those of the Writing Department courses. The instructors who teach these courses are each allowed to choose their own materials and assignments, but we have developed a suggested list of resources as well as a suggested syllabus, which incorporates the methods, materials, and assignments used in the Writing Department courses. Now that the new writing courses and the new ELS courses are in place, future ELS directors, in consultation with the Writing Department chair, will need to ensure that the courses remain equivalent. They will not use identical materials or assignments, but the curricular goals and learning outcomes ought to be in alignment.

A final step in realigning the curriculum with university requirements—approval of our undergraduate writing courses as general education credits—was completed in 2006. The proposal required identifying three integrated skills and justifying how those skills are developed in a given course. Integrated skills that the ELS writing courses focus on are reading complex texts, using information technology, and writing effectively. As the proposals for general education credit for these courses state,

The focus [in ELS 112] is on expository writing and the goal is to help students develop effective strategies for addressing different expectations and genres. Such a course naturally develops students' core skills in general education. They develop critical reading and writing skills, as well as the ability to access, organize and explain information.

ELS 122 [also] addresses core skills in general education. Because of the wide diversity of topics in reading and writing assignments, students become aware of the diversity of content in academic literature as well as the variety of contexts and audiences that can be addressed. They develop critical reading and writing skills, as well as the ability to organize and synthesize information.

We proposed that these courses carry general education credit for the same reason that they carry credit in the first place: Students should get degree credit for the work they do in our classes. If they are completing assignments that meet general education requirements, they ought to get general education credit for their work. In the long term, if students do not get this credit, they are less likely to take the courses; why take English classes that do not earn them English communication credits toward graduation? Getting approval for these courses, similar to the process for new courses, requires approval by the General Education Committee of the School of Arts and Sciences and then by the Faculty Senate. Both steps were completed by spring 2006. In the future, we may consider proposing the undergraduate listening/speaking courses for general education credit as well.

Sample Curricular Products

The new ELS Program curriculum includes two courses per semester for undergraduates and at least one course per semester for graduate students. The changes are shown in ELS Program Curriculum Before and After the Revitalization. All ELS courses are offered for credit, and all but one are graded (the graduate writing course is proposed as a pass-fail seminar). Courses meet 3 hours per week for 15 weeks, for a total of 45 contact hours in a semester.

Assignments and grading are up to the individual course instructor, but syllabi for each course must be given to the program director, and each syllabus must include the specific requirements. In a large program, such a decentralized curriculum might cause chaos, but in our program it is manageable. The program director teaches two courses per semester, and an adjunct faculty member teaches a third, in addition to working as the ESL

ELS Program Curriculum Before and After the Revitalization

Before	After
Undergraduate	
English as a Second Language I (fall): Designed to enhance students' speaking and oral presentation skills, as well as writing	Expository Writing in English (fall): Varieties and strategies of expository writing for different audiences and situations
English as a Second Language II (spring): Companion course to English as a Second Language I	Academic Writing in English (spring): Practice in writing assignments for introductory and general education courses across the curriculum
	Oral English Skills for the Public Sphere (fall): Focus on pronunciation, listening and speaking skills, and a variety of speaking projects; special emphasis on speaking freely in academic and social situations
	Oral English Skills for the Academic Sphere (spring): Intensive focus on pronunciation, listening and speaking skills, and a variety of communicative projects; development of oral presentation skills
Graduate	
Advanced Communication Skills for ITAs (fall): Focus on pronunciation, teaching skills, and cross-cultural differences in education; priority given to international teaching assistants	Unchanged
Oral Communication Skills for ITAs (spring): Intensive focus on pronunciation, listening and speaking skills, and an awareness of colloquial American speech	Unchanged
	Graduate Writing for International Students (proposed): Focus on the writing skills needed by international graduate students and on acquisition of knowledge of professional standards in rhetoric, style, and documentation

consultant in the Writing Center. With only two faculty members involved in grading and assessment, it is easier to maintain standards and consistency.

Sample Activities shows tasks from two courses in the program (for details on skills and topics covered, see University of Rhode Island, 2005). The program director will continue to monitor the content, materials, and assignments in these required courses, with the intention of keeping the focus of ELS courses in line with those in other departments. The ultimate goal is to have a variety of courses that are useful to students and that meet their academic needs.

Sample Activities

Advanced Oral English Skills

Task: Role play about academic dishonesty (Fragiadakis & Maurer, 2000, chapter 4)

Goals

- Analyze appropriate academic policies for dealing with cheating.
- Consider the consequences of cheating in a U.S. university.
- Practice appropriate register for communicating with university personnel.
- Improve turn-taking strategies so that everyone can participate.

Role-Play Scenario

One student plays the role of a student who was cheating on an exam. Another student plays the role of the professor who caught the student cheating. A third student plays the role of the dean of Arts and Sciences. They pretend they are at a hearing to discuss the case and decide an appropriate punishment.

Graduate Writing for International Students

Task: Write a grant proposal.

Goals

- Develop ability to communicate main purpose of a research program.
- Develop ability to write clear, concise, and effective grant proposals.
- Improve skills in analyzing goals and targets of funding sources.
- Improve skills in reviewing and discussing proposals with colleagues.

Steps to Take

1. Prepare a proposal for a universitywide grant available for graduate students.
2. Identify goals and targets of grant, and address those goals in a proposal summary.
3. Exchange proposals with a classmate, review them, and discuss the effectiveness of the writing.

Conclusion

At the time of writing, two courses had been added and two courses redesigned within the ELS Program curriculum. These adaptations were made to respond to changes in the student population as well as changes in university requirements. Further adjustments will likely be required to ensure that student needs are being met, but the greatest shift for us has been in the momentum of the program. After over a decade with no significant changes in curriculum, we were able to redesign the entire set of undergraduate offerings. This shift involved a major redefinition of what is possible within the program.

By realigning the curriculum to include core skills in oral communication and academic writing, we brought our small, marginalized program more into the center of the university. By making sure that courses covered material and skills similar to those covered by required general education courses in the university, we helped ensure that what we were teaching was central to students' academic success. To the extent that our program was marginalized before, so were our students. When what we teach is at the core of what the university requires, then our students have access to that core knowledge as well. Finding the institutional logic for change, in our case, has allowed us not only to expand our offerings but also to realign our curriculum to address the fundamental educational goals of the university. The process has been at once exciting and empowering.

Appendix: Needs Assessment Survey Completed by Students

Name:

E-mail:

Major:

YOUR LANGUAGE BACKGROUND

1. What language(s) have you spoken all your life (since childhood)?
2. Did you learn that language (those languages) at home, in school, or both?
3. How many years have you studied English?
4. Where did you study English? (the United States, another country, in school, private lessons, etc.)
5. What did your English classes focus on? (grammar, vocabulary, reading, writing, speaking, listening, pronunciation, etc.)
6. Are there any skills you did not learn in English class that you need now (professionally or personally)?

GOALS FOR LEARNING ENGLISH

What English skills do you need to learn most? (5 = need most, 3 = need sometimes, 1 = do not need)

Grammar:

Verbs forms/tenses _____

Prepositions _____

Articles (*the, a*) _____

Adjectives/Adverbs _____

Nouns (plurals, proper) _____

Numbers _____

Agreement (S-V, A-N) _____

Other: _____

Vocabulary:

Finding the right word _____

Right form of the word _____

Exact meaning of words _____

Root of the word _____

Words that go together _____

Other: _____

Writing:

Writing short assignments _____

Writing papers in your field _____

Writing essay tests _____

Making ideas clear _____

Using grammar correctly _____

Taking notes during class _____

Other: _____

Reading:

Understanding main idea _____

Understanding details _____

Analyzing themes _____

Interacting with the text _____

Remembering facts _____

Highlighting the text _____

Other: _____

Speaking:

Speaking during class _____

Giving oral presentations _____

Speaking with professors _____

Other: _____

Listening:

Hearing lectures clearly _____

Listening to TV, radio _____

Listening to Americans _____

Other: _____

Pronunciation:

Hearing correct pronunciation _____

Saying specific sounds _____

Using stress in words, phrases _____

Rhythm of English _____

Linking words together _____

Intonation to convey meaning _____

Other: _____

American Culture:

Typical American behaviors _____

Traditional American values _____

Important cultural trends _____

American business life _____

American family life _____

American education _____

Other: _____

Revitalizing an Established Program for Adult Learners

Innovation as a Curriculum Renewal Process in a Turkish University

YASEMIN KIRKGÖZ

This chapter highlights a major curriculum renewal project for adult learners of EFL in the context of Turkish higher education that resulted in innovative and improved practices and a more dynamic program. A 2-year longitudinal study revitalized the curriculum by directly involving all constituents: administration, teachers, current students, target students, and higher education faculties offering English-medium instruction.

The revised curriculum for Çukurova University's Center for Foreign Languages (CFL) is designed to reflect views espoused in the current literature, institutional expectations, a comprehensive needs analysis to reveal identifiable elements of students' target English language needs, current needs of the students, and expectations of the subject lecturers. Survey findings, discussed below, revealed the need to introduce innovation into the curriculum and have been used as the basis for meaningful curricular change.

The chapter also details the challenges that resulted in a successful curriculum renewal. We at the CFL introduced five major changes to the curriculum and put in place a process to manage the new curricular standards. Based on our experience, this chapter offers a set of principles to guide curriculum designers in their efforts to promote successful innovation as part of curriculum renewal.

Curricular Context

The English language plays a crucial role in Turkish education, politics, and economics. The strategic and geopolitical status of Turkey as a geographical crossroads between Asia and Europe has made the nation the cradle of many great civilizations throughout history. In Turkey, English, or rather EFL, is generally part of the educational curriculum and is widely employed in government and business sectors. Thus, the decision to introduce English as the medium of instruction in higher education has been largely motivated by the nation's political and economic ambitions. Indeed, the Higher Education Act states that the purpose of English-medium education is to

> *enable students to access scientific and technological information published in English in their related disciplines and equip them with the necessary skills to enable them to attend international conferences by discussions or publications. (Higher Education Act, No. 182701, 1984)*

Çukurova University occupies a prominent place among Turkish universities. In 1983, the university senate decided that 40% of the courses in the Department of Economics and Business Administration (DECOBA) would be taught in English. In the academic year 1990–1991, two more engineering departments, Mechanical Engineering (ME) and Electric-Electronics Engineering (EEE), following an official decision by the Higher Council of Education (Higher Education Act, No. 90.17.5352, 1990), began to teach all their courses in English.

To meet the university's expanded English language requirements, the CFL was established in 1990. Students attending the CFL are prospective members of their future English-medium academic discourse communities, which will require them to read specialized professional literature, follow lectures, hold discussions, and conduct laboratory experiments in their second language. Accordingly, the ultimate goal of the CFL's 1-year English for academic purposes (EAP) curriculum is to enable the students to participate effectively in that discourse community. In other words, EFL is a means, not an end—a prerequisite to academic study and successful academic performance. The CFL's crucial role in equipping students with the knowledge and skills necessary for future academic success is stated in the university declaration of 1995: "to bring the students enrolled in an English-medium program to a level where they can follow their English-medium courses and access relevant scientific information" ("Declaration on the Establishment of the Center for Foreign Languages," 1995).

Curriculum Framework

Students who have been admitted to the CFL receive 21 hours of instruction per week. An examination, which assesses a student's competence in reading, writing, listening, translation, grammar, and speaking, determines the English language proficiency of students entering the program. Students who pass this examination are enrolled directly in first-year undergraduate courses. Those who fail to pass take a placement examination and, based on their scores, are assigned to an appropriate level of language instruction. The program has three levels (see Curriculum Framework).

The teaching year is divided into four 8-week teaching blocks. During each block, students take two quizzes. An achievement test at the end of each teaching block measures the students' short-term language performance. To exit from the program, students must reach the upper intermediate level of proficiency as measured by the proficiency examination.

The core course, which is considered central, is designed to offer systematic language learning opportunities using a series of course books supported by additional teaching materials. Before the renewal, the textbooks used were structure focused. The weekly teaching schedule consists of 21 hours for all levels. No separate courses are designed for separate skill areas; reading, writing, listening, and speaking are taught as part of the core course, following an integrated skills program. During the third and forth blocks, students write a project on a topic of their interest.

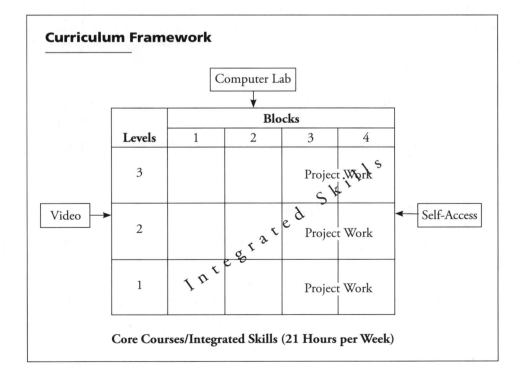

Curriculum Framework

Core Courses/Integrated Skills (21 Hours per Week)

As the Curriculum Framework shows, video, a computer lab, and self-access materials are additional components of the curriculum. Time spent in the computer lab is designed to reinforce the skills and strategies introduced in the core class. Video is an optional curriculum component with the aim of providing students with authentic listening practice and natural input for speaking and writing tasks.

The CFL is run by 60 Turkish instructors with teaching experience ranging from 6 to 18 years. All have received in-service teacher training mainly as part of a cooperative project between the university and the British Council in Turkey.

Motivation for Curriculum Innovation

Although the CFL's curriculum was originally based on research studies tailored to the university's needs, over the years the course content had deteriorated, becoming based largely on the intuition of faculty curriculum designers. Although the program's stated goal was to promote students' productive language skills, the course books and other instructional materials were structure focused and did not prepare students adequately for the final proficiency assessment exit examination, nor did they parallel the academic tasks required in future university course work. On the contrary, they were based largely on what the teachers and the curriculum team perceived to be good and useful for students.

This resulting mismatch, or lack of coherence, between the students' academic needs and what was taught in the program, along with informal faculty concerns about the difficulty many students were having in coping successfully with the requirements of their English-medium departments, showed us that the curriculum caused low morale and feelings of alienation among students. We knew we had to make major curricular changes and embarked on a comprehensive needs analysis, described in the following section. Ultimately, the findings of the needs analysis led to five major innovations.

Evaluating the Curriculum

The Curriculum Renewal Model, adapted from Richards (2001a), shows the process we used to bring about the innovations. The model illustrates the cyclical nature of curriculum development. It consists of a dynamic system of interrelated elements comprising needs analysis, the setting of goals and objectives, and the implementation and evaluation of the program.

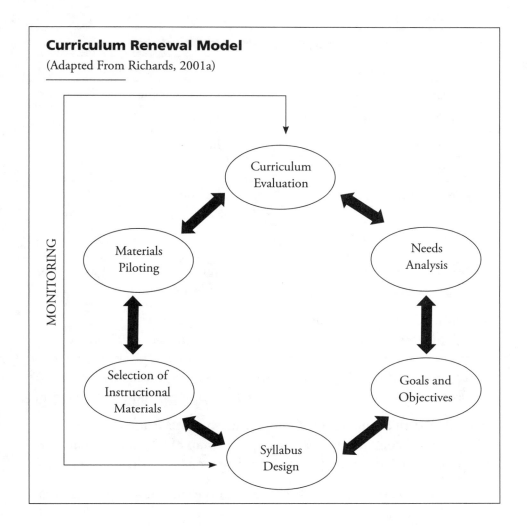

Curriculum Renewal Model

(Adapted From Richards, 2001a)

MONITORING

- Curriculum Evaluation
- Materials Piloting
- Needs Analysis
- Selection of Instructional Materials
- Goals and Objectives
- Syllabus Design

NEEDS ANALYSIS

Needs analysis forms the basis of curriculum design (Johns, 1991; Long & Crookes, 1992) and is the starting point for identifying students' communicative and linguistic needs and specifying language learning objectives. As noted by Johns, without such investigations, curriculum developers often tend to intuit the future needs of the students, which may result in limited success, as was the case in the former curriculum. In our curriculum renewal project, needs assessment served the following purposes:

1. We wished to obtain a wide range of input from administrators, teachers, and students in order to review and evaluate the existing program during the early planning stages.
2. We needed reliable information concerning the present and future needs of students in order to make informed judgments on goals and objectives for the new CFL program.

Needs Analysis Survey Respondents	
Respondents	**Instrument**
650 current EAP students	Evaluation form
82 students just completing the EAP program	Interviews
120 past EAP students	Interviews
220 past EAP students	Questionnaire
15 subject instructors	Interviews

Our first step was to develop a needs analysis survey, which included about 1,000 respondents (see Needs Analysis Survey Respondents).

Data From Current EAP Students
All 650 students enrolled in the EAP program completed a written curriculum evaluation at the end of the fall 2002 semester. The evaluation form focused on students' perceptions of their own language needs and wants, and aspects of the curriculum that the students thought should be changed.

Interviews With Students Just Completing the EAP Program
In May 2003, I conducted interviews with a group of 82 students who were about to complete the EAP program. The questions were the following:

1. Can you describe the effectiveness of the curriculum in relation to its goals and objectives?
2. What aspects of the curriculum do you like most?
3. What aspects of the curriculum do you think should be changed?
4. Can you describe your perceptions of your own language improvement in comparison with the time when you were enrolled in the program?

Other Data From Past EAP Students
We also wanted to know how students perceived the effectiveness of the EAP curriculum, what their objective needs from and expectations of the CFL program were, and what students had to know in order to function effectively in the university's academic departments. To this end, the third group of informants included past EAP students who had already completed 1 year of the English program at the CFL and were pursuing their academic studies in their respective university departments.

I conducted semistructured interviews with 120 volunteer students across the three English-medium departments of the university to discuss their first-semester experiences in regular university classes. Students were also invited to make a formal critique of the EAP curriculum and offer suggestions for the curriculum renewal process.

In addition, I contacted the heads of the three departments to request their cooperation in conducting a needs assessment in May 2003. Students from the three English-medium departments responded to a survey questionnaire (see Appendix A) aimed to find out (a) the frequency of the various academic tasks students were required to do in four macroskill areas in their subject-matter courses and (b) their perceived effectiveness in meeting those requirements. Each section of the questionnaire also included an open-ended question in which respondents could write about the difficulties they faced regarding a particular language skill. All data were analyzed statistically except handwritten comments, which were subjected to content analysis. The findings revealed the realities of discipline-specific courses, with significant implications for the development of instructional materials for EAP students.

Interviews With Faculty Lecturers
The survey findings were complemented by interviews with 15 subject instructors teaching content courses: 4 from ME, 5 from EEE, and 6 from DECOBA.

The questions focused on (a) course requirements, (b) students' performance in relation to these requirements, and (c) the subject instructors' suggestions for how to overcome the weaknesses identified in the four language skills.

NEEDS ANALYSIS FINDINGS

Students' Current Needs
The results of the needs analysis revealed that CFL students (a) needed more challenging instructional materials, (b) wanted more productive learning, (c) needed autonomy, (d) needed content-based materials, and (e) were experiencing acculturation difficulties.

More Challenging Instructional Materials
Eighty-six percent of the students enrolled in the program, as well as a majority of the exit group polled, expressed a gap between their expectations and their actual experience in the CFL program. They felt that the structure-focused course books used in the program were unchallenging and boring and demanded they be changed to ones with content that efficiently prepared them for the heavy demands of their academic content classes.

More Productive Learning

The students all stated that they had gained a solid knowledge of grammar but complained that, despite a year's hard work, they did not notice appreciable improvement in productive skills, particularly in speaking.

Autonomy

While emphasizing the importance of language-related needs, the learners regarded building positive attitudes to learning as a vital prerequisite to the acquisition of language learning skills. They also highlighted the need for assistance in developing and using independent learning strategies. Students strongly requested more challenging out-of-class tasks, such as projects and research-oriented activities, which would give them more responsibility and autonomy.

Content-Based Materials

Students complained about the heavy reliance on textbook-bound teaching in the curriculum, highlighting the need for change and innovation, particularly the need to align course content with their academic goals. Of the students enrolled in the program, 79% complained that the program did not familiarize them with subject-specific English and requested strongly that curriculum include such a component. Similarly, students who had exited the program noted the gap between the requirements of disciplinary courses and what they were taught in the EAP curriculum.

Help With Acculturation

A significant finding of the needs analysis interviews was that all exiting students had experienced difficulties in adjusting to their departments' discourse communities. A majority of the students initially underwent culture shock due not only to their lack of English but also to unfamiliarity with disciplinary knowledge. Students reported that they did not notice appreciable improvement at the end of their year in the EAP program. The students requested that the curriculum be redesigned as a bridge to their English-medium departments.

Students' Future Language Needs

To renew the program, we needed to learn which academic tasks were vital to the students' success in the three English-medium departments. As shown in Required Academic Tasks Mentioned by Students, lecturing was the dominant instructional method.

A large number of the students (75%) perceived their effectiveness to be low in following the lecturer's instructions, participating in class discussions by asking and answering questions, asking for clarification, and expressing opinions. This perception stemmed from lack of confidence in their language proficiency (i.e., a low level of vocabulary knowledge, lack of fluency,

Required Academic Tasks Mentioned by Students		
	Students Mentioning the Task	
Task	No.	%
Following the lecturer's instructions during the lesson	210	95.4
Asking and answering questions during lectures	180	81.1
Expressing opinions during class discussions	178	80.9
Reading various texts on a topic to express one's own opinion	176	80.0
Guessing the meanings of unfamiliar words from the context	192	87.3
Summarizing a text orally or in written form for an assignment	168	76.4
Writing summaries using notes taken in a lecture	180	81.8
Answering examination questions	208	94.5
Writing an essay on a topic incorporating ideas from various sources	212	96.4
Writing a curriculum vita/report	102	46.4

and lack of opportunity to practice English and pronunciation) and lack of familiarity with the discourse conventions of a lecture setting. Similarly, all professors commented that their students struggled most with in-class interaction and with asking or responding to questions and following instructions well.

All departments required students to read textbooks, articles, and lecture notes rapidly and effectively. Not surprisingly, social science majors needed relatively stronger English language skills in reading a variety of texts on a topic to evaluate information, in writing summaries, and in expressing the author's opinion in their own words.

The writing skills emphasized throughout the curriculum of the first-year undergraduates were answering questions in examinations and integrating information from different sources into different written modes, such as project writing. In addition, students in ME and EEE were expected to write laboratory reports.

Regardless of their academic departments, students complained that they lacked adequate academic and general vocabulary. This affected their speaking fluency and obstructed reading comprehension, causing slow reading and lack of concentration. Lecturers and students urged that an introductory course based on students' specific disciplines be incorporated into the curriculum, and subject instructors proposed collaboration between the CFL and the faculties.

IMPLICATIONS OF THE NEEDS ANALYSIS

Identification of the aforementioned problematic areas helped me, as the language program administrator, get directly involved in the curriculum renewal process, initiate programmatic innovation, respond to external and internal demands more effectively, and overcome areas of weakness identified through the needs analysis. Hamilton (1996, cited in Stoller, 1997) notes that innovation results from deliberate efforts intended to bring about new and improved practices. Thus, my major responsibility was to "serve as a catalyst for change and innovation" (Stoller, 1997, p. 33), introducing innovation as a fundamental component for a progressive program.

In her study of innovation (which used directors of language programs as respondents), Stoller (1997) identified dissatisfaction with the status quo as one of the incentives for curriculum innovation. This rang true for the CFL: The dissatisfaction of all parties concerned showed that the curriculum needed to be improved, upgraded, renewed, or replaced.

Renewing the Curriculum

Each step illustrated in the Curriculum Renewal Model shown previously was pursued in a structured, well-planned manner, with the goal of ensuring responsiveness to the linguistic, academic, and acculturation needs of EAP students in general and in ways specific to the academic disciplines to which they would be transitioning. We also wanted to achieve a more coherent curriculum by incorporating new insights from the relevant professional literature. The process aimed to maximize support for teachers, the key players in curriculum change. We devoted 1 month to orientation workshops that supported teachers' adjustment to the curricular innovations.

The curriculum renewal focused on five areas: revising curriculum goals and objectives, moving from a structure-focused to a task-based course book, innovating in assessment, introducing an EAP materials development project, and revamping the extracurricular program.

REVISING CURRICULUM GOALS AND OBJECTIVES (SHARED OBJECTIVES)

The findings of the needs assessment needed to be translated into a mission statement encoding CFL's beliefs and its curriculum goals and objectives. These were established with the participation of all teaching staff in September 2003, before the start of the academic year. Because any innovation offered for classroom practice from the outside is vulnerable to rejection, direct involvement of teachers in curriculum design is vital (Brown, 1995). Although in the past only the curriculum committee had made decisions, we now adopted an ownership model, with teachers given an opportunity to participate in the decision-making process to achieve a more effective program.

We held a 3-day orientation program whose aim was to

1. introduce teachers to the principles on which the new curriculum would be based
2. encourage teachers to establish goals and objectives so that they share in setting the philosophy of the program
3. introduce teachers to proposed innovations in the hope that this would increase their commitment to making the changes happen

For the program, we sought assistance from an expert consultant on curriculum development. First, teachers received a theoretical overview of the curriculum renewal process. Next, their role within the process was highlighted. This was essential to encourage their contribution, to help them build a sense of involvement in and ownership of curricular changes, and to ensure teachers' successful implementation of the innovations.

All 60 teachers took part in this process. In small focus groups, they analyzed how English was used in the students' respective departments and determined the varied needs of CFL students. Finally, through participatory decision making, teachers unanimously reached an operational definition of the mission statement.

Teachers then participated in designing goals and intended outcomes, based on their classroom experience and their beliefs about what students needed and could achieve in a 1-year period in the CFL. The next task involved stating objectives. Because the curriculum promoted skills-based learning, objectives were specified in four macroskill areas (reading, writing, listening, and speaking), each followed by a list of microskills.

The curriculum committee acted as a mediator between the administration and the teachers in bringing about the desired curriculum changes. The committee collected and revised the draft mission statement, goals, and specifications of objectives. The revised versions were then returned to the teaching staff for final comments. Based on teachers' feedback, the committee finalized the curriculum documents and turned them into a coherent statement of mission, goals, and objectives. The document provides an exact characterization of the target proficiency for CFL students (Johnson, 1989a).

To achieve coherence in the curriculum renewal process, the committee also took into account findings from the needs analysis on students' and departmental lecturers' expectations. The committee checked to see to the extent to which the aims identified by the subject lecturers coincided with those of the CFL teachers. Not surprisingly, there was a great deal of overlap. Aims unstated by the CFL teachers but included by the subject lecturers were added to the goal statements. For example, the survey conducted in the students' academic community identified answering examination questions and writing reports as frequently required tasks; these were added to the objectives.

We then needed to redefine the syllabi for each level (see Appendix B for a description of the new Level 3 syllabus); redistribute curricular elements, such as the language items to be taught in different levels; select new course books; and adopt supplementary teaching materials. For each level, program objectives indicated the level of proficiency students were required to attain in order to pass (see Appendix C for a description of reading goals and objectives for the new Level 3 syllabus).

MOVING FROM A STRUCTURE-FOCUSED TO A TASK-BASED COURSE BOOK

The next task involved choosing course materials. As mentioned, in previous years the program's core class had used structure-focused textbooks. Not surprisingly, when evaluated by a team of teachers in summer 2003, the course books were found not to correspond to learners' needs or to the goals and objectives of the new curriculum.

Because we had made a commitment to task-based and content-based learning, we examined a variety of course books to see how well they would meet the needs identified in the needs assessment. Sadly, commercial texts are written for a generalized international audience, not for a particular educational context, such as that of our Turkish learners. However, we chose the most appropriate course books that had a task-based philosophy. Following an examination of the congruence of the tasks with the objectives of the new curriculum, we invited a native-English-speaking teacher trainer to run another workshop on effective use of the new course books.

INTEGRATING PORTFOLIOS INTO ASSESSMENT

As suggested by Johnson (1989a), "evolution not revolution must be the aim in language curriculum development" (p. 10). The final day of the orientation program was therefore devoted to introducing the teaching staff to portfolios, purposeful collections of student work that show students' progress and achievements. We wanted to use portfolios not only to assess the students' performance but also to promote their autonomy and enhance their productive language.

With this in mind, we decided to use multiskill portfolios consisting of three components—reading, writing, and vocabulary—rather than the standard writing portfolio. We felt this could better help students track their language skills development. In September 2003, the curriculum committee worked intensively to prepare for each component of the portfolio.

Students were assigned various portfolio tasks connected with a theme relevant to the content of their core class. These tasks would enable the students to integrate and apply the knowledge and linguistic skills they had acquired in class. For example, the theme *report writing,* studied in the Level 3 core class, was followed by a portfolio task called Survey Report Project, which asked students to prepare a questionnaire and conduct a survey on a general topic of their choice. As part of this task, each student prepared a written report on a topic such as smoking, reading books, or youth problems and gave an oral presentation based on the report. In addition, students were introduced to certain academic skills.

Students were required to complete these tasks outside class and put the products in their portfolios. A further component of the portfolio was a Students' Reflections section, in which students were encouraged to evaluate their own work, express their opinions on the portfolio tasks, and compare several of their attempts to perform those tasks. In addition, teachers completed a reflection sheet expressing their views of students' progress and achievement.

Integrating portfolio assessment into the curriculum has been a major innovation for the CFL. Students and the teachers believe that it promotes students' language skills; fosters independent, self-directed learners; and allows the program to be responsive to students' needs.

The program has also revised its institutional English language assessment in line with curriculum changes. With the incorporation of portfolio assessment, the former Participation Scoring System (PSS), used from 1992 to 2003, was removed from the curriculum. The underlying reason for using PSS had been to increase student motivation and solve attendance problems. Each week, the teachers gave a mark out of 10 based on each student's attendance and attitude toward participating in the lesson. Although the PSS achieved the goals it was designed for, in time it turned out to be a mathematical burden for the staff, and many teachers could not apply it properly. Consequently, as part of the curriculum renewal, we decided to use the portfolio not just to replace the PSS but also to serve as an innovative and useful institutional assessment tool. In the current grading system, four achievement examinations account for 70% of a student's grade, eight quizzes account for 10%, and the portfolio accounts for 20%.

INTRODUCING AN EAP MATERIALS DEVELOPMENT PROJECT

The needs assessment showed that students wanted to see the immediate relevance of their studies in the CFL to their academic, content-based needs. This realization provided the program with the impetus to initiate an EAP materials development project. In December 2002, we obtained course syllabi from the university's three English-medium departments and examined their required texts and tasks for first-year undergraduates. We also received a list of major journals that were potential sources for materials development.

At the CFL, three teams of teachers were organized, each focused on producing content-based materials and developing instructional tasks in a specific disciplinary discourse (e.g., economics). For example, business was a required topic for DECOBA students. Therefore, teachers produced a text entitled "Advantages of Small Business Ownership" and developed the following tasks, which resemble the academic tasks students would need to do when studying business the following year:

1. listening task (guided note taking): Listen to a lecture, "The Advantages of Small Business Ownership," and take notes.
2. writing task (postlistening): Assume that you wish to go into business for yourself. Select the type of business you would like to own, and write a short report stating why you selected this type of business.
3. speaking task: In groups, discuss the disadvantages of going into business for yourself.

These materials were piloted, feedback was obtained from students and teachers, and necessary modifications were made in order to incorporate the texts into the student portfolio in the second semester of the academic year.

REVAMPING THE EXTRACURRICULAR PROGRAM

One of the major concerns raised by faculty instructors was that students did not fully comprehend the connection between the EAP curriculum and university classes. The need for familiarity with authentic lectures led to the incorporation in spring 2003 of a class visitation project, which required students to visit their intended academic department and attend an introductory lecture on a typical topic. Alternatively, I invited guest speakers from the students' intended academic departments to deliver 2-hour introductory lectures. Feedback from the students who attended was extremely positive, because it formed a bridge between the CFL and the students' academic context.

The aim of the Renewed Curriculum shown here is to provide students with a comprehensive course of study. The core course, still considered central, offers students systematic language learning opportunities 21 hours per week using a series of basic course books. The new curriculum follows an integrated skills– and task-based philosophy. Unlike the old curriculum, in which the course books were structure focused, in the new curriculum the course books all follow a task-based philosophy, in line with the curriculum goals and objectives. Though not shown in The Renewed Curriculum, project work is still part of the course of study in the form of the introductory lectures and content-based EAP materials described above. A portfolio is integrated into the curriculum from the beginning.

During the curriculum renewal, we also revised the three additional program components: the computer lab, video, and self-access materials. For example, computer lab instruction now not only reinforces the skills, tasks, and strategies introduced in the core class, as was the case previously, but also emphasizes the use of computers for information searches in which students access either specific Internet sites or materials on CD. Video was enriched by the purchase of new equipment and videocassettes to give the instructors a wider choice of material to complement themes explored in the core class or to introduce new subject matter. In addition, self-study materials in the self-access room were renewed by a team of teachers. This year, the facilities were expanded by the incorporation of computers and satellite TV to expose students to authentic TV broadcasts that may help improve their listening competence.

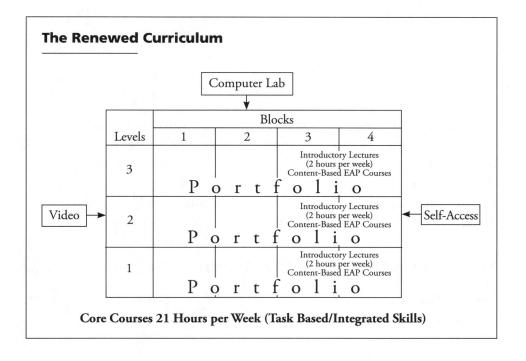

The Renewed Curriculum

Core Courses 21 Hours per Week (Task Based/Integrated Skills)

MANAGING COHERENCE BY MONITORING

The final step in curriculum renewal is the development of a system for frequent monitoring of organizational concerns as a way of obtaining formative evaluation. Johnson (1989a, p. 12) states that achieving and maintaining coherence requires the active engagement and cooperation of all the participants throughout the life of a curriculum. Communication among the teaching staff and the different program units is another requirement for the success of a curriculum.

We see this flow of communication as having horizontal and vertical modes. In our experience, the horizontal flow, which involved teacher-to-teacher communication, took place in weekly meetings also attended by one member each of the curriculum committee and the testing unit, who needed to be informed about the teachers' concerns in their respective areas. This instilled the cooperation necessary to help the curriculum achieve its goals. These regular meetings also served to

1. get curriculum changes running smoothly by maintaining the momentum of planned innovation and constant feedback
2. provide teachers with a teaching schedule to help standardize learning opportunities and ensure that teachers stayed on course in meeting curriculum goals and objectives
3. support teachers not only at the initial critical stage but also throughout the term by providing weekly supplementary materials that enabled them to accommodate innovation in their teaching practices
4. give teachers an opportunity to exchange information and share progress and practical difficulties with colleagues
5. achieve coherence, or, as stated by Johnson (1989a), demonstrate that the end specifications matched the institution's policy and that means and ends are compatible

To develop unity of purpose among all the participants, we also looked to communicate vertically. I held weekly follow-up meetings with members of different units involved in creating the curriculum (e.g., testing, materials production). We discussed and cooperated in solving issues such as the need for more cooperation between the curriculum committee and the test creators to ensure that the tests met curriculum objectives.

Evaluating the Curriculum Renewal Project

The perceptions of teachers and students served as the basis for a summative evaluation of the curriculum renewal.

TEACHERS' PERCEPTIONS

To obtain and quantify teachers' reactions to the curriculum renewal process, 5 months after the full implementation of the project I held semistructured, 15- to 20-minute interviews with individual teachers. I was interested in their perceptions of four aspects of the curriculum:

1. the in-service teacher orientation program, which encouraged teachers' involvement in establishing curriculum goals and objectives
2. the new course books
3. the portfolio as central to methodology and assessment
4. the extent to which teachers felt they received administrative support

Teachers' perceptions of the orientation program and their involvement in establishing curriculum goals and objectives were extremely positive. They accepted the program as an innovation of the system and stated that orientation added "professionalism" to their teaching. One teacher commented, "I felt myself valued. Since it is us, the teachers who put these new ideas into practice, I really appreciated my opinion being consulted in goal setting."

The teachers also believed that the timing of the orientation program (1 month before the start of the academic year) was very appropriate: It helped them refresh their knowledge of program aims. Teachers stressed that the guidance they received was useful and essential. Many felt strongly that such teacher training opportunities needed to be provided frequently. Thus, the orientation proved to be an important forum for a curricular dialogue between the teachers and me and essential for effective curriculum initiatives.

When discussing the new course books and their appropriateness for meeting curriculum goals and objectives, all teachers stated that no single book or series would entirely meet institutional needs. However, a majority found that, with supplementation, the course books appropriately promoted students' communicative skills.

When discussing the implementation of portfolio assessment, however, teachers were divided into three groups:

1. For a majority of teachers (43 of 60), portfolio assessment was a completely new experience. Therefore, as noted by Wedell (2003, p. 443), to achieve even a modified version of the expected outcomes, they had to make considerable adjustments to their professional beliefs and behaviors. Most felt they had succeeded in integrating portfolio assessment into their practices.

2. For a minority of teachers (14 of 60), innovation was compatible with their past practice; in other words, they stated that they had already been using collections of student work.

3. A few teachers (3 of 60) were reluctant to abandon the certainties of their educational status quo and fought innovation. Despite their reluctance, these teachers felt it necessary to assign the portfolio because they were aware that it counted toward an institutional assessment system and that the students would be graded on it.

The interview findings gave me insight into the extent of the adjustments teachers were expected to make. As noted by Stoller (1997, p. 39), innovations necessitate modifications in routine practices, often causing an increase in workload. Teachers acknowledged the powerful role of the portfolio innovation in developing students' writing skills. They felt it promoted student autonomy and found it compatible with curriculum goals and objectives, yet they mentioned its time-consuming nature. However, they agreed that, compared with previous years, students were developing better and more productive writing skills, the intended outcome of the shift in methodology. A further benefit of portfolio assessment was that it gave teachers a rare opportunity to critically reflect on the effectiveness of the new curriculum, particularly in assessing student performance in writing.

STUDENTS' PERCEPTIONS

A questionnaire gathered students' opinions on the centrality of portfolios in the new curriculum. The questionnaire focused only on the portfolio because I used other research tools to obtain students' perceptions of other aspects of the innovation. In response to the questionnaire, a majority of the students said that keeping a portfolio was useful and enjoyable. When asked what they learned most, all students stated that they had improved their writing skills, followed by vocabulary and reading skills. Students mentioned that they had a better idea of their specific achievements and progress; they could trace their own growth; and they were able to receive regular, systematic, and individualized feedback from their teachers. The results of this innovation, particularly for students' improvement in writing, suggest that the CFL curriculum is now fulfilling the students' learning needs. In short, portfolio assessment filled in a missing component in the curriculum.

To evaluate whether the EAP project and student in-class visits had achieved their intended aims, I held a focus-group interview with students across the three English-medium discourse communities. Students reported that they had greatly benefited from the project. The class visitation project clearly provided a bridge between the CFL and the students' respective departments, and the students strongly recommended that the innovation become permanent. As one student stated,

> *When I was told the idea I initially had some misgivings concerning the lecturer's style of delivery. However, after attending the lesson, I saw how much importance had been given to the lesson. I recommend it to continue.*

Lessons Learned

As Stoller (1997, 2001) points out, curriculum renewal is a complex process. The CFL, motivated by a strong desire to meet the needs of students, promote the professional development of its teaching staff, and raise the standards of the EFL classes we offer, has actively engaged in the hard work needed to achieve a dynamic curriculum. We strongly believe in the philosophy highlighted by White (1988): "Successful language programs are biased toward action and they avoid stultification by developing and changing rather than remaining reutilized and standardized" (p. 138).

We learned many important lessons during this challenging process:

- Innovation needs to be introduced gradually, systematically, and in the light of theoretical issues.
- Achieving coherence among the components of a foreign language curriculum requires effective organization and administrative engagement and support. We feel that the success of the current curriculum can be attributed primarily to congruencies between administrative and curricular priorities and teacher priorities.
- The administration and a group of teams must share the responsibility for innovation diffusion. For example, a strong team of committee members must be willing to promote and sustain the innovation from its early stages through diffusion to and implementation by the teaching staff.
- In an EFL environment, using a native-speaking expert consultant seems to have a great impact on teachers' responsiveness to innovation.
- All participants need to be involved in decision making, and there should be maximum provision for the development of consensus, commitment, and motivation.
- Teachers, as key players, need adequate administrative support not only during the earlier stages of the curriculum renewal process but also throughout the following teaching periods.
- Efficient internal communication is vital. Institutions are organizations, and the real challenge for them to survive lies in creating regular

feedback mechanisms. Ongoing dialogue and open lines of communication with potential adopters of innovation will facilitate acceptance of change.

- To ensure that innovation is relevant to the needs of the target students, innovators need to cooperate closely with university department faculty and be responsive to their input. In a language institution such as ours, which maintains close contact with the degree-giving departments, curriculum renewal can best be achieved through the collaborative efforts of the departmental faculty, the students, and the EFL teaching staff.

The final lesson we learned concerns the need to provide opportunities for teachers' professional development. Curriculum committee members and teachers need to be motivated to increase their responsiveness to, and acceptance of, innovation. In addition to receiving regular administrative support, teachers on the curriculum committee were encouraged to attend conferences and workshops to update their knowledge and experiences on this issue. We created further training opportunities by organizing seminars to reinforce the need for continuous staff development and to promote teachers' interest in curricular innovation.

Conclusion

Although the needs of EFL/ESL students might vary from country to country, the curriculum renewal project in the Turkish university described in this chapter can serve as a model for similar contexts. Over the course of 2 years, the project revitalized the program by directly involving administration, the entire teaching staff, current students, target students, and higher education departments offering English-medium instruction. In this challenging curriculum revitalizing process, courses are developed based on goals and objectives, teaching materials are regularly reviewed, and the curriculum is monitored and subjected to ongoing renewal. The effectiveness of the curriculum renewal process as a whole is based on student and faculty needs and perceptions, participatory decision making by the teaching staff, consensus building, and a continuous feedback mechanism incorporated into the system.

As a consequence, teachers appreciate receiving guidance in implementing curricular innovation and having direct involvement in curriculum development. The university faculty are pleased with the collaboration established with the CFL and with its responsiveness to meeting their expectations and ensuring the relevance of innovation to the needs of the target students.

As administration, we feel satisfied that students are better prepared for the communicative demands of their future academic disciplines. We are also satisfied that the revised curriculum better meets the goals stated by the promulgation: The needs analysis we conducted among current and target students has provided reliable information on which to base the new curriculum.

As illustrated throughout the chapter, implementing any kind of major educational changes and sustaining innovation (Fullan, 2001) is complex. Despite the complexities involved, the CFL undertook the challenge and succeeded. The new curriculum has been successful because students and teachers perceive it as different from previous ones and directly relevant to learners' academic needs. The evaluation process demonstrated that the renewed curriculum is coherent—the content represents a research-based approach to achieving the curriculum mission (Richards, 2001a).

Appendix A: Survey Questionnaire

Dear Student,

The following questionnaire constitutes part of a research project that investigates your English needs in your departments. The results obtained from this questionnaire will be used to help the Center for Foreign Languages make the necessary adjustments to its current curriculum. The questionnaire is anonymous and your answers will remain strictly confidential. Before you fill in the questionnaire, please write your department.

Your department: _____

Fill in the rest of the questionnaire by circling the relevant answer. In the first column of the questionnaire, you will find various tasks you carry out in your academic department. The second column shows how often you are required to accomplish a given academic task. Please circle the answer that characterizes your experience best. In the third column, please circle the most relevant answer that shows how effective you perceive yourself in fulfilling those tasks. Thank you for your help.

PART I. SPEAKING

Please circle the most relevant item in both columns.

	How often are you required to accomplish the following tasks in English in your departmental courses? 1 = never; 2 = sometimes; 3 = often; 4 = always				How successful do you think you are in accomplishing the following tasks? 1 = not effective at all; 2 = somewhat effective; 3 = quite effective; 4 = very effective			
1. Ask the instructor questions during lectures	1	2	3	4	1	2	3	4
2. Answer questions asked by the instructor	1	2	3	4	1	2	3	4
3. Make presentations/do demonstrations on a topic related to your field of study	1	2	3	4	1	2	3	4
4. Participate in pair or group activities in class in order to complete a task given by the instructor	1	2	3	4	1	2	3	4
5. Express your opinion and/or convince classmates of your opinion/negotiate meaning during class discussions/debates	1	2	3	4	1	2	3	4

Other (please specify)

_____

What difficulties do you face while speaking in English?

_____

PART II. READING

Please circle the most relevant item in both columns.

	How often are you required to accomplish the following tasks in English in your departmental courses? 1 = never; 2 = sometimes; 3 = often; 4 = always				How successful do you think you are in accomplishing the following tasks? 1 = not effective at all; 2 = somewhat effective; 3 = quite effective; 4 = very effective			
1. Go through a chapter, article, etc. quickly to decide whether the information it contains is useful for you or not	1	2	3	4	1	2	3	4
2. Summarize a text orally or in written form to fulfill an assignment	1	2	3	4	1	2	3	4
3. Read an article/text quickly to find the specific information that you are looking for	1	2	3	4	1	2	3	4
4. Answer comprehension/ discussion questions related to a text during an examination, during class work, or for an assignment	1	2	3	4	1	2	3	4
5. Read various texts on a particular issue to form and express your own opinion about the issue	1	2	3	4	1	2	3	4
6. Read a text and criticize the author's idea	1	2	3	4	1	2	3	4
7. Read a text and express the author's ideas using your own words	1	2	3	4	1	2	3	4
8. Interpret data in various forms (graphs, charts, etc.)	1	2	3	4	1	2	3	4
9. Guess the meanings of unfamiliar words without using a dictionary	1	2	3	4	1	2	3	4
10. Translate parts of textbooks/ journal articles into Turkish	1	2	3	4	1	2	3	4

Other (please specify)

_____

What difficulties do you face while reading in English?

_____

PART III. LISTENING

Please circle the most relevant item in both columns.

	How often are you required to accomplish the following tasks in English in your departmental courses? 1 = never; 2 = sometimes; 3 = often; 4 = always				How successful do you think you are in accomplishing the following tasks? 1 = not effective at all; 2 = somewhat effective; 3 = quite effective; 4 = very effective			
1. Take notes during a lecture given in English	1	2	3	4	1	2	3	4
2. Write summaries using notes taken in a lecture	1	2	3	4	1	2	3	4
3. Follow the instructions of the lecturer during class	1	2	3	4	1	2	3	4
4. Watch a video recording and comment on what you see	1	2	3	4	1	2	3	4
5. Communicate with classmates	1	2	3	4	1	2	3	4
6. Listen to an audio recording	1	2	3	4	1	2	3	4

Other (please specify)

_____

What difficulties do you face while listening in English?

_____

PART IV. WRITING

Please circle the most relevant item in both columns.

	How often are you required to accomplish the following tasks in English in your departmental courses? 1 = never; 2 = sometimes; 3 = often; 4 = always				How successful do you think you are in accomplishing the following tasks? 1 = not effective at all; 2 = somewhat effective; 3 = quite effective; 4 = very effective			
1. Answer questions in an examination	1	2	3	4	1	2	3	4
2. Write a report describing the steps and the result(s) of an experiment/ group project	1	2	3	4	1	2	3	4
3. Write an essay/paper on a topic incorporating ideas from a variety of sources and document these sources appropriately	1	2	3	4	1	2	3	4
4. Write a summary of an article	1	2	3	4	1	2	3	4
5. Design a questionnaire to gather information for an assignment	1	2	3	4	1	2	3	4

Other (please specify)

_____

What difficulties do you face while writing in English?

_____

Appendix B: Description of Level 3 Syllabus

Level 3 students already have an English language background but are still at a lower-intermediate level, with limited language skills and only basic grammar knowledge at the beginning of the academic year. They need to improve their language skills, subskills, critical thinking skills, and learning strategies during their 1-year CFL program.

In this level, the students are expected to

- read and understand various factual and scientific articles and magazine or newspaper texts of 500–600 words and use various reading strategies (i.e., skimming, scanning) effectively

- write texts of various genres, including formal and informal letters and descriptive, narrative, and argumentative essays of about 250 words
- listen to longer texts for comprehension and develop note-taking skills by fulfilling various tasks such as filling gaps, completing charts, and answering questions
- speak on realistic topics in formats that include narratives, discussions, and problem solving

Appendix C: Reading Goals and Objectives for Level 3 Syllabus

By the end of Level 3, the students will meet the following goals and objectives.

GOALS

The students will be able to

- read and summarize a text
- be aware of the process of pre-, while-, and postreading
- develop appropriate reading strategies
- read and comprehend texts and semitechnical texts
- read to support ideas
- read to learn technical terms
- read for pleasure

OBJECTIVES

The students will be able to

- understand grammatical items in context
- guess the meaning of vocabulary in texts
- increase vocabulary knowledge
- read for the gist
- outline a reading text
- do decision-making tasks
- scan for specific information
- skim for the main idea
- paraphrase texts
- read up-to-date materials relevant to their specific fields and interests
- read nonverbal information, such as tables, graphs, and charts

Satisfying Customers:
A Business Approach to
Curriculum Development

9

ROANN ALTMAN

The program discussed in this chapter could be considered highly success-ful. Students have always rated it 4.25 or higher on a 5.00-point scale. The faculty enjoy teaching in the program. The administration recognizes the quality of the program and the expertise of the staff. The client appreciates the work the program does in preparing the students for their upcoming studies. And many students participate in the program voluntarily, either as a result of word-of-mouth advertising or because they recognize its value.

Then why did a program such as this need revitalizing? First, the language program did not reflect changes made in the curriculum of the associated content area. Second, over the years, the level of the students' English language ability had risen. And, third, the hiring of new teaching staff with little background in this special kind of program, and the fact that the staff had no textbooks to depend on, led me to conclude that the curricular goals needed to be more clearly articulated. With approval from the unit's curriculum committee, I undertook a formative evaluation of the program (Altman, 2000).

Curricular Context

THE PROGRAM

The program under discussion is an intensive summer program for international students entering the University of Michigan's master of business administration (MBA) program (referred to here as the B-School).[1] The preparatory program, known as English for Business Studies (EBS), is one of three summer programs offered through the university's English Language Institute (ELI). (The other two are English for Academic Purposes, the original and largest program, and English for Legal Studies.) The ELI, an independent academic unit housed in the College of Literature, Science, and the Arts, provides English language instruction to international students at the graduate (over 90%) and undergraduate level. Its summer programs are run independently of the academic-year programs and have their own coordinator. I have served as coordinator of EBS since 2000.

The summer EBS program was first established in 1986 at the suggestion of John Swales, the newly appointed director of the ELI. Instead of taking a 28-hour advanced-level summer intensive program with an elective in business for 5 hours weekly, students enrolled in an 18-hour-a-week intensive preparatory program for the MBA. ELI faculty taught courses in analyzing business cases and in oral and written communication skills; a B-School doctoral student taught a course called Business Topics (particularly covering organizational behavior; see Initial EBS Program for a list of courses and hours allotted). Classes were held from approximately 9:00 a.m. to 3:00 p.m. Monday through Friday for 6½ weeks.

For many years, the teaching staff consisted of two veteran ESL instructors (one of whom coordinated the program) and the doctoral student from the B-School who taught the business topics component. It was most likely the departure of the EBS coordinator in 1998 that precipitated the changes described here. The appointment of a coordinator who had never taught in the program, along with the hiring of two new teachers, highlighted the difficulties of teaching in a program with no clear curricular objectives. Over the years, highly experienced professionals had developed their own materials. New instructors, who were often brought in to teach just during the summer term, did not receive materials to use and were thus often unsure how to proceed.

The University of Michigan's B-School offers degrees at all levels

---

[1] At the time of the revitalization, the school was referred to as the University of Michigan Business School. The name was later changed to Michigan Business School, and in 2004 the school was renamed the Stephen M. Ross School of Business.

Initial EBS Program (Circa 1986)	
Course	**Hours per Week**
Case Readings	4
Business Writing	4
Listening (not specifically geared to business)	3
Pronunciation	3
Business Topics (organizational behavior)	4
Total	18

Note. Course titles and number of hours allotted are approximate.

(bachelor's, master's, and doctorate), though the MBA program is clearly the largest and most important. The B-School prides itself on the high rankings it receives in the annual ratings of MBA programs across the country, with three major curricular reforms that had been instituted over the preceding 10-year period likely contributing to its success:

- Leadership Development Program: In this 5-day workshop, participants assess their managerial strengths and weaknesses, formulate an action plan for self-development, and produce results by working effectively in teams.
- Executive Skills Program: This half-day, noncredit workshop teaches skills (e.g., teamwork, time management, interpersonal communication, networking) needed by business leaders.
- Multidisciplinary Action Project (MAP): In this full-time, team-based project for first-year MBA students, scheduled for the second half of the winter term, students help firms solve problems by making recommendations for process improvement.

MAP is central to the first-year program. In this field-study program, teams of students apply what they have learned during their first semester of study to solving real business problems at sponsoring companies. The objective of the intensive, hands-on project is to develop the knowledge and personal and professional skills that will help students succeed in the MBA program and, subsequently, in their careers. The challenge to perform well in teams faced by international students, who have to contend with language and cultural differences as well, is tremendous.

International students make up some 25–30% of each incoming MBA class. The Office of Admissions relies on a variety of measures (including an interview either in person or by telephone) to determine whether to require or recommend the summer preparatory program. The minimum Test of English as a Foreign Language (TOEFL) score for B-School admission is 600 (250 computer-based). Some students decide to enroll of their own accord as a result of having received either a brochure or a recommendation from former participants from their country. Very rarely do non–University of Michigan students apply.

CHALLENGES

The most pressing challenge I became aware of was the lack of curriculum or materials, a problem that surfaced only with the hiring of new teaching staff. Although the staff was highly experienced, the intense summer teaching schedule precluded extensive course development during the program.

Another challenge concerned staffing needs. Although doctoral students from the B-School normally taught the business topics component, they were often too busy during the summer either studying for exams or writing their dissertations to take on a 50% position. Moreover, they were rarely available for more than 2 years.

A third challenge was the advanced level of the participants' English. Not only was the TOEFL cutoff high, but many students who voluntarily attended the program scored much higher than the cutoff. The students enrolled in the MBA program had always been capable of handling material at a much higher level than that found in business English textbooks for ESL students. Now, their increased ability made finding—or designing—materials appropriate to their level even more urgent.

Evaluating the Program

Because the goal was to better prepare the international MBA students, I decided that we should conduct a formative evaluation to ascertain what the program's strengths were, how the program could build on them, and how the offerings could be improved. (For a discussion of formative and summative evaluations, see Brown, 1989; Richards, 2001a.)

UNDERLYING CONSIDERATIONS FOR THE REDESIGN

Because the program in place was already quite successful, it was important to honor what had gone on before—the work of the previous coordinators, the materials that had been developed, and the expertise of the existing faculty. That also meant honoring the expertise and teaching styles of the highly experienced faculty by providing a flexible curriculum.

And the participants themselves needed to be honored for the language background and business expertise they brought to the program. They would likely not require a full-fledged language skills program. Rather, they would need opportunities to practice what they already knew, receiving instruction in new skills as needed. The most critical skill they would likely need would be interacting with others as a successful team player.

NEEDS ANALYSIS

The underlying premise in redesigning the program was to satisfy the customers. But who exactly were they? Although the primary customers were, of course, the students, our ultimate customer was the B-School's Office of Admissions: To require or recommend our program, they would have to be confident that participants were being well prepared for successful participation in the MBA program. The teaching staff would also have to be satisfied with the program, or they would not be willing to teach in it. Clearly, the needs analysis would have to focus on more than just end-of-course measures of student satisfaction.

To best determine the needs of our various customers, I gathered data from multiple sources: (a) from the students on what did and did not work; (b) from the instructors in the program on their perception of student needs and their own needs as professionals; and (c) from the B-School curriculum, materials, faculty, and staff on skills the entering students would need. This triangulation would also allow us to more accurately identify the needs, focusing particularly on those common to all three constituencies.

The EBS participants had always completed evaluations immediately following the program. As program coordinator, however, I felt that additional feedback sometime later would provide even greater insights about the relevance and value of the program for their studies. Therefore, following their first semester and a half in the MBA program, students were invited back to participate in a focus group. I expected that the focus groups would provide a richer source of data than would surveys or interviews with individual students. (See Krueger, 1988, for details on conducting focus groups.) In fact, although only two students were able to attend the focus group, the session, which had been originally scheduled for 2 hours, lasted more than 3. In addition, two students responded by e-mail, and one came in for an individual interview.

The EBS faculty provided input at the end of the summer in the form of written journal entries and individual follow-up interviews. One of the instructors, a doctoral candidate in the B-School, provided valuable information on how the two programs relate to each other. As both the researcher and an instructor in the program, I was able to offer insights on how the ELI program fits into the total MBA program.

The third source of data consisted of materials and people from the B-School. I conducted situated discourse research (Jacoby, 1998) to determine the tasks students would be expected to perform. Data included course descriptions, curricula, syllabi, and handouts along with job-search skills materials from the B-School's Office of Career Development. A summary of the different genres extrapolated from the data appears in Genre Descriptions Extrapolated From B-School Syllabi.

The print data were enhanced by interviews with B-School faculty, staff, program directors, consultants, and students not enrolled in the ELI program, and by observations of classes, project presentations, and student interactions with their professors and peers.

FINDINGS OF THE NEEDS ANALYSIS

The rich data sources—students, ELI faculty, and B-School faculty and course materials—indicated where improvements might be made. Some of the suggestions concerned adjustments to specific courses; others, to skills needed for business school; and still others, to ways of reorganizing the curriculum to make the offerings more coherent. Specific requests from the students for each course appear in Course-Related Requests From Program Participants. Overall, the students seemed to want to spend more time practicing their language skills, with a greater variety of tasks, and less time on the business content itself.

In the case studies component, which is very common in most business schools today, students read published cases based on real business

Genre Descriptions Extrapolated From B-School Syllabi	
Genre	**Description**
Case study (prose/bullet/outline)	Identification of problem, opportunity, theme, or issue Identification of potential solutions Analysis and evaluation of alternatives Final recommendation
Project (usually group: research paper, proposal, report)	Executive summary Introduction and background information Current process/situation and problem definition Analyses and recommendations Appendixes Bibliography
Reaction paper (personal reactions, learning logs)	Self-reflection Examples from students' own experience: understanding of consequences of values, attitudes, style, behavior, and other factors on themselves, others, and the organization Students' thoughts about what they did Conceptual understanding Application (plans for action)

Course-Related Requests From Program Participants	
Course	**Request**
Case Studies (also known as Case Readings)	Fewer cases
Business Communication (i.e., business writing)	Shorter, more frequent writing (rather than a research paper)
Listening	Lectures by nonnative-English-speaking professors
Fluency (formerly Pronunciation; later Oral Presentation Skills and Oral Communication)	Pronunciation instruction only for those who need it
Business Topics	More skills-based activities; increased time for discussion

Note. Although some course titles had changed, the components were essentially the same as those shown in Initial EBS Program on p. 163.

situations, discuss them in teams, and then present their analyses in class, either by volunteering or when called on by the instructor. Because much of the work in business schools is conducted in teams, effective participation in teams is a key skill for success. Although the Case Studies course was already team based, the students would benefit if teamwork were an essential component elsewhere in the program as well. Greater coordination throughout the program (an interest expressed by the teaching staff) would help reinforce what the students were learning. And if the oral and written communication skills were coordinated with the content from the Case Studies course, then the number of cases they would have to read could be reduced, fulfilling one of the students' requests.

Redesigning the Program

INITIAL STEPS

For several reasons, the recommendations from the needs analysis were not immediately implemented. First, the curriculum needed to be specified before materials could be developed. Second, all members of the teaching staff would need to agree to the changes, which would necessitate a great deal of discussion and time. And, third, because the program was already going well, we needed to be aware of the impact that any changes might have on the program. Consequently, during the summer immediately following the needs analysis, the program made only the few changes listed here. They were, however, important changes for the future success of the program:

- acculturation: For the first time, classes were held at the B-School.
- course and program evaluations: A qualitative, end-of-course evaluation form (with a 1–5 rating scale) was designed based on the one used during the academic year. Another form was designed to evaluate the general aspects of the program (e.g., orientation, guest speakers, extracurricular activities).
- coordination: Some assignments were coordinated between the Business Topics class and the Business Communication (writing) class.

With the departure of the coordinator in summer 2000, the coordination was turned over to me. Having conducted the initial needs analysis and having had 2 years' experience teaching in the program, I could now more easily implement the recommendations.

INCREMENTAL IMPROVEMENTS

My first goal was to design a task that allowed the students to practice their teamwork skills while working on their language skills. The ideal solution seemed to be to create a project modeled on the B-School's MAP, which students work on during their second semester in the MBA program. Following a brainstorming session with the teaching staff, I decided to adopt the suggestion made by the doctoral student teaching the Business Topics course: Students would develop a plan for an online business. This instructor introduced the project and provided information on business plans. The students then worked on the oral presentations and write-ups in teams of four or five as part of their English skills classes. What made the project particularly successful was the attendance at the oral presentations of two venture capitalists, who asked insightful questions and gave feedback on the viability of the business plans.

To give students more opportunities to practice the language and obtain feedback on their performance, all presentations in the fluency course (now called Oral Presentation Skills, to reflect the new focus) were videotaped (see Oral Presentation Skills Assignments). Following the presentation on companies in the news, presenters were asked to review the videotape together and complete a worksheet indicating what went well, what they noticed on the videotape, and what went less well. Reviewing the videotapes allowed students to assess their own performance and become aware of what they would need to do to improve.

Despite the apparent success of the business plan project, it was problematic in one significant respect: It was time-consuming. The teams worked

---

Oral Presentation Skills Assignments

- **Companies in the news:** 5- to 7-minute presentations by pairs of students on current business issues
- **Project proposal:** Written by one or two group members
- **Project progress report:** Written by one or two group members
- **Project final presentation practice:** Attended by all members of the group
- **Project final presentation:** Given by all members of the group in front of classmates, instructors, and guests from the B-School

---

Note. All assignments were videotaped.

so hard on it that they had little time left to prepare for their other courses (particularly Case Studies). Coordinating the schedule of assignments, deliverables, and presentations was challenging for the staff as well. In the end, the students said they would have liked more guidance in developing the plan and would have preferred the opportunity to do shorter, more frequent writing assignments.

MAJOR REDESIGN

A confluence of factors in the summer of 2001 provided a rare opportunity to redesign the program. A new faculty member highly experienced in writing in the business context was hired to teach Business Communication, and a new doctoral student was available to teach the Business Topics course. Because the original instructor of the e-commerce business plan was no longer teaching in the program, the Case Studies instructor and I decided to develop a new project. In addition, the program needed to respond to student requests for more varied and shorter writing assignments with explicit grammar instruction and instructor feedback. The listening component was also in need of change: It had received a relatively low evaluation even though it was taught by the same person who taught Case Studies, the course that always received the highest rating. To comply with students' requests for more opportunities for language practice and less focus on the business content per se, I asked the instructor to incorporate listening activities (videos), speaking practice, and short written exercises into the Business Topics class.

My first step in the redesign was to construct a curricular framework that would represent what was happening in the program. The framework needed to be clear enough for anyone to be able to understand it, yet flexible enough to be used year after year, even with changes in teaching staff. (See Hull, 1996, for a similar approach taken with curriculum design for corporate language programs.)

The cornerstone of the framework I designed (see Curriculum Framework for EBS) is the business content, located in the inner circle; the outer circle represents the skill areas. The business content is divided into a sampling of core business topics, case studies, and a hot topic. The skill areas appear as a two-by-two matrix: oral versus written, and receptive (materials for gathering information) versus productive (communication via project presentations).

Conceptualizing the curriculum in this way allowed program staff to more easily see the relationship between the business content and the language skill areas. Although clearly separate, the skills could conceivably be addressed in the delivery of the business content. To overcome the problems of the separate listening component, we integrated its objectives and materials into the case studies, oral communication (renamed again to encompass

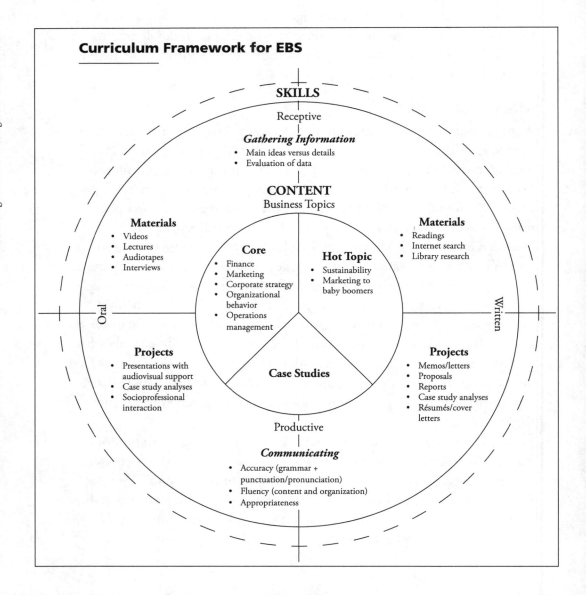

Curriculum Framework for EBS

SKILLS
Receptive

Gathering Information
- Main ideas versus details
- Evaluation of data

CONTENT
Business Topics

Materials
- Videos
- Lectures
- Audiotapes
- Interviews

Materials
- Readings
- Internet search
- Library research

Core
- Finance
- Marketing
- Corporate strategy
- Organizational behavior
- Operations management

Hot Topic
- Sustainability
- Marketing to baby boomers

Oral

Written

Projects
- Presentations with audiovisual support
- Case study analyses
- Socioprofessional interaction

Case Studies

Projects
- Memos/letters
- Proposals
- Reports
- Case study analyses
- Résumés/cover letters

Productive

Communicating
- Accuracy (grammar + punctuation/pronunciation)
- Fluency (content and organization)
- Appropriateness

Courses From 1986 and 1999–2004

1986	1999	2000	2001	2002	2003	2004
Case Readings	Case Studies	Case Studies	Case Studies	Case Studies	Case Studies	Case Studies
Business Writing	Business Communication	Business Communication	Business Writing	Business Writing	Business Writing	Business Writing
Listening	Listening	Listening				Video Lab
Pronunciation	Fluency	Oral Presentation Skills	Oral Communication	Oral Communication	Oral Communication	Oral Communication
				Pronunciation	Pronunciation	Pronunciation
Business Topics (taught by B-School doctoral student)	Business Topics (taught by B-School doctoral student)	Business Topics (taught by B-School doctoral student)	Business Topics (taught by B-School doctoral student)	Business Topics (taught by B-School doctoral student)	Business Topics (with guest presenters)	Business Topics (with guest presenters)
		E-Commerce Business Plan	Sustainability Project	Sustainability Project	Sustainability Project	Marketing-to-Baby-Boomers Project

the addition of some listening skills), and business topics components. (For a historical perspective on the courses from 1986 through 2004, see Courses From 1986 and 1999–2004, page 171.)

At this time, I compiled a list of study and interaction skills that the students were expected to be able to perform (see EBS Study and Interaction Skills). The list was designed to serve as a guide to instructors for what to cover in their courses; the *how* was left up to the individual instructors. Students were also informed of the criteria for evaluating their performance in the program:

- timely attendance and completion of assignments
- clear evidence of preparation
- active, quality participation
- ability to work in a team

As in the MBA program itself, students do not receive grades. Rather, at the end of the summer session, students receive brief descriptions of their performance in the program compiled jointly by all members of the teaching staff.

The project was introduced into the curriculum to give students the experience of working in teams on a project similar to the B-School's MAP. The topic chosen for the new project was *sustainability* (efforts by organizations to eliminate the negative environmental and social impacts resulting from their business activities while also seeking to maximize the economic benefits). With the approach of the new millennium, many people were expressing concern about the future of the world in terms of protecting the environment and ensuring sufficient natural resources for future generations. The B-School and the School of Natural Resources and the Environment were recognized as leaders in the area of sustainable resources and had cosponsored a series in 1999 on sustainability in business development:

EBS Study and Interaction Skills

Study Skills	Interaction Skills
Listening • Taking notes • Identifying discourse markers • Requesting clarification	Interview skills • Getting started • Obtaining information • Acknowledging contributions
Reading • Recognizing discourse markers • Guessing vocabulary from context • Speed reading • Highlighting text	Presentation skills • Giving impromptu talks • Making short, informal speeches • Producing long, formal presentations

Businesses that concerned themselves with sustainability were shown to be able to increase their profits. Faculty specialists were available for consultation, the campus libraries held the most up-to-date books in the field, and videotapes from the conference (18 titles) were available.

In preparation for the project, students received a sustainability project packet including an introduction to the concept of sustainability; a description of the project, which was to be completed in teams of four or five; five project suggestions; a calendar of due dates for the deliverables (proposal, progress report, oral presentation, and final written report); and an annotated bibliography of 10 key books and 11 articles from the Web (all of which were available on reserve in the library).

The Business Topics instructor also provided coaching on effective teamwork. Videotapes from the sustainability conference were shown during the Business Topics and Oral Communication classes, thus providing background information on the topic of sustainability as well as opportunities for practicing listening. The ELI instructors coordinated assignments and due dates for the deliverables and, as a team, provided feedback on the oral proposals. Again, two specialists in sustainability attended the oral presentations, asking relevant questions and providing valuable feedback on the viability of each project.

Positive Outcomes

The redesign was extremely successful in helping us achieve our main goals—promoting teamwork and coordinating instruction. The project required students to work in teams throughout the program. Although difficult and time-consuming, generating the final project reports (oral and written) gave the students a great sense of accomplishment. Receiving feedback on their oral presentations from specialists in the field was especially gratifying to them.

Introduction of the project also marked a turning point for the teaching staff: We began working as a team, each member working on a different skill area with the students. This coordination among instructors was easier than in previous summers because, with the elimination of listening as a separate component, the number of teachers was reduced from five to four.

An additional positive outcome from the redesign was the extensive feedback we received from the expanded and standardized course and program evaluations and the follow-up focus groups. An unexpected byproduct of the initial needs analysis was increased collaboration with the B-School: The consultants for MAP provided material on training effective teams; the Office of Career Development (part of the Office of Admissions) gave presentations to the group on preparing résumés and applying for internships.

Drawbacks

Unfortunately, some of the same items that were successful also proved to be problematic. The project, although modeled after the B-School project, turned out to be too ambitious. Although the problems to be solved in the B-School project are assigned, the summer project required students to select a topic to investigate, a time-consuming process that necessitated a great deal of negotiation. Students also complained that unlike during the academic year, when they could devote half a semester to the project, the summer project had to be accomplished while they were taking three additional courses. The students also found the project time-consuming because, instead of writing 20-page reports as assigned, they procured extensive background material from the Web, which resulted in 40-page reports. They reported that they would have preferred doing shorter, more frequent writing assignments.

Although the project helped us focus the students' energies and coordinate skills instruction for the project, the coordination did not extend to the remainder of the program. For example, the remaining courses were still being taught independently, with just a few instances of coordination of writing assignments with the Case Studies course.

Although the turnover in faculty (50%) in 2001 facilitated the redesign, it also resulted in difficulties managing the program. Swales (1989) has recognized the fact that many problems affecting the success of a program are structural or managerial, and such was the case here. Not only was a new writing instructor hired, but a new doctoral student joined the program. Although quite eager to work with us to develop the program, he was not as experienced as the previous one had been. It was also a challenge for him to integrate English language skills into the Business Topics class; manage the new project, for which he had no background; and integrate the project videos with the remainder of the traditional Business Topics content.

Despite these difficulties, the average scores of satisfaction continued to be quite positive: The averages in 2000 were 4.48 for courses and 4.49 for faculty; in 2001, they were 4.38 for courses and 4.60 for faculty. Clearly, the program was fine just as it was—but the instructors were well aware that, with a little tweaking, the program could be even more successful. Annual evaluations from students and staff, along with the follow-up focus-group feedback, were crucial in helping us identify the gaps and areas for additional improvement.

REDESIGNS REVISITED

2002

With the same faculty anticipated to return in 2002, we were looking forward to the opportunity to run the program using the same curriculum again, perhaps with a few minor adjustments. But in 2002, we were surprised to have 25 students enrolled in the program: In recent years, the highest enrollment had been 20. The new challenge was not just to tweak the curriculum but also to solve a managerial problem: how to hire additional, qualified staff at the last minute. Furthermore, with the budget predicated on a class size of 16, splitting a group of 25 into two groups was not financially feasible.

Therefore, some compromises had to be made. Because the normal class size in the B-School is 70, I decided that all 25 could be taught in the Business Topics course. That would mean that the Business Topics instructor would not be able to focus as much on skills development as the students had requested. On the other hand, keeping the students together for this one course would enable us to offer two sections of the language skills courses.

Feedback from 2002 identified areas to work on for 2003. Feedback on the sustainability project was consistent with that from the previous year. Although some students found the project interesting and relevant, others felt it was not very interesting and not related to business school work. Most found it too broad, ambitious, and time-consuming. Students again requested more, shorter writing assignments than just the group writing for the project. Clearly, the project needed to be made more manageable.

Participants in the focus group 6 months later were extremely positive about the summer program experience and contributed thoughtful ideas for improving the program. Because they had become very much aware of how difficult it was to participate effectively in MBA class discussions, they provided several recommendations for the highly rated case studies component of the program:

- Include more cases.
- Challenge the students more through cold calling (a common technique in courses based on the case-study approach wherein professors call on students at random to answer questions about a case they were to have prepared for class) and by asking *Why?* more often.
- Provide background issues on cases in order to focus the discussion.
- Show videos of professors leading case discussions.
- Have Americans participate in the case discussions in class.
- Have students build their own cases.

Interestingly, now students were asking for more cases, whereas in 1999 they had asked for fewer. Apparently, we would need to find a balance.

2003

Increased networking with contacts from the B-School (apart from the Office of Admissions) allowed us to address some recurring problems. To make the project more manageable for 2003 and help the students understand the business application of sustainability, a specialist in the field from the B-School was invited to give an introductory lecture on sustainability and assist the students with their proposals. To provide students with more listening materials and a sample case study discussion, we were fortunate to obtain a videotape of a class taught by a nonnative speaker of English.[2]

With the doctoral student no longer available to teach the entire business topics component, and with new contacts made at the B-School, we decided to invite guest speakers to provide the Business Topics content. The advantage was that the students would be able to experience courses taught by professors as well as by doctoral candidates. The disadvantages were that it would not be a coherent course (the guests would teach in their specialty areas) and that we could not expect the guests to focus on language skills or take responsibility for managing the integrated project. Coordinating these guest presenters also turned out to be labor intensive. Presentations needed to be scheduled around vacation time; feedback needed to be elicited from the students following each session and communicated to the presenters in a constructive, nonevaluative way; and arrangements needed to be made for honoraria.

Dealing With the Unexpected

The biggest challenge for 2003 was that we could not predict how many students we would have—or whether there would even be a program at all. The introduction of federal guidelines in the form of the Student and Exchange Visitor Information System (SEVIS) following the terrorist attacks of September 11, 2001, combined with an outbreak of the SARS virus, meant that all decisions had to be delayed.

Enough students eventually enrolled for one section, but the group was unusual: Although most of those students who were required to attend the program enrolled, none of those who had been recommended to attend did so. Fortunately, enough students volunteered to attend, resulting in a group of 14 students. With fewer students enrolled than usual and with almost 25% arriving late (including one almost a month late), the teachers found that the group lacked energy. The staggered arrivals (and one 10-day

---

[2] Students had previously requested samples of speech by nonnative speakers. Perhaps they realized something that the research has only recently begun to show: If they could watch videotapes of a speaker with a particular foreign accent, they would be able to more easily understand other speakers with that particular accent (Bradlow & Bent, 2003).

unavoidable departure midsemester) also affected the class dynamic and required repeated adjustments to the syllabus.

Going Back to the Drawing Board

The 2003 group provided valuable feedback for future development of the program. What became apparent was that some of the requests the students were making had already been made the previous year—which meant that, even with a specialist in the field assisting with the sustainability project, the problem had yet to be resolved. For example, the students again found the project time-consuming and would have preferred a variety of shorter writing assignments and opportunities to write under time pressure; they also wanted to have a logical framework for discussing the cases and to be able to discuss them with native speakers. One student requested intensive work in listening, particularly in a format where the material could be listened to multiple times. And several students asked that the work be practical (i.e., less theoretical) and focus on more informal language use.

These requests were all addressed in the 2004 program. Background material for discussing the cases was provided. Many lectures and videotapes were digitized and posted on the course Web site. Students received a variety of weekly writing assignments (e.g., memos, thank-you letters, summaries, case analyses). Most important, however, the sustainability project, which had been problematic in so many ways, was retired, and a new project was designed.

A recurring topic in the media was the baby-boomer generation and ways to market products to it. Therefore, with the assistance of an intern, we developed a project on marketing to baby boomers. A search of the Internet provided a plethora of sites with relevant articles and background information; the B-School librarian helped identify the latest books and chapters addressing the topic.

This marketing-to-baby-boomers topic was a great improvement over the sustainability topic in several respects. First, the concept was much more accessible. Second, marketing was more closely aligned with concepts being covered in the Case Studies course. Third, students immediately grasped the need to develop something practical—a project or service—thus avoiding the pitfalls of a more academic search of the literature. And, finally, the students enjoyed coming up with what they hoped were unusual ideas and presenting them to their classmates and two outside evaluators.

Lessons Learned

From the evaluations and focus group feedback collected from 2001 to 2004, I can make several generalizations and pose some additional questions to guide the program in its successive attempts at revitalization.

First, despite continuous attempts to refine the program and meet customer needs, we cannot satisfy everyone all the time. Sometimes, requests were contradictory: One year, more cases; another year, fewer cases; one year, a focus on job-search skills; another year, no focus on job-search skills. Perhaps students' skills and needs vary from year to year, or perhaps we have moved too far in one direction in response to the feedback. How can we continue to meet student needs year after year when those needs may change?

The solution seems to be to look at requests that keep recurring. Reviewing a program after a minimum of two, preferably three, iterations provides the advantage of perspective. In this program, the recurring requests were

1. practical content and exercises
2. multiple opportunities to practice skills and receive feedback (preferably individual)
3. oral and written skills practiced using cases from the Case Studies course
4. case discussions based on a theoretical framework and involving native speakers
5. a customized program of skill development based on students' individual needs

Of the five requests listed, the program has addressed the first three. The fourth—to base case discussions on a theoretical framework—was introduced with great success in 2004 and was to be further refined and developed in 2005. The request to have native speakers participate in the case discussions is an ongoing, if elusive, goal. The fifth request—to develop customized programs based on individual needs—has been addressed in an ad hoc manner and was expected to be addressed more systematically in 2005.

How do we know what modifications to make each year? Although no changes were ever required, some particular element of the program drew our attention. The other core teacher and I always felt that responding to student feedback would enable us to build an even better program. This ongoing process of making incremental changes is what kept the program new for us. It also allowed us to take pride in knowing we were doing the best job we could.

Conclusion

The approach taken since 2001 to redesign the EBS program was one of constant refinement. I started with what I knew about the program and its issues and then, based on my expertise, decided what to do next. The direction for the project evolved as a result of this interaction, much like the process of problematizing described by Graves (1996). Redesigning the program was—and still is—an ongoing process. The initial course evaluations showed us that we were on the right track. The extremely capable teaching staff knew how to provide a program that satisfied the students. Beyond that, however, we knew there was room for improvement.

The curricular revisions described here were highly successful in several respects. The core skill the students needed—teamwork—was reinforced through the addition of the project to the Case Studies course. The highly experienced teachers worked collaboratively (see Nunan, 1992, for a more complete discussion of the role of collaboration) to set up the project each summer and evaluate the outcomes. And developing mechanisms for eliciting data for the formative evaluation (e.g., standardized course and program evaluations; focus groups; interviews with B-School faculty, class observations, and syllabi analysis; reflective feedback from the instructors in the program) were positive outcomes.

We learned much that will inform our future efforts. First, if the focus group is small, the results may not be representative. One solution might be to provide a survey option for students who are interested but whose schedule precludes their participating in the focus group. In addition, students might not be aware of the relevance of the skills acquired by doing the project because the B-School project is assigned only in the second half of the second semester—after the focus groups are held. Similarly, students might not recognize the value of other skills practiced during the summer (e.g., case write-ups) if these activities take place primarily during their second semester, if not the second year, in the B-School. An easy solution would be to request additional feedback at the end of the first year and then again toward the end of the students' MBA studies.

We also learned that any activity introduced would require that one of the instructors assume responsibility for it. The integrated project was a great idea, but the topic of sustainability was too complicated for the time allotted and too challenging for an instructor without adequate background or support material. And, finally, only so much can be accomplished at any one time. Limited resources and staffing make extensive development extremely difficult. Prioritizing needs is essential.

Some problems affecting the program—enrollment size, availability and experience of teaching staff, funding—may be either unpredictable or uncontrollable. All we can do is take care of the managerial problems to the best of our ability and then depend on the highly dedicated and qualified teachers to do the best they can. Being flexible is one of the overriding factors in the program's success.

Despite the challenges, we know that we are still on the right track and that the students are benefiting not just from the stated curricular goals and objectives but in other ways as well. When asked on the end-of-program evaluations what they like best about the program, students often mention the friends they made. Later, after completing their first year of B-School (or perhaps even the entire program), they can articulate additional benefits. Either through e-mail or chance meetings, we hear how confident they felt at the beginning of the MBA program because they knew their way around the B-School, were familiar with the computing environment, and had covered during the summer some of the same cases that were presented in their first-year program. They are relieved that their personal lives were already settled: They had a place to live, a social security number, a bank account, a car, and a driver's license—all of which would have been challenging to deal with at the onset of the rigorous MBA program. And there is a social benefit, too: The students feel more connected when seeing their classmates from the summer program. They are satisfied with their success in the MBA program and recognize the role played by the summer program in that success.

Then the process begins again: Former students pass the word on to their friends; the most recent set of feedback is analyzed; another aspect of the program is selected for refinement. Students recognize the dedication of the instructors, and this commitment to excellence contributes significantly to the program's ongoing success.

Acknowledgments

I thank the EBS faculty and students for their eager participation in the program and intern Larysa Cherner for compiling the materials for the marketing-to-baby-boomers project. I especially thank colleague Brenda Imber for her invaluable input and support, John Swales for reviewing an earlier version of the chapter, and Diane Larsen-Freeman and Carolyn Madden for their continuing help and encouragement.

Partnering With Students in Curriculum Change: Students Researching Students' Needs

10

DIANE POTTS AND PUNAHM PARK

Fundamentally, curriculum must serve students' needs. Although new ideas, materials, and technologies generate energy and enthusiasm, truly successful redesign never loses sight of the students, who are the heart of all programs.

Yet understanding the centrality of students' needs is much easier than crafting a process that opens a space for meaningful student involvement. Designing such a process is further complicated when the surrounding academic culture is characterized by traditional hierarchical relations between students and professors, and when those responsible for redesigning a program's curriculum do not speak the students' first language (L1). This was the context in which the redesign of the noncredit English curriculum at the Language Education Center (LEC) of Chonnam National University (CNU) in South Korea took place.

This chapter describes the use of student-led focus groups conducted in participants' L1 as a method of meaningfully involving students in the redesign of an established EFL program. Through an innovative process that involved training local fourth-year English education students in the techniques of conducting focus-group interviews, we as the curriculum designers were able to obtain students' candid opinions about their learning within the existing program and the needs that they believed were not addressed. Because critiquing those in positions of responsibility and leadership is culturally and socially inappropriate in South Korea, the education students' knowledge of the pragmatics and content of student conversations about English allowed us to more effectively refine the interview protocol. Though time-consuming, the process yielded insights that could not otherwise have been obtained within this educational setting.

Curricular Context

THE UNIVERSITY

CNU is a large public university located in Gwangju, South Korea, a city of more than 1.4 million people and the major urban center in the southwest of the country. Emerging from its origins as a series of colleges opened during the Japanese occupation, the university was formally constituted in June 1952 during the latter half of the Korean War.

With over 20,000 undergraduate students, more than 3,000 graduate students, and 1,500 faculty and staff, it is now the leading postsecondary institution in the region and, like most postsecondary institutions in Korea, is highly focused on preparing students for the global context. In 2003, just over 20% of the student body was enrolled in the College of Engineering, with the remainder distributed broadly throughout the sciences, business, medicine, the humanities, and the arts. The university is the site of a number of pure and applied research institutes in engineering, electronics, polymer science, agriculture, biotechnology, and medicine. In the past several years, the university has been aggressively pursuing partnerships with foreign universities, and extensive ties have been developed with universities in China, Japan, and the United States.

THE LEC

The LEC has operated as an independent institute within CNU since 1969 and currently offers noncredit courses in English, Japanese, Chinese, German, Russian, and French. In addition to its course offerings, it provides a wide variety of language services to the university and local community. These include language proficiency assessments, translation services, academic seminars, and publications, such as the *LEC Language Journal* and other books related to the field of language studies. The core of the English language program is a six-level oral skills program, which is complemented by an intensive English program offered between university semesters, English for specific purposes courses developed for the local business community, professional development programs for English teachers in local school systems, and writing programs. In support of the university's expansion of programs for international students, the center also offers Korean as a second language courses for visiting scholars and professionals.

The majority of the course offerings in the oral skills program are taught by non-Koreans, typically a mix of Americans, Australians, British, Canadians, and New Zealanders. Most of them have master's degrees in a related field; the remainder have TESL certification. Turnover among the foreign staff is relatively high, as is typical of many institutes in Korea outside Seoul. Some sections of Levels 1 and 2 are taught by Korean nationals who have lived in English-dominant cultures and received master's or doctoral degrees in second language education outside South Korea.

The oral skills program is offered six times per year. For 7 weeks, students attend a daily 50-minute class focused on speaking and listening. Enrollment in the lower levels of the program has traditionally been much greater than in the upper levels. Progression through the levels is not automatic; course instructors evaluate students' preparedness for the next level. All students completing Level 6 are assessed using common instruments jointly prepared by instructors teaching at this level. The maximum class size is 20 students, and most courses have an average enrollment of 15–20 students. The number of students enrolled in the program averages over 700, with enrollment substantially higher during peak sessions. Although the majority of individuals who enroll in the courses are CNU students, the municipal government uses the program for employee development, as do some corporations or *chaebol* (Korean industrial conglomerates such as LG and Samsung) with major industrial operations in the immediate geographic area.

Students pay for their studies session by session. There are no requirements for students to study continuously. As a result, it is not unusual for students to stop their English studies for a session or more while they focus on their degree programs. The School of Engineering grants a 100% subsidy for engineering students studying at the LEC with the proviso that attendance in the class must exceed 90%. No other subsidies for the institute's programs are available to university students.

Although it is a stand-alone, non-degree-granting institute, the LEC has by virtue of history, employment standards, and university affiliation a reputation as the highest quality language institute in Gwangju. The certificate granted to students who successfully complete Level 6 is recognized regionally by businesses and public institutions.

Economic Impetus for Change

In 2002, instructors and administrators at the LEC had a daily window on the impact of the external context on their students' lives. Toward the end of their degree programs, students took off semesters to study English as part of preparing for their job search. Students who had completed their degrees remained on campus to improve their English skills while simultaneously seeking employment. Students who were not taking courses at the LEC haunted the language labs, working to improve their listening skills. Student discussion boards were filled with invitations to form English study groups. Applicants to on-campus English clubs faced fierce competition during club recruitment drives, and it was not unusual for students to let their grades suffer in order to meet club requirements. Bulletin and notice boards were filled with advertisements for off-campus English courses and English study aids. It was impossible to be on campus and not feel the omnipresence of English.

Although Korean employers have used proficiency in English as a screening criterion for graduates of postsecondary institutions for some time, the relative importance of English proficiency has been increasing since the Asian economic crisis in 1997. For the first time in many people's memory, a postsecondary degree is no longer considered a guarantee of employment. Unemployment rates among young adults remain high, with 7.6% of youth with undergraduate degrees unemployed in May 2004, up from 4.0% in June 2002, the first time such statistics were collected by the Korean National Statistics Office (Park, 2004).

In this competitive employment market, English proficiency can determine whether a student gets a job interview or a job offer, regardless of whether the job responsibilities entail the use of English. Job applications are usually submitted digitally, and a "safe" Test of English for International Communication (TOEIC) score of 900 (out of a possible 990) prevents applicants from automatically being screened out of contention. Internationally, language educators have seen the impact of these shifts in employment patterns in an increase in the number of Korean students studying ESL in private and postsecondary language institutes and, more recently, in the number of Korean students registering as foreign students in public secondary systems ("More Study Abroad," 2004). Students who cannot afford to study English abroad often feel they are systemically disadvantaged by current education and employment systems. This, too, increases the drive for English studies as parents and students begin to consider emigration as a solution to their employment situation ("Suffering in Korea," 2003).

The president of the university took a direct interest in students' achievement in English, challenging the director of the LEC to find better ways to ensure the university's graduates gained entry into their desired fields. At approximately the same time, one of us (Park), the English program coordinator, toured the Language Centre at La Trobe University in Melbourne, Australia, a partner university of CNU. She was impressed by the digitalized organization of the program's curricula, particularly the breadth and depth resources at each instructor's fingertips. In the summer of 2002, external circumstances, interest from the university administration, and ideas from foreign programs coalesced into a resolve to revise the LEC's curriculum.

Revision Process

INITIAL PLANNING

Although the LEC and the university were committed to improving opportunities for English language learners to hone and develop their language competency, there was no single vision of where to begin. In one arena, the university moved to have the LEC develop and implement a compulsory for-credit, first-year English course for all university entrants. Creating this course, a mix of introductory oral English and TOEIC preparation, still left unanswered how to revise the curriculum for the existing six-level program.

The curriculum was loosely guided by a collection of teacher-prepared syllabi and, in Levels 1 and 2, by the scope and sequence of *New Interchange I* (Richards, 2001b), the recommended textbook for these levels. Teachers had significant latitude to adapt the materials as they saw fit, and the upper-level courses were often designed independently by individual teachers. From the director's perspective, the priority was to develop standardized lesson plans across all six levels to ensure consistency within and between levels and instructors. As coordinator for the program, Park had a somewhat different perspective on the priorities. Envisioning a curriculum that was less grammar dominated than the syllabi sometimes prepared by individual teachers, she sought to mitigate the heavy influence of the standard scope and sequence of EFL textbooks that colored many instructors' perceptions of curricular possibilities. She wanted a curriculum that spoke directly to the communicative needs of students in the region, a program that students perceived as leveling the playing field between themselves and those who could afford to study overseas. Such a program had to use content derived from the South Korean context and prepare students for global, not U.S., contexts. She believed that the LEC could achieve such a program only by putting appropriate resources at teachers' fingertips.

For many instructors, a curriculum would impinge on their freedom to teach what and how they chose. There was muted support for revising the existing instructional framework; however, there was little strong emotion for or against its development and little interest in the needs analysis process. Because most instructors signed 1-year employment contracts, a term determined in part by Korean visa regulations governing foreign language instructors, a significant number recognized that their employment would end before the curriculum was put into place. Those potentially affected by the change chose a wait-and-see approach.

When approached to develop the revised curriculum, I[1], as one of the

---

[1] The academic coordinator speaking in this chapter is Diane Potts. Punahm Park was the LEC program coordinator.

program instructors, hesitated for many reasons. Language was my greatest concern. Although Park spoke English fluently, others within the LEC's administration did not, and I do not speak Korean. Negotiating expectations, finalizing project plans, and carrying out the curriculum development would all be complicated by language and cultural barriers. In addition, the timeline would of necessity be short. I was first approached to carry out the project in September 2002, and I was scheduled to commence my doctoral studies at the University of British Columbia in less than a year.

Although some staff members initially conceived of the curriculum redesign as the creation of a shared databank of lesson plans, it was quickly apparent that a detailed needs analysis was a critical first step, followed by the establishment of performance standards and assessment instruments for each level in the program. As a means of communicating my ideas, I created a project overview that included activities and timelines for each stage of the curriculum revision process (see Excerpts From the Curriculum Project Overview). The administration's approval of the plan was an important signal of its commitment to a thoughtful approach to curriculum change, and I set aside my concerns to undertake the project.

The student focus groups described in this chapter were part of a larger needs analysis. That analysis included a written survey of the teaching faculty at the university, including tenured and tenure-track professors as well as lecturers, interviews with key personnel responsible for curriculum development and management at five language centers on three different continents, and a written survey of LEC students' current English study habits. Thus, the focus groups were central to the process from the project's initial design, reflecting the administration's commitment to learning about the needs of CNU's current student body from the students as well as other informants.

FOCUS-GROUP RESEARCH

From the outset, the focus groups were a critical component of the curriculum redesign. The LEC's administration was dedicated to advancing the English language proficiency of CNU's students; however, most members of the program's senior administration staff were tenured education professors whose key research interests lay in the fields of linguistics and EFL. Their teaching and research activities provided little opportunity to explore the English language demands placed on CNU's general student population. Understanding the pressures students were experiencing in their daily lives required talking to students, and these conversations had to take place in the students' L1 in order to yield the rich understandings needed for effective curricular design. Time did not allow for individual interviews or for translation of interview transcripts for my use. Further, given existing cultural

---

Excerpts From the Curriculum Project Overview

Establish Program Objectives and Pedagogical Stance

1. Company/employer contacts
2. Desk research
3. Textbook selection
   - Make initial contact with suppliers
   - Hold initial meetings with selected suppliers
4. Review of other language institute curricula
   - Identify institutes to contact (one British, one Australian, one Canadian, two U.S.)
   - Make initial contacts (writing)
   - Review institute Web sites
   - Conduct telephone interviews
   - Review materials
   - Make follow-up contacts (including by telephone if required)
5. Survey of professors and university teaching staff
   - Create survey document
   - Translate survey
   - Prepare survey for distribution
   - Input survey results
   - Analyze findings
6. Student focus groups
   - Select and train facilitators
   - Develop interview guide
   - Hold focus groups
   - Hold results meeting
   - Write focus-group summaries
   - Write report

Develop Curriculum Overview

1. Establish program objectives
2. Create program scope and sequence
3. Create course objectives, scope, and sequence
4. Develop performance benchmarks for program and courses
5. Identify or develop assessment standards and instruments
6. Test assessment instruments
7. Coordinate with systems analyst of software design and support

---

practices, it was thought that students were more likely to be truly engaged in the topic if the discussions took place with peers as well as interviewers. We also believed that students would be more successful as interviewers or facilitators in challenging their peers to go beyond the general discourse of the demands of English. The LEC administration accepted this rationale and the need for focus groups.

My proposal was to train fourth-year English education students to conduct the focus groups. No one associated with the LEC, not an instructor or anyone employed in administration, would be present. This setup was difficult for some people to accept. The use of students as facilitators challenged deeply held cultural assumptions about expertise and hierarchy. There were suspicions that students participating in the focus groups would use the opportunity to gossip about individual teachers. LEC employees were uncomfortable trusting the selected student facilitators to honor the confidentiality promised to students who participated in the focus groups. Employees who trusted the student facilitators to honor the commitment to confidentiality did not always trust their ability to keep the discussions on track and to prevent the focus-group participants from wasting time on topics that would not benefit the development of the curriculum.

The administration staff were willing to override these concerns as long as they were confident that the resulting information would lead to a stronger curriculum. If the needs analysis process guaranteed that a formal curriculum would be delivered within the established time frames, then it was desirable. Thus, the focus groups as outlined in the original project proposal were approved.

The information gathered from the focus groups would help achieve the goals set out for the needs analysis process, which were

- to uncover commonalities in students' needs that could be addressed in core programming
- to identify special needs of significant subgroups of students that might profitably be addressed in specialized or tailored programs
- to reduce student dissatisfaction that resulted from courses that failed to assist students in meeting their personal language goals

These goals would ground the development of the focus-group interview protocol developed in concert with the education students selected to train as facilitators.

Selecting Student Facilitators

Before the work plan for the project had been accepted, I had already begun recruiting students to assist me in conducting the focus groups. It was not unusual for fourth-year English education students to enroll in LEC classes. Although public school English teachers are expected to use a communicative approach to English instruction, teacher education courses are frequently conducted in Korean. To prepare themselves for their future classrooms, English education students regularly sought out LEC courses to supplement their credit-bearing course work.

I selected two fourth-year education students from classes that I was teaching, intermediate-level users of English who had on several occasions sought me out after class to discuss methodologies, task design, and ESL/EFL theory. Their eagerness to learn and the quality of their questions singled out both as students who could effectively contribute to the quality of the revised curriculum and who would benefit personally from their involvement. The students, both female, were asked to commit to attending four preparation and training sessions, to conduct a minimum of three focus groups, and to assist in the translation and analysis of the results. There was no money available for salaries or honoraria. The students accepted the role because of their interest in learning more about their chosen profession.

The students were asked to identify and approach two additional education classmates that they thought would be interested in participating as facilitators. They recruited classmates using criteria I had provided, but on their initiative added criteria related to increasing the demographic diversity of the facilitators. They selected one of the few male students in their program as well as a third-year female student who had spent several years living in the United States as a child. Their two peers also had different visions of themselves as future teachers; the male student was comfortable with traditional Korean educational values and roles, and the female student was an advocate for change and innovation. Thus, the students immediately increased the quality of their contribution to the project by broadening the perspectives held by those who would facilitate the focus-group discussions. Far from being technically weak and detracting from the quality of the process, the students began to create value from the moment they became involved.

Developing the Questions

The student facilitators and I worked collaboratively to develop the focus-group questions. From my own teaching, I was acutely aware that concepts in English did not map neatly onto concepts in Korean and that a direct translation of my intended questions might not yield the information that I needed for curriculum development. The process for developing the focus-group interview protocol had to address this issue.

Developing the questions was more difficult than the student facilitators had anticipated and more time-consuming than I had planned. Although I had prepared questions before our first meeting, I began by asking the facilitators what questions they thought they should ask to learn about students' past, present, and future language learning needs. The students then edited their questions, using resources I provided on question types and the use of open, closed, probe, and confirmation-check questions. As they revised their questions, I asked the student facilitators to keep in mind whether the question would provide useful information for developing a curriculum. We then compared the four sets of questions created by the facilitators and the questions I had previously prepared, examining them for common themes and challenging each other on the types of information the questions might yield. This process was vital if the students were to effectively translate the questions as they were written in English into questions that fit the pragmatics of Korean conversation. Only through working through the questions in this manner were we able to ensure that all five of us had a detailed, shared understanding of the information we were seeking. The students then took home to translate the list of questions we had compiled as a group.

At the next meeting, the students compared their translations of the questions. Additional differences surfaced in how the facilitators understood the questions' intent, and the facilitators set about reconciling the differences. Much of this meeting took place in Korean. Occasionally the students would switch to English to test two possible interpretations of a question. I had to trust that the students were capable of resolving the differences and coming to a correct decision.

Through this process, the manner in which concepts are structured within the Korean language surfaced, and the concepts were examined for their implications. We could then make informed decisions about the appropriate question. For example, Question 10 evolved as the facilitators moved back and forth between the two languages. *Thinking* and *feeling* are not distinct in the Korean language; they are experienced as a single action. We struggled with a question that would have students talk about their perceptions and beliefs as to the importance of English in their lives and the way these beliefs influenced their educational choices. We wanted a question that would not result in students' telling us what everyone was telling them, that English was important to their future. As the facilitators worked between languages, they consistently rejected the way I phrased the question in English. My use of the word *think*, when translated, they said, would result in students' telling us the correct answer, not what the students personally believed. Working from two bases of knowledge, their knowledge of Korean and their knowledge of their peers' language, they developed the question in Korean first and then gave me the translation, assuring me that it matched my intentions.

Sample Questions From Student's Working Copy of Interview Protocol represents the work-in-progress on the focus-group interview protocol. The students expressed their understandings in both languages, sometimes, as in Question 6, including notes on the intended meaning rather than the translation. The final draft was in Korean. It was prepared by one of the facilitators, circulated electronically among the others for comment, and then presented to Park for comments. No changes were required.

Thus the student facilitators contributed much more than simple

> ## Sample Questions From Student's Working Copy of Interview Protocol
>
> [...]
> 6. Is English important in your plans for your life?
> How (how use and in what situations) will you use English in the future?
>
> (아주 구체적으로) 여러분의 인생에서 영어가 중요하세요?
>
> 왜 중요한가요? (앞으로 영어를 어떻게, 어디에 사용하는지)?
>
> [...]
> 10. Describe your feelings and attitudes toward English.
> How does this impact upon your English studies?
>
> 영어에 대한 느낌이 어떠세요? (바로 대답을 요구함) 이것이 영어 공부에 어떤
>
> 영향을 끼치나요?

translation. In addition to their rich understanding of the pragmatics of the Korean language, they contributed their situated understandings of current student discussions on English language learning. By working with the language of an insider, we as the curriculum designers believe we were better able to go beyond answers that students considered appropriate and to obtain a truer understanding of their personal thoughts, beliefs, and experiences.

Training Students as Focus-Group Facilitators

Once the questions had been developed, the student facilitators had to be prepared to conduct the focus groups. As none had any research experience or had previous knowledge of focus groups, the first step was to help them become comfortable with their concepts of expertise. The onus of their responsibilities in the redesign of the curriculum weighed on them, and they held themselves to high standards. The challenge was to help the facilitators understand that their expertise lay in their ability to gather good information, not in their knowledge of second language education or their English language competency.

As part of their training, I developed a package of materials on facilitation techniques. The handouts stepped the facilitators from general understandings of research through to specific techniques for eliciting and managing the discussion, focusing only on those dimensions that would be useful to them as facilitators. Facilitator Training: Sample Handout (page 192) shows one of the first handouts in the series, which was intended to demystify the notion of research. It develops the metaphor of research as

---

Facilitator Training: Sample Handout

Conducting Research in a Conversation

Conducting research in a conversation means choosing to learn more about what the other person is saying rather than communicating your own thoughts and ideas. It means making sure that you clearly understand the message being sent, letting the person expand on the subject, and creating an atmosphere in which the person is comfortable communicating their emotions regarding the subject under discussion, be it anger, enthusiasm, doubt, etc.

Research involves asking questions and providing feedback. Asking the right questions at the right time takes practice. This study is one opportunity for you to practice these skills.

As much as research involves asking questions, you will sometimes need to make some statements or the people may feel like they are being interrogated. Paraphrasing or repeating can help break the questioning rhythm and make people comfortable.

Another technique of effective listening is to acknowledge the feelings behind the person's statement. This gives the speaker "permission" to openly address how they feel as well as how they think. It is possible that the speaker will feel it is inappropriate to discuss their emotional response unless they are specifically given permission to do so. Expressions of empathy consist of three parts:

1. a tentative opening phrase
2. a definition or identification of the feeling
3. a context or a reason for the feeling

An example of such a statement is "It seems to me that you're concerned about the quality of the instructors." "It seems to me" makes the statement tentative. There are lots of other alternatives. You'll need to identify a few in Korean. The important thing is that the listener doesn't feel like he or she is being told.

"That you're concerned" is the feeling part of the statement. Given the heart/mind connection in Korean, you may need to think carefully how you craft this part of the statement.

Demonstrating empathy keeps people talking by giving them confidence that you are really listening to them and that you understand what they are saying. These statements allow you to confirm feelings and thoughts.

---

conversation in which the facilitator's primary roles are questioning and listening. Handouts served as prereading assignments and as supports for training activities. Because I cannot speak Korean and the students' English language proficiency varied across skills, subject matter, and context, providing these prereading materials was a useful step. It allowed the facilitators to read the materials several times and prepare questions for us to discuss as a group.

The next step in the training focused on preparing the students to conduct focus groups and took the form of role plays. The focus groups were organized so that the facilitators could work in pairs, with one person taking the lead questioning role. The second person took notes and asked follow-up or probe questions when they thought it appropriate. The role plays mirrored the structure of the upcoming focus groups. Two individuals facilitated a mock discussion using the questions we had developed together, and two individuals acted as student participants while I acted as observer. Each facilitator had a turn in each of the two facilitation roles.

False starts were not unusual. In the beginning, the student facilitators focused on the questions, not on an individual's responses, often cutting off the speaker without realizing it. Follow-up questions were inadvertently asked as yes/no questions, and the facilitators would become frustrated by their failure to elicit a lengthier response. The facilitators had been given the rough interview formula of 80% student talk and 20% facilitator talk. They quickly became aware of how difficult it was to maintain this ratio.

However, the student facilitators were also ready learners. They became aware of their tendency to rush and practiced becoming less uncomfortable with pauses between a response and the next question. They began to use silence as a probe to elicit additional information from an individual. By this time, the student facilitators and I had become comfortable working together. The two individuals who had role-played focus-group participants provided detailed feedback, pointing out when they had been cut off, when they had been prevented from raising an important issue because of a change in the line of questioning, and when they had been confused by questions. Those who had role-played facilitators paraphrased back their understandings of their peers' responses to their questions, checking their comprehension and thinking through the clarification questions, which might have prevented any misunderstandings that had arisen. Although the role plays were conducted in Korean, it was not difficult for me to provide feedback as the rhythms of the conversation and the physical responses of individuals made it easy to read the subtext if not the content of the discussions. At the end of several hours of role-playing and feedback, the student facilitators were confident that they were ready.

An additional benefit of the role plays was that we were able to create better facilitation teams. Through the process, the student facilitators became aware of their individual strengths and weaknesses as facilitators and paired themselves with someone whose skills complemented their own.

The student facilitators also received support in managing the logistics of the focus groups, both as training and through the provision of checklists to assist them during focus-group sessions. As the student facilitators had complete responsibility for managing the process, from setting up the room to welcoming the participants to closing the session, training and development also needed to address these responsibilities.

Conducting the Focus Groups

Four focus groups were held on-site with LEC students during core class times in an attempt to ensure a broad-based representation of the LEC student body and to prevent scheduling problems that would have inevitably arisen if the focus groups had been held at another time. Each focus group was intended to last 1–2 hours. Participants were provided with pastries or pizza, depending on the time of the session, but there was no other remuneration. LEC instructors were asked to invite or select two students from each of their classes, representative of different types of students (i.e., talkative and quiet, enthusiastic and uninterested). Most classes had two willing participants. The focus groups ranged in size from 12 to 18 students.

Two focus groups contained a broad representation of LEC students. Of the two remaining, one contained only undergraduates, and the other consisted of graduate students and individuals from the community. Given existing cultural practices, the concern was that young students might be unwilling to speak in front of or contradict senior students or businesspeople. Also, the makeup of the groups allowed for issues and concerns specific to different subsets of the LEC's student population to emerge.

Two additional focus groups were held with CNU students who were not enrolled in the LEC at the time of the study. The majority of the participants were solicited from campus clubs. A small number of participants were reached through word of mouth. These two focus groups ranged in size from 8 to 12 participants.

Coping With Challenges

After preparing carefully to conduct the focus groups, the student facilitators were nervous but confident that they had anticipated and thought through the difficulties they might encounter in the sessions. Interestingly, the challenges that arose were in areas not fully anticipated by the facilitators. Despite their preparation, they found that the identity of teacher as modeled in their public school and postsecondary education had more strongly influenced their behavior than they had previously realized. When participants' comments ran counter to their own notions of good language learning or teaching, their instinct was to teach, correct, and amend. They wanted to talk. Only by drawing on their facilitation training and working as a team, they reported, were they were able to maintain their nonjudgmental stance and draw out the findings that would assist me in revising the curriculum.

Outside the focus groups, the greatest problems encountered by the student facilitators could always be traced back to notions of hierarchy and place. For example, they were scolded for using the photocopier in the teachers' room without asking permission after I had told them they were free to make copies of any materials they required. In another situation, a focus group terminated early when a faculty member from outside the LEC demanded to use the room without checking the booking. Although none of these events had a significant impact on the quality of the results, they were a constant reminder to the student facilitators of their place in the academic hierarchy. For them, it was further motivation to prove they could make a meaningful contribution to the curriculum revision process.

Analyzing the Focus-Group Outcomes

After the focus groups were completed, the student facilitators prepared two summaries of the interaction, one in English and one in Korean. The summaries became the basis of our discussions of the findings.

The initial process for analyzing the focus-group outcomes mirrored the process used to develop the question guide. As a group, we reviewed the English summaries, questioning each other for details and understanding, working back and forth across languages as the facilitators sought to ensure that they were communicating what the focus-group participants had intended when they spoke. Because of the time invested in question development, the process of reviewing the results was smoother and less time-consuming than the initial preparation had been. I soon had the information I needed to assist me with the revision of the curriculum.

Focus-Group Findings

The investment in conducting student focus groups could be justified only if they contributed information not already available to the LEC. The conclusion of the LEC administration was that the investment had not been wasted.

The student survey conducted as part of the needs analysis process provided a snapshot of the time LEC students were investing in English language studies (see Students' Study of English Outside the LEC, page 196). Much of that time, though not all of it, was spent preparing for the TOEIC. Although a minority of focus-group participants enrolled in the six-level program in order to improve their TOEIC scores, most came to talk. They had studied English in public school for 6 (now 10) years and achieved grades that allowed them to enter the most prestigious postsecondary institution in the region, but they could not talk. While they struggled to define what they meant by *talk* or who they might talk to or with, they came to the LEC to improve their ability to talk.

This key finding was not as obvious as it may seem. Instructors at the LEC saw students obsessed with TOEIC scores and asking highly technical questions regarding English grammar, and they worked from assumptions

Students' Study of English Outside the LEC			
Time	**No.**	**%**	**Cumulative %**
Less than 7 hours per week	58	20.2	20.2
1 hour per day	101	35.2	55.4
1–3 hours per day	75	26.1	81.5
3–5 hours per day	11	3.8	85.4
More than 5 hours per day	5	1.7	87.1
No additional study	37	12.9	100.0

about the relevance of highly patterned lessons centered on increasingly complex grammatical forms. The students in the focus group reported that they wanted more talk, and they wanted to know how to talk. On this point alone, the results of the focus groups provided a rationale for shifting the content of the program and a foundation for orientation programs for new instructors.

The program also needed to provide the students with a working definition of success. The students drew direct connections between the current economic climate, the demands of the workplace, and their personal reasons for enrolling in the LEC's programs. Many also brought firsthand experiences of failing in the simplest English conversations after years of language study. The students' comments on the existing curriculum fell into three broad categories:

1. the need to establish and manage realistic expectations
2. the need to meaningfully measure one's language learning progress
3. the need for greater continuity and flow across levels within the LEC's core curriculum

Although everyone associated with the curriculum revision had anticipated the third issue, neither of the first two issues raised in the focus groups had previously been discussed. The students were frustrated by having invested time and money in English language study and having no means of assessing their success. They wanted a program that prepared them to use language outside a classroom and one that told them whether or not they were succeeding. They were critical of the quantity and quality of assessment they received in the LEC's programs and in their previous language studies. They needed the LEC and instructors to create an environment that was not inherently demotivating and that did not reinforce their perceptions of themselves as unsuccessful language learners.

Changes to the Curriculum

A program about talk was going to be communicative. Practically speaking, it would have been difficult to defend any revision of the curriculum that did not adopt a communicative approach, as that approach continues to be pushed within English instruction and teacher training in South Korea. *Communicative,* however, has become a loosely defined term for a classroom that removes the teacher from the front of the room and involves extensive pair and group work. The LEC needed to create its own working definition of *communicative,* one that took into account how long the program was and what a student could reasonably expect to achieve within that time. The students' focus on talk, and on what we came to understand as conversation, both personal and professional, became the backbone of the revised curriculum and that contributed to the Primary Recommendations Arising out of the Needs Analysis.

LEC students were not going to be nativelike speakers of English at the end of the program. Neither their desire and hard work nor the efforts of instructors were going to compensate for the short duration of the courses and the diverse demands on their time. The program could, however, teach courses in a way that prepared students to manage the communicative contexts in which they found themselves and not to be silenced when encountering English in their personal and professional lives. The LEC began to make that commitment to its senior classes.

Primary Recommendations
Arising out of the Needs Analysis

1. Program Goals: The goal of the LEC's six-level English conversation program should be "to prevent students from being silenced when conversing in English with people from other countries."

2. Multiple Competencies: The LEC's program should address the discourse, sociolinguistic, grammatical, and strategic competencies required by language learners to maintain their place within a conversation, and educate learners on the contributions that each of these competencies make to their overall ability to communicate.

3. Clear Benchmarks: Clear benchmarks must be established in the four core competencies—discourse, grammatical, strategic, and sociolinguistic—for all six levels of the conversation program.

4. Program Orientation: Over the course of the six levels, the focus of the LEC's program should shift from conversational English to English conversation.

The results of the focus group influenced the decision to use Canale and Swain's (1980) definition of *communicative competence* as the frame for defining the curricular objectives. The four dimensions of communicative competence (discourse, grammatical, sociocultural, and strategic) give students a language for discussing their language needs and progress with their instructor. They encompass the range of skills that students must develop if they are to talk successfully. The four dimensions could scaffold the extension of instructors' thinking as to what might be taught and what might be assessed. By working on all four competencies, LEC instructors could help students not to be silenced. For each level of the program, I developed objectives for each of these four communicative dimensions. We also used the students' notion of talk to define a shift that would take place over the six levels, a shift from conversational English to English conversation, as illustrated in Shifting the Program Focus From English to Conversation.

This shift was not simple wordplay. There is a very real difference between teaching English as a subject and teaching students to communicate in English. If the LEC focused solely on English, the best its students could hope to achieve was an intermediate knowledge of language that might or might not help with the conversational needs described in the focus groups and surveys. Conflating goals for knowledge of language with knowledge of language use could have resulted in establishing goals that students could never achieve. By gradually shifting to a focus on English conversation and shifting the relative weight of the four dimensions of communicative competence, the LEC could better equip students for the communicative contexts they had described in the focus groups. Understanding questioning strategies, recognizing communication breakdowns caused by ideas deeply embedded in language, using body language, and maintaining high levels of conversational interactivity were skills that would better serve students in reaching their objective of talk.

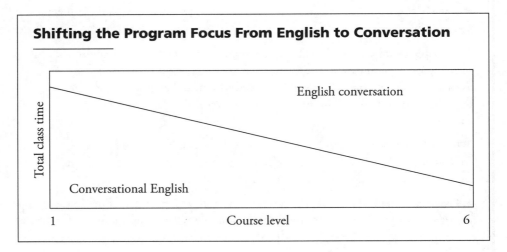

Shifting the Program Focus From English to Conversation

English conversation

Total class time

Conversational English

1   Course level   6

Without the focus groups, it is unlikely that the revised curriculum would have placed the same degree of emphasis on learning strategies or systematic self-assessment. Potts drew heavily on the work of Oxford (1990) while revising the program objectives and writing lessons. The Instructional Handout Excerpt shown here also included a checklist of the objectives for Level 4, roughly grouped by the four dimensions of communicative competence. Every level included increasingly complex goal-setting activities, and students revisited their goals systematically at every level.

In the revised curriculum, detailed lesson plans directed instructors to provide explicit instruction in the course's objectives and rationale in the early lessons of each level. Pedagogical tasks involving students in personal goal setting and self-evaluation were incorporated into the early lessons, and tasks linked course objectives to individual student needs. By seeing direct connections between the course objectives and their needs, students could better understand the *why* of the instructional content and design. Thus, the revised curriculum was better able to address the information needs of students because of the understandings developed through the focus-group process and the contributions of the education students who acted as facilitators.

Instructional Handout Excerpt From Level 4, Lesson 2

Goal Setting

Throughout Levels 2 and 3, you have been involved in setting goals and measuring your progress. When goal setting was introduced in Level 2, you were taught that setting a goal and measuring your progress is important. It is the one process that has been proven to consistently improve learners' learning.

You will continue to set goals and measure your progress as you study at the LEC. You may find that it's sometimes a little more frustrating. As you change from a beginning to an intermediate-level learner, it becomes more difficult to "feel" your progress. You'll probably have days in which you feel like you're not getting any better. You may even have days in which you think you're getting worse! Don't worry! Even if you can't tell the difference, there's all sorts of things going on in your brain. Eventually, when your brain has saved enough information and had enough practice, you'll feel a difference again.

That's why goals are important. Set goals that are small steps. Add some words. Quit overusing an expression. Focus on one verb tense. Think about one aspect of pronunciation. Improve your body language when you listen. Pick a goal that's specific to you. Pick something easy to improve. Pick something that you think is important even if no one else cares. Make it small and make it manageable and watch yourself learn!

Other Benefits of the Focus Groups

As described, program objectives, performance standards, assessment instruments, and detailed lesson plans were heavily influenced by information gathered in the focus groups. The focus groups had additional benefits, though, which, though not directly related to the goals of curriculum revision, were equally powerful in their own context.

The focus groups provided a basis for dialogue with students about their expectations and language learning experiences as well as the benefits that would accrue to them through their successful participation in the program. Some students who participated in the focus groups took a direct interest in the project's progress, stopping us in the halls to ask about its development. Portions of the curriculum were piloted in the upper-level classes as the curriculum continued to be revised. In those cases, the instructor (sometimes myself) often pointed out how the materials were linked to the concerns and needs that had been expressed by the focus-group participants. The course content consistently received above-average student satisfaction scores regardless of the instructor or of the students' evaluation of the quality of the instructor. The report on the findings of the needs analysis, including the summary of the focus-group discussions, was circulated among the teaching faculty. Although the potency of the focus-group findings will decline over time as circumstances continue to evolve, they continue to open the door to dialogue if an instructor chooses to use them in that manner.

The focus groups caused the four education students working as facilitators to think deeply about their own professional development and the principles that would guide their decision making in their future classrooms. They found that material from their degree program came alive in the focus groups. Although their course content emphasized communicative language teaching, cooperative learning, and the role of the teacher as facilitator, as students they had experienced little other than teacher-fronted transmission of information. The time they investigated in question development, the unexpected responses of their peers in the focus-group role plays, and the sometimes frustrating responses they encountered in the focus groups caused them to rethink what it meant to use the communicative approach so freely discussed and ascribed to in their education classes. By the time the results of the focus groups had been translated, the male participant stated that he could not see himself teaching English other than in the way he had been taught. The identity of change agent and teacher as researcher had been firmly rejected as incompatible with his historical and cultural understanding of *teacher* and with the identity he wished to assert in the classroom.

For the remaining three facilitators, the process raised their interest in the continuing evolution of English language education in South Korea.

The focus groups engaged the facilitators as apprentices in the profession of language educators, demystifying research and building truer understandings of what it means to engage in praxis. They found that their commitment to researching their practice strengthened, and they chose to submit a conference paper on the impact of their participation on their identity construction as English language educators to the Korean Association of Teachers of English International Conference. The acceptance of their paper caused great consternation when faculty and senior administrators in English language education discovered that the students had not completed their undergraduate degrees, as no one could remember a paper by anyone with less than a graduate education being accepted. Not only were they the only undergraduate presenters at the conference, but they were also the only undergraduates in attendance. Curiosity resulted in above-average attendance for the session; their work was thoughtfully received. The disruption in the social order of the profession was likely temporary; however, their work opened avenues for revisiting how English language teaching professionals apprentice student teachers.

Needed: Student Participation in Curriculum Design

The points we raise call for creativity in the processes English language teaching professionals use to revitalize a curriculum. All responses to the challenge of curriculum change are situated in their unique context, and the opportunities for student consultation and student engagement that were employed at CNU may not be appropriate in all situations. However, the experience described in this chapter argues for the importance of revisiting student needs at the beginning of the change process and of integrally involving students in such efforts. The investments in time and effort yielded results that many programs seek when revitalizing their curricula.

Self-Portrait: Capturing Curriculum in Black and White

11

ELIZABETH BYLEEN

Revitalizing curriculum can inspire creativity and innovation while invigorating a program and its teachers. Is it any wonder, then, that the next task—documenting the new curriculum—often seems flat and laborious? The magic of classroom interaction is much more appealing than trying to capture curriculum on paper, and once the curriculum is on paper, will teachers actually use the document to guide their instruction?

Despite these concerns, curriculum documentation has been an important step in curriculum change at the Applied English Center at the University of Kansas, in the United States. In a complex center with a large teaching staff, the process of creating curriculum documents has helped the program staff ensure that the program is clearly sequenced and that multiple sections of the same course receive comparable instruction. Our curriculum documents are maps that tell us where we have been, where we are, and where we might go in the future.

Motivation for Documenting the Curriculum

Changes in the program called for three distinct curriculum documentation projects with different audiences, formats, and levels of participation from the staff. Through these experiences, we have learned that curriculum documentation is a work in progress, influenced by changes in teaching philosophy, research, testing and assessment, teaching staff, textbooks, methods, materials, and technology. We have also learned that it is important to begin with a staffwide investment in reflecting on, researching, analyzing, debating, negotiating, and restructuring the curriculum; otherwise, the resulting curriculum document may lack substance and usefulness. In fact, this dynamic process can often be just as valuable as the curriculum document product and, in some cases, perhaps more so.

This chapter begins with a brief description of the structure of the program followed by the details of three curriculum documentation projects undertaken over the span of 15 years. The chapter ends with seven strategies to guide curriculum documentation. Although our first project now seems like a trial run, it was part of our evolution toward the most recent design. Our experiences are a window on the potential of curriculum documentation to solidify and invigorate a program. The various processes and formats we have used demonstrate that curriculum documentation needs to be tailored to the specifics of each program.

Curricular Context

The Applied English Center is both an intensive and a semi-intensive ESL program. After initial proficiency testing, we place students in semester-length courses with a strong focus on English for academic purposes. Although lower-level intensive students study only English, upper-level semi-intensive students can often take one or two university courses while they are enrolled in advanced-level ESL classes.

Since 1964, we have gone through many fluctuations in enrollment, hitting a high in the early 1990s of 475 students per semester and then settling comfortably into an enrollment of about 275 per semester. The composition of the teaching faculty has also changed. At one point, the Applied English Center employed 20–25 graduate teaching assistants (GTAs), most of whom taught for 2–4 years before receiving their degrees. The program currently employs only 1 or 2 GTAs and a group of 7 language specialists and 16 lecturers who have at least a master's degree in TESL or a related field, most with permanent positions.

In addition, the curriculum has gone through many changes (see Basic Class and Level Structure During Curriculum Documentation Projects). Whereas the program once had four levels, with separate classes called Reading, Writing, Speaking/Understanding, and English Structure, it has evolved into a five-level program with three core courses: Reading and Writing for Academic Purposes, Speaking and Listening for Academic Purposes, and Grammar for Communication.

Curriculum documents over the years have reflected these changes in student population, teaching faculty, and course and level configuration. Life in an intensive English program is busy, and there are always compet-

Basic Class and Level Structure During Curriculum Documentation Projects		
Project 1 (1987)	**Projects 2 (1992–1993) and 3 (2001–2002)**	
Levels 1–4	**Levels 1–4**	**Level 5ᵃ**
Reading Writing	Reading and Writing for Academic Purposes	Advanced English for Academic Purposes (capstone)
Speaking/ Understanding	Speaking and Listening for Academic Purposes	**Labs** Pronunciation Grammar
English Structure	Grammar for Communication	**Special Studies** Reading/Writing Speaking/Listening Grammar

ᵃLevel 5 students are generally part-time and take one or more labs or classes.

ing priorities, so finding the time, staff, and interest to begin a curriculum documentation project can be challenging. Sometimes, as in the case of the most recent curriculum documentation, the accreditation process provided the impetus to begin. However, once the project is well begun, momentum usually carries it.

Designing and Evaluating the Curriculum Documentation

DOCUMENTATION PROJECT 1: SUMMER 1987

An ESL program can appear to run quite smoothly without an official curriculum document, but often there comes a point at which curriculum documentation is necessary to focus the curriculum and staff in a positive way. The Applied English Center had been in existence since 1964, and although the curriculum had been described and changed many times, there had been no formal unifying curriculum documents. As noted previously, when we began the first curriculum documentation project, in 1987, the program had four levels of instruction and a very traditional curriculum with separate skill classes: Reading, Writing, Speaking/Understanding, and English Structure.

The impetus for the first curriculum documentation project was the idea that we had to know what the current curriculum was before we could change it. The student population had grown quickly, and the program was understaffed. In 1986, with the addition of three more permanent staff members, two course coordinators, of which I was one, began to document the curriculum of the skill areas of reading and writing to get a better sense of the big picture and the relationships among the levels of instruction.

Format

To get started, we developed a list of common elements in the writing and reading courses. For example, for the writing courses, these general categories were mechanics, process, skills, forms, and methods of development. Starting this way helped us get a handle on the aspects of our curriculum.

Under each of these general categories, we filled in the blanks with what was being done at each of the four levels of instruction. We were not looking for the ideal, or what we wanted the curriculum to be, but rather the reality of what the curriculum was. We wrote it down whether or not it seemed to make sense or to be properly sequenced with the other levels. The bulk of both curriculum reports consisted of about 35 curriculum features delineated for each level of instruction.

The final sections in each report included a brief analysis based on discrepancies found within the curriculum and some suggestions for curriculum and course changes. Finally, we included a section entitled Questions to Consider with about 15 items. These examples come from the questions for writing and reading:

Writing Curriculum Report (1987)
Should we explore the idea of combining structure and writing or reading and writing into one class? At what level(s)? How soon could we be ready to test out one such combination course? Would we start with only one section of the course?

Are we too focused on the essay? Should we be providing more opportunities for other kinds of writing that students will encounter in their university courses? What are the main types of writing they'll need? Will undergraduates get this instruction in English 101 and 102? How much should we provide?

Reading Curriculum Report (1987)
At present, there is very little individualization done in the reading classes. Should we do more? If so, how? Is a weekly lab day a good idea?

All of the reading classes seem to have too much material to deal with. Sometimes this is cumbersome. Is there any way we could achieve the same goals with fewer texts, especially at the first and second levels?

We completed these two reports of more than 50 pages each rather quickly—in about 6 weeks in the summer. These reports helped lay the groundwork for future reports. In the second curriculum project, we wrote a report for the Speaking/Understanding curriculum, and the final course, English Structure, was included in the third project.

Analysis

Looking at these 1987 reports now, I find that their impact seems inconsequential in some ways. They did not result in immediate curriculum change, they had a very small readership, and the Questions to Consider were never given a forum for serious consideration. The reports suffered the fate of many curriculum documents: They ended up gathering dust on a shelf. In hindsight, I realize that the key point we learned from this project is that curriculum documentation should not just be words on paper but the culmination of a dynamic process in which teachers and administrators improve and revitalize the curriculum. For this project, the other course coordinator and I did not even have much face-to-face interaction, with most of the work completed by exchanging and refining drafts.

However, these reports were significant in at least three ways. First, finishing them gave us the confidence that curriculum documentation was something we could accomplish. In addition, though the results were not of great value to the entire staff, the process proved professionally important to the writers and contributors. Finally, it helped solidify our work in course supervision and gave us something concrete to build on.

Finally, the reports paved the way for positive changes. Looking back on the Questions to Consider in both reports 20 years later, I see that we had inklings of positive changes about a decade before we brought them to fruition. For example, now the courses have a much stronger focus on the academic skills students need to succeed in the university, and the program has combined skill courses in a content-enhanced curriculum. Undoubtedly, the program would have evolved faster if we had allowed ourselves the time and space to digest these reports fully and create a plan of action, but perhaps on some unconscious level they were a foundation for future curriculum changes.

In this earliest curriculum documentation project, we attempted to paint the big picture by putting together all the pieces of the curriculum puzzle. Although we only defined what the program offered, the results provided the background for the second project, in which we had a better perspective on shaping the curriculum. In addition, for the second project, we used a format that would make the document much more widely used within the program.

DOCUMENTATION PROJECT 2: 1992–1993

Often the changes in ESL programs are subtle, but occasionally a change requires a major shift in the curriculum and in how it is documented. The

Applied English Center experienced phenomenal growth: In the early 1990s, about 25 GTAs were teaching in the program. We had also created an additional level of instruction, making a total of five. We needed a way to update the curriculum and move forward with a clearer vision. Most important, we needed a way to provide structure for the growing number of relatively inexperienced teachers in the program.

At that time, coordinators oversaw the curriculum and teachers of individual courses. The Speaking/Understanding teachers and coordinators had formed a network, holding regular meetings to revise the curriculum and the content and format of the listening component of the proficiency test. They discarded a multiple-choice, grammar-based listening test and created an English for academic purposes test requiring students to write short answers as they listened to several interconnected conversations and two lectures. Networks for the Writing and Reading courses followed, with a primary focus on relating these two skills in the separate classes. As a result, at these meetings we developed a greater sense of teamwork and a wider perspective of courses in the program and their interrelationships.

Out of this confluence of ideas and the pressing need to provide more structure for the GTAs, we began writing in-house curriculum/teaching guides for Reading, Writing, and Speaking/Understanding that presented both what to teach and ideas about how to teach. They proved very useful for inexperienced teaching staff, some of whom were teaching their first ESL classes, and for the coordinators of this revolving staff.

Format

These curriculum/teaching guides had a teacher-training focus, a user-friendly format, and a collegial tone, and they varied in length from 30 to 130 pages. The shorter Speaking/Understanding guide incorporated more charts in its format, whereas the Reading and Writing guides relied primarily on prose. Although different in format, the guides each included

- an overview of the skill and very basic theoretical background
- a description of texts, materials, and students' abilities at each level of instruction
- priorities, major components, and suggestions for specific activities and practices
- expectations for working with other teachers and coordinators

As an example of the process for creating one of these three guides, another writing coordinator and I collaborated in writing *A Guide to Teaching Writing at the Applied English Center* (for the table of contents, see Appendix A). We kept our audience, the GTAs, in mind at all times, asking ourselves, What do GTAs need to know about the curriculum and teaching philosophy to teach effectively? It was easy to decide on the elements to cover because it was the information we conveyed to teachers at presemester meetings, team meetings, individual consultations, and postobservation conferences. Some of the sections were "Characteristics of Student Writing," "Texts and Materials," "Responding to Students' Writing," "Individualizing Instruction," "Increasing Writing Fluency," "Midsemester Evaluation Process," and "Testing."

As we wrote, we were each other's best critics, and we held numerous discussions to shape our thinking and presentation of ideas. Many members of the program staff read preliminary drafts and made valuable comments. At the same time, their involvement helped them become more invested in the project. Producing the guides to teaching Reading and to teaching Speaking/Listening followed a similar collaborative process.

These guides gave the GTAs solid support and helped teachers realize their responsibilities and place in a large intensive English program. This proved important to keep inexperienced teachers from becoming so absorbed in the microcosm of their own classrooms that they had difficulty seeing beyond them. These curriculum/teaching guides helped include all teachers in a shared curriculum, teaching philosophy, and mission.

Analysis

At this stage of the Center's history, the curriculum/teaching guides proved very beneficial. Coordinators within a skill area collaborated and got a firm grasp on the teaching of that skill. The guides were instrumental in course coordination, as the staff discussed various sections at teachers' meetings, establishing common ground. Teachers now had a ready reference and an overall philosophy, and it was easier to ensure consistency among different sections of a course from year to year, text to text, and teacher to teacher. The guides were also a very efficient way to distribute information. New GTAs could get an overview of their skill area instead of focusing only on their particular course. The shared knowledge these guides provided was also helpful in maintaining quality control in a busy program with a rotating staff and with a high student enrollment that taxed the program's staff and resources.

Interestingly enough, these curriculum guides were top-down documents. Although the course coordinators collaborated in producing them, only a few GTAs were involved in their creation. However, the GTAs, who were new to the field, strongly appreciated this guidance and felt secure knowing the expectations of the job. These guides were a good match for the program's teacher-training and supervision focus at this time. Later, with a different staff composition, we did not even consider this top-down dissemination as a possible approach to curriculum documentation.

DOCUMENTATION PROJECT 3: 2001–2002

The Center started to restructure its curriculum about 5 years after the curriculum/teaching guides were written. In addition, the composition of the teaching staff changed markedly, making us choose an entirely different format for the third curriculum project. The program had gone through many changes: Enrollment was not as high, and the program no longer employed a large number of GTAs. In fact, the staff was composed almost completely of teachers with at least an MA in TESL or linguistics and only one or two GTAs. This change in the composition of the teaching staff caused a major shift away from teacher training and supervision.

Besides changes in enrollment and teaching staff, the curriculum had changed to provide stronger academic preparation for the students, most of whom would be pursuing an undergraduate or graduate degree. Instead of offering four discrete-skill courses, we created three core courses in a new content-enhanced curriculum: Reading and Writing for Academic Purposes, Listening and Speaking for Academic Purposes, and Grammar for Communication. At the most advanced level, Level 5, we added a multiskill capstone course with supporting labs in grammar and pronunciation. Other auxiliary courses in the program included an international teaching assistant (ITA) training course, remedial online grammar and reading/writing courses, and labs for reading and pronunciation. Another positive curriculum change was that the College Assembly had approved a proposal to make the upper-level ESL courses credit bearing.

We had also made substantial additions to the in-house proficiency test to reflect this stronger focus on academic skills. In the grammar section, we added a 30-minute timed essay to the existing paraphrase production test. For the reading/writing portion of the test, in addition to a traditional multiple-choice test over short reading selections, we added a passage that students read and take notes on for 20 minutes. The passage is then taken away, and students answer five questions about the reading based on their notes.

Revitalizing the curriculum and proficiency test in these major ways took a great deal of time, research, discussion, and healthy debate as well as some trial and error. We had countless meetings, committees and subcommittees, retreats, and water-cooler discussions. And as the program staff adjusted to the new paradigm, there was the expected defending of turf and redefining of boundaries. As with any change, people found their comfort zones at varying rates, but within about 3 years, all the new courses were in place, we were pleased with the direction the curriculum had taken, and we had settled comfortably into the courses.

During the initial stages of the curriculum change, we started the process of becoming accredited by the TESOL Commission on Accreditation (TCA). Although some of the accreditation standards were easy to address, the curriculum standards were difficult to document because the curriculum was in transition. As it turned out, TCA disbanded, and we rested for a few years before we took up the accreditation process with the Commission on English Language Program Accreditation (CEA). In the meantime, the new curriculum had solidified. Prompted by the requirements for CEA accreditation, we knew we had to create a document that reflected the revised curriculum.

In the earlier curriculum documentation projects, we had written separate documents for each skill. This separation reflected our thinking at the time, but the years of curriculum discussion and debate had helped us see the curriculum more holistically. The new perspective was reflected in new integrated skill courses. It made good sense to create a unified curriculum document. Practically speaking, it was also easier to contemplate creating only one curriculum document while going through the time-consuming accreditation process.

Format

The program devoted a 1-day presemester teachers' workshop to beginning this project, so we needed to design tasks to take full advantage of the teaching staff. The key was to be able to visualize the completed document before we started it and design a standard format or template that could be used to document all courses at all levels. A two-page template was tested with the information from a few courses to be sure that it would work. With a very controlled format that would fit all the courses (some with slight variations), we could make maximum use of the staff's time and effort.

Key course coordinators were asked to serve as discussion leaders for small-group sessions during our workshop. Teachers were asked to bring course materials, such as course policy sheets, syllabi, or course notebooks, that would help the groups complete the workshop tasks. When the workshop began, participants selected one of the three areas of expertise (reading/writing, grammar, or speaking/listening); it turned out that the groups were fairly balanced. At this workshop, we had a captive workforce and full participation. With about 25 teachers and coordinators working 5 hours each, by the end of the day, we were 125 hours into the project.

The workshop was divided into two main parts, Guided Discussion and Delineation of Goals and Objectives.

Part 1: Guided Discussion

In the morning session, the three groups met in separate classrooms for a guided discussion (see Discussion Questions for Curriculum Documentation Project). The stated purposes of this session were

- to develop a sense of community and purpose among teachers of the same skill
- to brainstorm information for a one-page overview of the skill (See Appendix B for the overview for the Grammar for Communication course.)
- to start working on the major goals of the skill area to use in the afternoon task

The fourth question gave participants a head start on the afternoon workshop.

Part 2: Delineation of Goals and Objectives

In the afternoon session, each of the three groups broke into pairs or triads to work on completing the Form for Delineating Goals and Objectives for their skill and level. This form was heavily based on Question 4 in the morning's guided discussion. See Appendix C for a completed description of the Level 4 (low advanced) Reading and Writing for Academic Purposes course.

By the end of the workshop, we had the makings of a rough draft of a curriculum document. Although accomplishing so much in a day was a great boost, it would take months of refinement to feel that we had a solid document. Throughout that academic year, teachers and coordinators refined the document through meetings and exchanged drafts. A few (non-core) courses that were not covered in this session were documented later.

Discussion Questions for Curriculum Documentation Project

1. What are the strengths of our current curriculum in this skill area?
2. What is the general teaching philosophy?
3. What should teachers know and be able to do to teach this skill the most effectively?
4. What are our main **goals** for courses in this skill area? This question will help you with the afternoon task. Try to limit yourself to no more than six main goals, which should be in this format:
   - To prepare students for academic listening
   - To teach research skills
5. What are some areas of concerns, or things that we may need to look into more carefully later?

Form for Delineating Goals and Objectives

Level: Course:

Goals and Objectives
Course goals guide the development of meaningful and achievable instructional objectives.
Objectives: What will students know and be able to do as a result of course instruction?

Goal 1:
    Objectives:
    a.
    b.
    [etc.]

Goal 2:
    Objectives:
    a.
    b.
    [etc.]

[etc. for remaining goals]

Content Themes (list, e.g., Success, Consumer Behavior):

Methods:
Typical in-class activities:

Typical homework activities:

Means of assessment:

Instructional Materials

The final 50-page document had three main sections, one for each of the core courses (see the table of contents in Appendix D). Each section began with a one- or two-page prose overview followed by the individual characteristics of the courses in each of the five levels of instruction. At the end of the document, we reported on courses that fell outside the three main core courses, such as the ITA training course.

Analysis

This workshop generated a lot of raw material for the curriculum document in a short time. Although this jump-right-in approach is not everyone's preferred work style, it certainly helped launch the project. We could then adopt a more reflective pace to fine-tune the document. Doing this task in teams gave the entire teaching staff an investment in the curriculum. One goal of the CEA accreditation is full staff involvement, and because the staff now consisted almost entirely of teachers with advanced degrees, many with at least 15 years of experience in the field, it was extremely important to tap into the collective experience and wisdom of these stakeholders. The top-down approach of the previous documentation project was not appropriate for this one.

This full staff involvement led us to publish the document as an appendix to the Applied English Center Teachers' Handbook. Each teacher thus had a copy of the current curriculum guide and could refer to it and suggest changes if necessary. As mentioned, the first curriculum document had a very low readership, and the second was widely read by teachers of each individual skill. It seemed logical that this curriculum document would be easily accessible to all teachers.

Of the three projects, this one was the culmination of years of curriculum redesign and revitalization. That important link between dynamic curriculum change and documentation was absent in the first documentation project, in which we merely reported on the current state of the curriculum. In the second project, we made some changes to the curriculum before writing the curriculum/teaching guides, but these changes were made by course coordinators without programwide input, and they were made in particular skill areas in isolation from the other skills. The third project included the staffwide exchange needed to make these major curriculum changes and staffwide investment needed to document them. In addition, the entire staff committed to reviewing the curriculum every November, a procedure we had not formalized in previous projects. This step is necessary to keep the curriculum and its documentation current. We are moving in the right direction.

The current curriculum document reflects the program at the time of writing. If we follow the trend we have established in curriculum documentation, in less than 10 years the curriculum will undergo more changes, which will warrant a new document and possibly a new format. The current document will have become history, and we will look back on how the program used to be structured. To stay vital, an ESL program must constantly evolve, and this evolution will be reflected in the next curriculum document.

Strategies for Curriculum Documentation

Over the course of three projects, the Applied English Center staff developed effective ways to accomplish curriculum documentation and experienced the benefits it can bring to a program. Every program will create its own tailor-made document, but the following general strategies may help focus your curriculum documentation project.

CREATE SOLID CURRICULUM CHANGES

Curriculum change can be quite time intensive, but through this process of reflection, research, analysis, and creativity, the program develops a solid curriculum that staff will be proud to document. Doing a thorough job here is important, as you may discover a few inconsistencies when you begin documenting this new curriculum.

INVOLVE AS MANY PEOPLE AS POSSIBLE

Full participation and collaboration of the teaching staff is important to build consensus and to have a curriculum teachers are invested in. Because producing a curriculum document can be very time-consuming, it makes sense to have many people share the load, whether by contributing content or refining it. Having one editor or project leader makes the orchestration of the many contributors easier to manage.

REALIZE THAT CURRICULUM IS A PROCESS

The curriculum may undergo changes even as you are working on the curriculum document, so it is at best a snapshot of the curriculum at a particular point in time. As the program evolves, you may need to do more than simply update the current document; you may need to totally revamp it to reflect the changes. However, once you have completed the first curriculum document, writing subsequent ones will be much easier.

GET STARTED EVEN IF THE TASK SEEMS OVERWHELMING

Initially, it is easy to feel overwhelmed by the task, but my recommendation is simply to jump in. We found that a workshop was a successful format. Another good way to start is to set up files for each class at each level. Individual teachers can be responsible for submitting key course information, which serves as the raw material you need to begin.

PLAN THE FORMAT CAREFULLY

Decide whether you want separate documents for individual courses and skills or a unified document. When you decide on a format for recording the curriculum of individual courses, test it out on a few courses to see if it is workable. Once you have determined the template, the actual content starts to fall into place. Be sure to choose a user-friendly format.

STRIVE TO MAKE THE PRODUCT A WORKING DOCUMENT

Involving the teaching staff and making careful choices in the document's format increases the chances that teachers will refer to it often. Publish the in-house document to make it accessible to everyone. It is also productive to establish the rhythm of annual or semiannual dates for curriculum review or document revision.

PLAN FOR REVISIONS

The document will need to be revised often, but by not including names of teachers and textbooks or other information that goes out of date quickly, you reduce the speed of obsolescence. You may want to develop a procedure for who will make the changes, how often the changes will be entered into the document, and how these revisions will be distributed to the staff.

Appendix A: Table of Contents to *A Guide to Teaching Writing at the Applied English Center*

Introduction

PART I: WITHIN THE AEC PROGRAM

Coordinating Writing Instruction
Teachers
> Teachers and Students
> Teachers and the Curriculum
> Teachers and Team Members
Coordinators

Characteristics of AEC Student Writing
Level 1–5 Writing
Special Studies in Writing: AEC 008 & 064

Texts and Materials
Function and Use of Assigned Texts
Incorporating Supplementary Materials into the Writing Class

PART II: IN THE CLASSROOM

Writing Practice
Process Approach to Writing
Timed Writing

Responding to Students' Writing
Guidelines and Approach
Tips for Responding Efficiently to your Students' Work

Individualizing Instruction
Three Basic Areas of Individualization
Lab Days

Increasing Writing Fluency

Utilizing Student Writing
Analyzing Student Writing
Creating a Publication of Student Writing

Midsemester Evaluation Process
Comment Sheets
Conferences

Testing
Practice Prefinal Writing Test
Final Proficiency Test

Interrelatedness of Skills in a Writing Class
Relationship to Reading Classes
Relationship to Structure Classes

Appendix B: Overview of the Grammar for Communication Course

Our purpose is to help students gain control of grammatical structures so that they can meet their academic goals. To do this, we stress an individualized approach and encourage students to be responsible for their learning. We do not emphasize learning grammar as an isolated activity but strive to integrate it with speaking and writing for the express purpose of using grammar effectively and accurately in communication.

Typically, students progress through the following steps in learning structures:

- understanding the form, meaning, and function of the structure
- using the structure in guided oral and written practice
- and using the structure to communicate

One of the main strengths of our curriculum is the variety of activities and opportunities used to help students produce accurate grammatical structures in their oral and written communication. For writing, students progress from grammar/editing exercises and sentence-level writing to paragraphs, essays, reports, and long-term projects such as guides and newsletters. For speaking, this is achieved through a sequenced approach of class discussions, asking questions, going over homework, encouraging and grading oral participation, and activities with small groups and partners, such as role plays, games, debates, and oral reports.

A variety of forms of technology are used in this active environment, such as the Applied English Center Computer lab, video equipment, and personal computers. Students also go into the university and local community to gather and develop material for projects, get topic ideas for writing, see and hear grammar in action, take polls, and conduct interviews.

Structure teachers in our program must have a strong grasp of English structure, both structures in isolation and their interrelationship. Equipped with this knowledge, teachers must be able to give clear explanations and think quickly to handle the many questions that arise. In addition, teachers must be able to evaluate the errors students make, identify error patterns, and give constructive feedback that helps students take risks and move to greater control of the structures. We feel that a systematic examination of grammar patterns helps develop the awareness necessary for the production and use of correct clear grammar in writing and speaking. We believe that ESL students want and need help with grammar accuracy.

At the same time, our classes are not teacher dominated. We attempt to engage the students' desire to learn. Teachers must make the grammar come to life and use creative approaches and activities to motivate students to use the grammar structures in speaking and writing, providing sufficient practice in class and as outside assignments.

Appendix C: Course Description for Level 4 Reading and Writing for Academic Purposes

Goal 1 Objectives	**To prepare students for academic reading** a. Increase reading fluency, comprehension and proficiency b. Expand strategies for critical thinking c. Read within several academic disciplines (psychology, anthropology, sociology, mathematics, history and business)
Goal 2 Objectives	**To prepare students for academic writing** a. Increase the fluency, accuracy, organization, support, and cohesiveness of writing b. Learn strategies for writing paraphrases, summaries, critical reactions, answers to essay questions, essays, and research papers
Goal 3 Objectives	**To broaden and deepen vocabulary** a. Develop strategies to manage the vocabulary demands of introductory undergraduate courses b. Learn theme-based vocabulary c. Increase vocabulary by learning the associated word forms d. Develop increased insight into which words to look up in a dictionary and which to attempt to understand by context
Goal 4 Objectives	**To teach research skills used in the American educational system** a. Gather information from a variety of sources, improve ability to take and organize notes on readings, write paraphrases and summaries and use quotations in writing b. Become familiar with library and online resources c. Evaluate sources for credibility and appropriateness d. Learn the key features of citation systems (order, punctuation, capitalization, etc.) and how to use APA style e. Understand what constitutes plagiarism and how to avoid it
Goal 5 Objectives	**To teach students to be independent readers and writers** a. Analyze academic reading and writing assignments from a variety of academic disciplines to determine academic expectations b. Gain insight into writing weaknesses and increase ability to analyze, edit and proofread c. Develop strategies to manage assignments and work under time pressure d. Predict, analyze, and interpret test questions e. Generate questions a reading will answer or generate questions the reader expects to be answered in a paper
Content themes	Success Academic skills Addictive behavior Food and lifestyles Mathematical literacy Consumer behavior

Methods	**Typical in-class activities**
	a. Prereading activities and postreading discussion of texts
	b. Writing tasks directly related to readings, including generating ideas and planning organizational structure of writing assignments
	c. Short writing assignments for fluency
	d. Supplementary videos and discussions
	e. Instruction in key research points, reading or writing strategies, or key grammar points
	f. Peer editing
	g. Vocabulary study
	Typical homework activities
	a. Assigned readings with follow-up comprehension and writing assignments
	b. Writing tasks related to readings
	c. Rewrites of assignments
	d. Outside research using the library and/or Internet
	Means of assessment
	a. Answering questions on a reading under time pressure using only students' notes on the text
	b. Vocabulary, reading comprehension, or essay tests
	c. Final drafts of essays, summaries/reactions, research paper
Instructional Materials	Core textbook; basic college reader; supplementary articles; CNN video clips related to content themes; supplementary worksheets and handouts

Appendix D: Table of Contents for the Curriculum Guide

Introduction

Reading and Writing for Academic Purposes

Grammar for Communication

Overview
Level 1 Grammar for Communication
Level 2 Grammar for Communication
Level 3 Grammar for Communication
Level 4 Grammar for Communication
Special Grammar for Communication (126)
Grammar Lab (109)

Speaking and Listening for Academic Purposes

Overview
Level 1 Speaking/Listening
Level 2 Speaking/Listening
Level 3 Speaking/Listening
Level 4 Speaking/Listening
Special Speaking/Listening (122)
Pronunciation Lab (109)

Advanced English for Academic Purposes (110)

Classroom Communication for International Graduate Teaching Assistants (082)

References

Altman, R. (2000, March). *Customer-oriented program design for business students.* Paper presented at the 36th Annual TESOL Convention, Vancouver, British Columbia, Canada.

Benesch, S. (2001). *Critical English for academic purpose: Theory, politics, and practice.* Mahwah, NJ: Lawrence Erlbaum.

Bradley, S., Dyer, W., Hayman, J., with Soars, J., & Soars, L. (1996). *Headway Australasia intermediate.* Oxford: Oxford University Press.

Bradlow, A. R., & Bent, T. (2003). Listener adaptation to foreign-accented English. In M. J. Sole, D. Recasens, & J. Romero (Eds.), *Proceedings of the XVth International Congress of Phonetic Sciences* (pp. 2881–2884). Barcelona, Spain: International Congress of Phonetic Sciences.

Brown, J. D. (1989). Language program evaluation: A synthesis of existing possibilities. In R. K. Johnson (Ed.), *The second language curriculum* (pp. 222–241). New York: Cambridge University Press.

Brown, J. D. (1995). *The elements of language curriculum: A systematic approach to program development.* New York: Heinle & Heinle.

Burton, J. (1998). Current development in language curriculum design: An Australian perspective. *Annual Review of Applied Linguistics, 18,* 287–303. Cambridge: Cambridge University Press.

Canale, M., & Swain M. (1980). Theoretical bases of communicative approaches to second language teaching and testing. *Applied Linguistics, 1,* 1–47.

Capra, F. (2002). *The hidden connection.* New York: Doubleday.

Chamot, A. U., & O'Malley, J. M. (1987). The cognitive academic language learning approach: The bridge to the mainstream. *TESOL Quarterly, 21,* 227–249.

Council of Europe. (2001). *Common European framework of reference for languages.* Cambridge: Cambridge University Press. Retrieved April 17, 2007, from http://www.coe.int/t/dg4/linguistic/CADRE_EN.asp

Cummins, J. (1996). *Negotiating identities: Education for empowerment in a diverse society.* Ontario: California Association for Bilingual Education.

Curtis, A. (1999). Changing the management of change in language education: Learning from the past, lessons for the future. *PASSA, 29,* 92–100.

Davis, B., & Sumara, D. J. (2000). Curriculum forms: On the assumed shapes of knowing and knowledge. *Journal of Curriculum Studies, 32,* 821–845.

De Lano, L., Riley, L., & Crookes, G. (1994). The meaning of innovation for ESL teachers. *System, 22,* 487–496.

Declaration on the establishment of the Center for Foreign Languages, No. 22241.3. (1995, March 28). *Official Gazette.* Ankara: General Directorate of the Turkish Ministry.

Delphi Group. (2006, March). *Innovation: From art to science.* Boston: Author.

Everard, K. B., & Morris, G. (1985). *Effective school management.* London: Harper & Row.

Fragiadakis, H., & Maurer, V. (2000). *Tapestry listening and speaking 4.* Boston: Heinle & Heinle.

Freeman, D., & Richards, J. (Eds.). (1996). *Teacher learning in language teaching.* New York: Cambridge University Press.

Friedman, T. (2006, October 6). Big ideas and no boundaries. *New York Times,* p. 25.

Fullan, M. G. (2001). *The new meaning of educational change* (3rd ed.). London: Cassell.

Grabe, W., & Stoller, F. (1997). Content-based instruction: Research foundations. In M. A. Snow & D. M. Brinton (Eds.), *The content-based classroom: Perspectives on integrating language and content* (pp. 5–21). White Plains, NY: Longman.

Graves, K. (Ed.). (1996). *Teachers as course developers.* New York: Cambridge University Press.

Harschi, K., & Wolf-Quintero, K. (2001). *Impact listening 3.* London: Longman.

Higher Education Act, No. 182701. (1984, June 7). *Official Gazette.* Ankara: General Directorate of the Turkish Ministry.

Higher Education Act, No. 90.17.5352. (1990, January 26). *Official Gazette.* Ankara: General Directorate of the Turkish Ministry.

Hoppenrath, C., & Royal, W. (1997). *The world around us: Canadian social issues for ESL students.* Toronto, Canada: Harcourt Brace.

Hull, L. (1996). A curriculum framework for corporate language programs. In K. Graves (Ed.), *Teachers as course developers* (pp. 176–202). New York: Cambridge University Press.

Hutchinson, T. (1992). The management of change. *The Teacher Trainer, 3*(1), 19–21.

Jacoby, S. (1998). How can ESP practitioners tap into situated discourse research—and why should we? *ESP News* [TESOL Interest Section Newsletter], *7*(1), 1, 4, 9, 10.

Johns, A. M. (1991). English for specific purposes (ESP): Its history and contributions. In M. Celce-Murcia (Ed.), *Teaching English as a second or foreign language* (pp. 67–75). Boston: Heinle & Heinle.

Johnson, R. K. (1989a). A decision-making framework for the coherent language curriculum. In R. K. Johnson (Ed.), *The second language curriculum* (pp. 1–23). Cambridge: Cambridge University Press.

Johnson, R. K. (Ed.). (1989b). *The second language curriculum.* Cambridge: Cambridge University Press.

Kennedy, C. (1988). Evaluation of the management of change in ELT projects. *Applied Linguistics, 9,* 330–342.

Krueger, R. A. (1988). *Focus groups: A practical guide for applied research.* Newbury Park, CA: Sage.

Long, M., & Crookes, G. (1992). Three approaches to task-based syllabus design. *TESOL Quarterly, 26,* 27–56.

Markee, N. (1997). *Managing curricular innovation.* Cambridge: Cambridge University Press.

More study abroad without parents. (2004, January 3). *Joongang Ilbo.* Retrieved January 3, 2004, from http://joongangdaily.joins.com/

Murphy, J. M., & Stoller, F. L. (2002, March). *Defining parameters of sustained-content language teaching.* Paper presented at the 36th Annual TESOL Convention, Salt Lake City, UT.

Nunan, D. (1988). *The learner-centred curriculum.* Cambridge: Cambridge University Press.

Nunan, D. (1992). Toward a collaborative approach to curriculum development: A case study. In D. Nunan (Ed.), *Collaborative language learning and teaching* (pp. 230–253). New York: Cambridge University Press.

Nunan, D. (2002, March). *Performance-based approaches to the design of ESL instruction.* Plenary presentation given at the Spain TESOL conference, Madrid. Retrieved March 3, 2007, from http://www.nunan.info /presentations/performance-based_approaches.pdf

Oakes, J. (1985). *Keeping track: How schools structure inequality.* New Haven, CT: Yale University Press.

Oxford, R. (1990). *Language learning strategies: What every teacher should know.* New York: Newbury House.

Pally, M. (Ed.). (2000). *Sustained content teaching in academic ESL/EFL: A practical approach.* Boston: Houghton Mifflin.

Park, J. (2004, July 20). Youth unemployment rate rises. *The Chosun Ilbo.* Retrieved August 23, 2004, from http://english.chosun.com/w21data/html/news/200407/200407200048.html

Parlett, M., & Hamilton, D. (1977). Evaluation as illumination: A new approach to the study of innovatory programmes. In D. Hamilton, B. MacDonald, C. King, D. Jenkins, & M. Parlett (Eds.), *Beyond the numbers game* (pp. 6–22). London: Macmillan.

Pennycook, A. (2001). *Critical applied linguistics: A critical introduction.* Mahwah, NJ: Lawrence Erlbaum.

Pinar, W. (1995). *Understanding curriculum.* New York: Peter Lang.

Price, D., & Smith, J. (2003, May). *Educational quality and the curriculum.* Paper presented at the Seventh DoS Management Conference, Sydney, Australia.

Richards, J. C. (2001a). *Curriculum development in language teaching.* Cambridge: Cambridge University Press.

Richards, J. C. (2001b). *New interchange book 1.* Cambridge: Cambridge University Press.

Rodgers, T. S. (1989). Syllabus design, curriculum development and polity determination. In R. K. Johnson (Ed.), *The second language curriculum* (pp. 24–34). Cambridge: Cambridge University Press.

Rogers, E., & Shoemaker, F. (1971). *Communication of innovations.* New York: Free Press.

Sartre, J.-P. (1955). *No Exit and three other plays.* New York: Vintage Books.

Stoller, F. L. (1995). *Managing intensive English program innovations* (NAFSA Working Paper No. 56). Washington, DC: NAFSA: Association of International Educators.

Stoller, F. L. (1997). The catalyst for change and innovation. In M. A. Christison & F. L. Stoller (Eds.), *A handbook for language program administrators* (pp. 33–48). Burlingame, CA: Alta Book Center.

Stoller, F. L. (2001). The curriculum renewal process in English for academic purposes programmes. In J. Flowerdew & M. Peacock (Eds.), *Research perspectives on English for academic purposes* (pp. 208–224). Cambridge: Cambridge University Press.

Stoynoff, S. (1991). Curriculum change and programming innovations in ESOL programs: Making it happen. *TESL Reporter, 24*(1), 9–15.

Suffering in Korea leads rising numbers to pursue emigration. (2003, September 17). *Joongang Ilbo.* Retrieved August 23, 2004, from http:// joongangdaily.joins.com/article/view.asp?aid=2031867

Sumara, D. J. (1996). *Private readings in public: Schooling the literary imagination.* New York: Peter Lang.

Sumara, D. J., Davis, B., & Kapler, L. (2000). *Engaging minds: Learning and teaching in a complex world.* Mahwah, NJ: Lawrence Erlbaum.

Swales, J. (1989). Service English programme design and opportunity cost. In R. K. Johnson (Ed.), *The second language curriculum* (pp. 79–90). New York: Cambridge University Press.

Tyler, R. W. (1949). Achievement testing and curriculum construction. In E. G. Williamson (Ed.), *Trends in student personnel work* (pp. 391–407). Minneapolis: University of Minnesota Press.

University of Rhode Island. (2005). *University of Rhode Island catalog.* Retrieved August 10, 2006, from http://www.uri.edu/catalog /cataloghtml/index.html

van Lier, L. (1996). *Interaction in the language curriculum: Awareness, autonomy and authenticity.* New York: Longman.

Vertesi, C. (1995). *Program for Renewal report.* Vancouver: University of British Columbia, English Language Institute.

Waters, A., & Vilches, L. C. (2005). Managing innovation in language education: A course. *RELC Journal, 36,* 117–136.

Wedell, M. (2003). Giving TESOL change a chance: Supporting key players in the curriculum change process. *System, 31,* 439–456.

White, R. V. (1987, July). Managing innovation. *ELT Journal, 41,* 211–218.

White, R. V. (1988). *The ELT curriculum: Design, innovation and management.* New York: Basil Blackwell.

White, R. V. (1991). Managing curriculum development and innovation. In R. White, M. Martin, M. Stimson, & R. Hodge (Eds.), *Management in English language teaching* (pp. 166–195). New York: Cambridge University Press.

White, R. V. (1993). Innovation in curriculum planning and program development. *Annual Review of Applied Linguistics, 13,* 244–259.

About the Editors and Contributors

Roann Altman has a PhD in applied linguistics and is a lecturer at the University of Michigan's English Language Institute, in the United States. She teaches English for academic purposes to advanced-level learners, specializing in teaching academic writing and pronunciation. During the summer, she coordinates the English for Business Studies program for entering international master of business administration students.

Rebecca Belchamber has been teaching English since 1994. Currently, she teaches in the English Language Intensive Courses for Overseas Students program at La Trobe University Language Centre, in Australia. Her particular interests are teacher training, computer-assisted language learning, curriculum design, sociocultural linguistics, and teaching in other settings.

Vivette Beuster is an intensive ESL instructor at Green River Community College, in the United States, and has taught ESL/EFL in South Africa and China. She has designed curricula and taught courses for ESL teachers in China and the United States. She is currently working on her PhD dissertation.

Phil Bonfanti is the director of admissions and scholarships at Mississippi State University, in the United States. He served as manager of the English as a Second Language Center from 1999 to 2001.

Elizabeth Byleen, associate language specialist at the Applied English Center of the University of Kansas, in the United States, was a designer and author for three documentation projects there. She is the author of *Looking Ahead: Developing Skills for Academic Writing* (Heinle & Heinle, 1998).

Jennifer Graupensperger teaches ESL and coordinates the Writing Center at the Annie Wright School, in the United States. She has served on the intensive ESL faculty at Green River Community College and taught EFL in Germany. She holds master's degrees in TESOL and mass communication.

Kathleen Graves is a professor of second language teacher education at the School for International Training, in the United States. She is the editor of *Teachers as Course Developers* (Cambridge University Press) and author of *Designing Language Courses: A Guide for Teachers* (Heinle & Heinle). In addition to curriculum development, her professional interests include helping teachers create learning communities in their classrooms and collaborative professional communities with fellow teachers.

Yasemin Kırkgöz was previously a director of the Center for Foreign Languages at Çukurova University, in Turkey. She completed her PhD at Aston University, in England. She has published on designing curriculum, teaching English to young learners, and integrating computers in English language teaching, and she has reviewed several book chapters. She currently works as a lecturer in the English Language Teaching Department of the Faculty of Education at Çukurova University.

Heather McIntosh teaches in the Certificate in TESL Program in the Faculty of Education at the University of Manitoba, in Canada. She holds an MA in applied linguistics and was a member of the curriculum development team at the English Language Institute, University of British Columbia.

Punahm Park is the program coordinator at Ducksung's Womens' University, in South Korea, and is pursuing a PhD in applied linguistics. Her research interests are in pragmatics, sociocultural competence and EFL pedagogy, and curriculum design.

Allison N. Petro served as director of the English Language Studies Program at the University of Rhode Island, in the United States, from 2003 to 2005 and as coordinator of the International Teaching Assistant Program from 1995 to 2001. She has taught ESL/EFL courses in the United States and abroad, including as a senior Fulbright lecturer in Russia. She is currently assistant professor of English at the Community College of Rhode Island in Newport.

Diane Potts is a PhD student in the Department of Language and Literacy Education at the University of British Columbia, in Canada. Her research interests are centered on multiliteracies and multimodality, the use of technology in ESL students' first and second language development, and teacher education. She taught in South Korea for 2½ years in the late 1990s and at Chonnam National University from 2002 to 2003.

Lee Ann Rawley is associate professor emerita in the Intensive English Language Institute (IELI) at Utah State University, in the United States. She has published on teacher development, teacher voice, and the shaping of policy for international students in higher education. Her research interests include systems change, building and sustaining collaborative communities, and understanding teacher knowledge through an ecological, systems perspective. She served as assistant director of IELI from 1986 to 2000.

Alison Rice is the director of the International English Language Institute at Hunter College, City University of New York, in the United States. She has worked in the field of English language teaching for over 30 years as a teacher, textbook author, teacher trainer, and administrator. She strongly advocates taking a creative and innovative approach to both classroom teaching and program management.

Ann Roemer is associate professor in the Intensive English Language Institute at Utah State University, in the United States. She is author of *College Oral Communication 2* in the Houghton Mifflin English for Academic Success series. Besides materials development, she is involved in teacher training, content-based instruction, and cross-cultural communication.

Wendy Royal is an instructor and codeveloper of the English Language Proficiency Diploma at Kwantlen University, in Canada, where she has worked since 1999. She was an instructor and part of the curriculum development team at the English Language Institute at the University of British Columbia (UBC). She is coauthor of *The World Around Us: Social Issues for ESL Students* (Harcourt Brace, 1997). She has an MA from UBC.

Molly Watkins is the manager of international education at Mississippi State University, in the United States. She was appointed manager in 2002 after serving on the ESL Center faculty since 1999.

M. Joyce White is an instructor at the English Language Institute, University of British Columbia, in Canada, where she has worked since 1988. She has also been involved in teacher training programs at the English Language Institute and at Vancouver Community College. She holds an MA in education and was part of the curriculum development team at the English Language Institute.

Index

Page numbers followed by an *f* or *t* indicate figures or tables.

A

Autonomy

    needs assessment and, 142

    teacher, 22–23

Avian flu, 73

B

Baby-boomers, marketing to, 171*t*, 177

Backlash, Intensive English Program revitalization and, 77

Basic Mastery Program, 48–49

Beliefs, examination of, 28–30

Benchmarks, Language Education Center curriculum project and, 197

B-School. *See* English for Business Studies program renewal

Business

    content-based instruction and, 90–91, 96

    English for Business Studies program renewal and. *See* English for
        Business Studies program renewal

    Language Education Center curriculum project and, 183

Buy-in, change and, 3

C

Cambridge exams, 74

Canadian Language Benchmarks, 74

Capstone, defined, 84

Case studies, English for Business Studies program renewal and, 166*t*, 167*t*,
    170*f*, 171*t*, 175, 178

CBI. *See* Content-based instruction

CEA. *See* Commission on English Language Program Accreditation

Center for Foreign Languages renewal

    conclusions, 154–155

    curricular context of, 136

    curriculum evaluation and, 138–144, 139*f*, 143*t*

    curriculum framework and, 137–138, 137*f*

    curriculum renewal and, 144–150, 149*f*

    evaluation of, 150–153

    goals/objectives for, 160

    lessons learned from, 153–154

D

Documentation projects
    class and level structure during, 205*t*

    curricular context of, 204–205

    design/evaluation of curriculum documentation and, 205–215

    motivation for, 203–204

    overview of, 203

    overview of Grammar for Communication course and, 217–218

    sample course description for, 219–220*t*

    sample table of contents and, 216–217, 220–221

    strategies for, 215–216

Drama, Intensive English Program revitalization and, 58*t*

E

Earth sciences, content-based instruction and, 90–91, 96

EBS. *See* English for Business Studies program renewal

Educational context, curriculum and, vi*f*

EFL. *See* English as a foreign language programs

eGrammar Series, 35, 52

Electives, needs assessment and, 20, 24–25*t*

ELI. *See* English Language Institute

ELICOS. *See* English Language Intensive Courses for Overseas Students

ELS. *See* English Language Studies Program revitalization

E-mail response systems, 40–41

English as a foreign language programs, 1. *See also* Language Education Center curriculum project

English as a second language programs, 1, 203. *See also* Content-based instruction; English Language Studies Program revitalization; ESL Center revitalization

English for academic purposes, 136. *See also* Center for Foreign Languages renewal

English for Business Studies program renewal
    conclusions, 179–180

    course examples from, 171*t*

    curricular context of, 162–164

    genre descriptions and, 166*t*

    incremental improvements to, 168–169

    initial program, 163*t*

H

I

L

model design and, 64, 65*f*

renewal process and, 63

Logic, institutional. *See* English Language Studies Program revitalization

Long-term results, evaluation of, 10–12

Loss/gain calculation, 8

M

Management, 5, 10, 12–13

Mandates, change and, 5

MAP. *See* Multidisciplinary Action Project

Market demand, change and, 5

Marketing

elements of needs analysis and, 64*t*

English for Business Studies program renewal and, 171*t*, 177

needs assessment and, 63

revitalization and, 37–38, 38–44, 47–51

Master of Business Administration programs. *See* English for Business
Studies program renewal

Materials

Center for Foreign Languages renewal and, 148

content-based instruction and, 97–99

cultural considerations and, 104

curriculum action plan and, 24–25*t*

Curriculum Renewal Model and, 139*f*

documentation projects and, 209, 213

English for Business Studies program renewal and, 170*f*

evaluation processes and, vi

innovation and, 9

Intensive English Program revitalization and, 75

model design and, 64

needs assessment and, 63, 141, 142

planning process and, v

for student facilitators, 191–192

syllabus design and, 108–111, 109*t*

systematic approach to designing/maintaining language curriculum and,
61*f*

teaching/learning processes and, vi

O

S

T

Testing. *See also specific test names*

    Center for Foreign Languages renewal and, 137

    curriculum action plan and, 24–25*t*

    documentation projects and, 209

    model design and, 65*f*

    systematic approach to designing/maintaining language curriculum and, 61*f*

Textbooks

    Center for Foreign Languages renewal and, 146

    Intensive English Program revitalization and, 70–71, 75, 76

    model design and, 64, 65*f*, 66

    New Interchange I, 185

Themes

    challenge and, 104

    content-based instruction and, 82

    documentation projects and, 213

    syllabus design and, 109*t*

Time allotment, needs assessment and, 20

TOEFL. *See* Test of English as a Foreign Language

TOEIC. *See* Test of English for International Communication

Training, student, 191–193

Trialability, acceptance of new curriculum and, 7

Tuesdays With Morrie, content-based instruction and, 96, 97–98

U

University Bridge Program, 46–47, 46*t*

University of Kansas, 203. *See also* Documentation projects

University of Michigan, 162. *See also* English for Business Studies program renewal

University of Rhode Island, 119, 121

Utah State University (USU), 79. *See also* Content-based instruction

V

Vocabulary

    content-based instruction and, 83

    documentation projects and, 219–220*t*

    Intensive English Program revitalization and, 58*t*

    needs assessment and, 134

    syllabus design and, 106–107*t*

W

Web advertising, 41

Web site development, 40, 96, 98

Workability, documentation projects and, 216

Working groups, model revisions and, 68*t*

Writing skills

    Center for Foreign Languages renewal and, 159

    content-based instruction and, 85*t*, 93*t*, 96

    core curriculum and, 47–48

    curriculum action plan and, 24–25*t*

    documentation projects and, 205*t*, 206, 209, 219–220*t*

    English for Business Studies program renewal and, 171*t*, 178

    English Language Studies Program revitalization and, 125–126, 131*t*, 132

    Intensive English Program revitalization and, 58*t*

    needs assessment and, 20, 134

    sample schedule and, 43*t*

    sample table of contents and, 220–221

    syllabus design and, 105*t*, 106–107*t*

    University Bridge Program and, 46*t*

Also Available from TESOL

Bilingual Education
Donna Christian and Fred Genesee, Editors

Bridge to the Classroom:
ESL Cases for Teacher Exploration
Joy Egbert and Gina Mikel Petrie

CALL Essentials
Joy Egbert

Communities of Supportive Professionals
Tim Murphey and Kazuyoshi Sato, Editors

Content-Based Instruction in Primary and Secondary School Settings
Dorit Kaufman and JoAnn Crandall, Editors

ESOL Tests and Testing
Stephen Stoynoff and Carol A. Chapelle

Gender and English Language Learners
Bonny Norton and Aneta Pavlenko, Editors

Language Teacher Research in Asia
Thomas S. C. Farrell, Editor

Literature in Language Teaching and Learning
Amos Paran, Editor

More Than a Native Speaker: An Introduction to Teaching English Abroad
revised edition
Don Snow

Perspectives on Community College ESL Series
Craig Machado, Series Editor
Volume 1: Pedagogy, Programs, Curricula, and Assessment
Marilynn Spaventa, Editor
Volume 2: Students, Mission, and Advocacy
Amy Blumenthal, Editor

PreK–12 English Language Proficiency Standards
Teachers of English to Speakers of Other Languages, Inc.

*Planning and Teaching Creatively within a Required Curriculum
for School-Age Learners*
Penny McKay, Editor

Professional Development of International Teaching Assistants
Dorit Kaufman and Barbara Brownworth, Editors

Teaching English as a Foreign Language in Primary School
Mary Lou McCloskey, Janet Orr, and Marlene Dolitsky, Editors

Teaching English From a Global Perspective
Anne Burns, Editor

Technology-Enhanced Learning Environments
Elizabeth Hanson-Smith, Editor

For more information, contact
Teachers of English to Speakers of Other Languages, Inc.
700 South Washington Street, Suite 200
Alexandria, Virginia 22314 USA
Toll Free: 888-547-3369   Fax on Demand: 800-329-4469
Publications Order Line: 888-891-0041
or 301-638-4427 or 4428
9 am to 5 pm, EST

ORDER ONLINE at www.tesol.org/

T E S O L